THE WORLD OF SEX
VOLUME 1: SEXUAL EQUALITY

Also by Iwao Hoshii (in English)
THE ECONOMIC CHALLENGE TO JAPAN (1964)
THE DYNAMICS OF JAPAN'S BUSINESS EVOLUTION (1966)
JAPAN'S BUSINESS CONCENTRATION (1969)
A FINANCIAL HISTORY OF THE NEW JAPAN (Co-author with T.F.M. Adams, 1972)

PERSPECTIVES ON JAPAN AND THE WEST

THE WORLD
OF SEX

Volume 1
Sexual Equality

IWAO HOSHII

PAUL NORBURY PUBLICATIONS LIMITED
Woodchurch, Ashford, Kent.

First published 1986 by
PAUL NORBURY PUBLICATIONS LTD
Woodchurch, Ashford, Kent.

ISBN 0-904404-54-5

British Library C.I.P. Data
Hoshii, A. Iwao
The world of sex: perspectives on Japan
and the West.
Vol. 1 : Sexual equality
1. Sex——Philosophy
I. Title
306.7'01   HQ21

ISBN 0-904404-54-5

Set in Bembo 10 on 12 by Visual Typesetting, Harrow.
Printed and bound by A. Wheaton & Co. Ltd, Exeter, England.

Contents

Foreword

THE MANIFESTATIONS OF SEXUALITY may not be too dissimilar within the same cultural environment but there is no uniformity in the moral and legal rules observed in different societies, and the views on sex professed by diverse groups or individuals have been influenced by disparate ideologies, customs and conventions. The conflict of ideas has become more confusing by the exaggerated publicity given to sexual phenomena, and the basic meaning of sex has been obscured by the polemics on practical issues.

I intend to explore the philosophical, ethical and legal aspects of sex by examining contemporary experience on the basis of a consistent philosophy of man. The first four chapters of this volume contain an inquiry into the philosophical and physical foundation of the equality of the sexes and a discussion of the essential sameness and specific peculiarities of men and women. The sameness of men and women is implied in the identity of human nature, their diversity in their existence as persons. The core problem of sexual equality, therefore, is to give the same recognition to men and women as human beings and to ensure to them the social, economic, legal and political conditions required for their existence as persons.

The feminist movement may not have been the most spectacular ramification of the sex revolution but it questioned basic assumptions of the social structure and led to a re-examination of the position of woman in society and her role in the family. For men, the message of the sex revolution was the possibility of sexual gratification without the burden of matrimony; for women, feminism promised liberation from institutionalised as well as indiscriminate oppression.

Although men have not accepted the demands of the feminists, male attitudes towards women have been changing. The patriarchal prejudices have not entirely disappeared but men are beginning to recognise independent women, they are resigned to women's work outside the home and even admit that women can be qualified to fill executive positions. But 80 per cent of the men in the United States and Europe and almost 100 per cent of Japanese men still think that a mother should stay at home when a child arrives and that it is the husband's job to earn the family's living expenses and not to change the infant's nappies. In the intrafamily work distribution, the vast majority of men cling to the traditional sex roles and want women to do the household chores, cooking, washing, ironing, cleaning and shopping while men should be responsible for repairs and taking care of the family car. Even if both partners are working, men retain their aversion to domestic work and are particularly allergic to cleaning.

In the public sphere, Japan may appear as the prototype of a male-dominated society but the matriarchal strains in Japan's tradition indicated by the position of Amaterasu-ô-mikami in the Shintoist pantheon have been influential throughout history. Amaterasu bears no resemblance to the fertility goddesses of the Near Orient and she has never been represented by statues like those of Aphrodite (only the Buddhist temples are adorned with sculptures). She taught her subjects to plant rice and to weave cloth but her chief attribute was that of ancestress of Japan's imperial dynasty.

Despite the institutionalisation of concubinage and hedonistic sex, the most stable position of the Japanese woman was that of wife and mother. But women were not excluded from public life. A number of empresses have occupied the imperial throne, and an imperial princess watched over the three treasures, the mirror, the sword and the jewel, transmitted by Amaterasu to her descendants and kept in the shrine of Ise, the first sanctuary outside the imperial palace. After the introduction of Buddhism, members of the imperial family and women from the ranks of the nobility became heads of nunneries.

The Japanese woman has never lost her status as mistress of the house and has always taken part in running the household economy and supervising the education of the children. A woman could be head of the 'house'; when the head of the house died and the male heir was a minor, the widow (*goke*) took over the administration of the house. It was only in the Edo period that the status of women suffered a decline.

The distinction of rank is a characteristic of the Japanese language and some common terms indicate the implication of male ascendancy in the position of the husband and the strong role of the wife in the domestic sphere. While *otto* (husband) and *tsuma* (wife) refer merely to the sexual distinction, *shujin, teishu* and *danna* stress the status of master and lord. *Oku*, the interior, can mean a wife, *oku-san* or *oku-sama* serves as a polite designation of the wife of somebody other than the speaker. When referring to his own wife, a man may say *kanai* (the inside of a house — family), *nyôbô*, originally the room of a female official (*nyôbô kotoba*, language of a court lady) or *saikun* (little lord). The mistress of a boarding house or inn is called okami (*kami* means head and things above, gods, lords and hair, but *okami* is written with the characters for woman and general) and *okami-san* is often used for wife in the working classes. *Shufu*, now used for housewife, meant a woman in charge of religious rites, the female head of a house and the wife of the head of the house.

Legal equality is the indispensable prerequisite for any valid form of sexual equality, in particular equality of rights in marriage, divorce, and property relations, but woman's actual condition depends greatly on the access to education and employment. These two aspects are given special emphasis in the last two chapters of this book. An official description of the position of women in Japan is *Fujin no Genjô to Shisaku* (literally, Present State and Policies of Women), published by the Prime Minister's Office. The 1985 edition, the fourth in a series, bore the subtitle 'Report Concerning Domestic Action Plans' and was meant to mark the final year of the United Nations Decade for Women. Much statistical material is contained in *Fujin Rôdô no Jitsujô* (Actual Situation of Female Labour) compiled yearly by the Women's and Minors' Bureau of the Ministry of Labour.

Although much of the information contained in this book concerns Japan, the situation in other countries has also been considered — not so much for the sake of comparison but rather to indicate the universality and complexity of the problems. Some aspects of the situation of women, such as marriage and prostitution, are treated in later volumes.

A discussion of the biological and physiological aspects of sex is beyond the scope of this book. I have borrowed a certain amount of anatomical and physiological information where I thought it necessary for explaining the meaning of sex but my concern is not with biology or other natural sciences but with the significance of their data for understanding the development and experience of sexuality. Some problems, however, involve ideology and their elucidation requires an exposition of their intellectual implications.

Demographic factors influence the entry of women into the labour force but the social environment may be more important. I have indicated some of the conditions that have encouraged or obstructed women's access to the labour market without attempting an exhaustive inquiry into this subject.

IWAO HOSHII
April 1986

1

Man's Unity and Diversity

THAT THERE ARE MEN AND WOMEN seems so trite that we seldom think about it; nevertheless, that man exists in two forms is of the deepest significance. The individual human being necessarily exists either as a male or as a female. A 'neutral' or 'asexual' human being is impossible. The same, of course, applies also to other organisms whose propagation is linked to sexuality. This, however, does not diminish the wondrousness of the fact, all the more so since so far, the natural sciences have not been able to give a plausible explanation of the transition from asexual multiplication (in simple organisms such as the unicellular algae and bacteria) to sexual propagation and the change from undifferentiated sex cells to differing forms and distinct male and female organisms. Together with the potentiality of growth and the capability to react to external stimuli, the possibility of reproduction constitutes a basic characteristic of life, and the phenomenon of propagation is one of the many unsolved problems of evolution.

Man and Woman

No matter how or when *homo sapiens* appeared, we must assume that he existed as man and woman right from the beginning of the race. That originally there was only man who begot offspring with a female primate (gorilla) has never been more than a bad joke. Man constitutes an element of the cosmos but, as far as we know, he occupies an altogether unique place in this universe. As an organism, man has a body, but this body is an animated body, and man's life is not only organic life but also spiritual life. Man's life involves the connection and interaction with nature as well as the independence of the person. Personality includes the capacity of self-consciousness and self-determination. As a person, the human being necessarily exists as a 'he' or 'she,' as a man or woman, and self-consciousness, self-expression and self-fulfilment are necessarily characterised by sexual differences. Right at the beginning of the human race, therefore, there must have existed a man aware that he was a 'he' and a woman aware that she was a 'she' and both conscious that they existed for each other.

The dignity of man is based on the uniqueness of the human person. As a person, every human being is different from everybody else. The person is not only something singular, but something unique and original that cannot be replaced because there is nothing the same. A true understanding of personality reveals the fallacy of egalitarianism and the special nature of the relations between man and woman.

Human sexuality means that one and the same human nature exists in two sexually differentiated forms. Human nature is not divided into a male and a female nature but the same human nature exists as man or woman in a different mode of existence. No human being is a perfect realisation of the essence 'man.' As a man or a woman, every human being is, so to speak, only a one-sided specimen of the human race. Sexual differentiation is only possible if the same nature can exist in different modes. The two sexes are not two mutually complementary halves of man (although it must be recognised that man and woman complement each other). Sex does not imply a one-sidedness to which something essential to man is missing. Human nature which essentially is a unity of body and soul, exists in different persons who are either male or female, but the plurality of human persons includes and presupposes the sameness of the human nature. Human nature is neither male nor female, neither unisexual nor bisexual; human nature is unrelated to sex. Sexuality is inseparable from the different mode in which human nature (the essence 'man') exists.

Existence is also the category to which personality belongs. Personality means man's existence as an independent being capable of self-consciousness and self-determination, sexuality is a mode of existence related to the continuation of the existence of the human race. Both, personality and sexuality, therefore, are related to man's existence, not to his essence. Existence as a personal being includes existence as a sexual being. Man or woman does not mean masculinity or femininity but a person of male or female sex.

The difference between man and woman cannot be reduced to differences in anatomy and biological functions, but pervades the totality of existence, self-consciousness and attitude to oneself and the environment, feeling and thinking, desires and actions, relations to other individuals and to society.

Nevertheless, masculinity and femininity do not constitute opposite or contradictory forms of human existence, but rather some kind of polarity. Polarity means diversity in unity. The polarity of man and woman presupposes the commonness and identity of human nature. The qualities attributed in western culture to the male, such as activity, rational thinking and aggressiveness cannot be denied to woman, just as man can possess intuition, warmth, emotionality and other characteristics considered typically feminine.

The essence of sexuality, therefore, consists in the twofold mode of existence of the same nature, in the duality of the form in which homogeneous beings are related to each other and the propagation of the species, the difference implied in the specific functions in their union for the transmission of life.

Masculinity and femininity are inseparable from man's ontological reality. That human sexuality is sometimes obscured by flaws and failures in the development of an individual and the sex changes based on such irregularities in no way prove that sex is an adventitious determination of man.

The statics of the human skeleton necessary for man walking erect and the corresponding musculature cannot be explained by any or all of the factors on which evolutionism relies in its theory of man's origin, and these factors also fail to account for the physiological characteristics of man required for his spiritual nature. As far as we know, only man is capable of mental processes such as reasoning, free decisions (denied by determinists but taken for granted in everyday life) and higher emotions. Evolutionism has not found an even remotely plausible hypothesis to trace man's acquisition of his spiritual capacities and functions.

Psychophysical Interaction

Many evolutionists have tried to evade this problem by embracing materialism and denying any essential difference between spirit and matter, or mind and body, and equating man's mental activities with the functions of the brain. While both body and soul are essential to man, the mind is not identical with the brain. Because of the oneness of man, no psychic process goes on without a corresponding brain function (there is some controversy whether this applies to all mystical experiences) while, conversely, it is less sure that all brain functions are registered in man's consciousness (this question involves the difficult field of the subconscious).

Bodily factors can greatly affect psychic functions, and man's mental state can influence his bodily well-being. Scientists have traced some mental illnesses to a substance that controls the level of an enzyme in the brain. The enzyme, *monoamine oxidase* (MAO), breaks down chemicals known as neurotransmittors which help to send nerve signals through the body. Unusually low levels of MAO may be a factor in schizophrenia and hallucinations; too much MAO seems to contribute to depression.

Other researchers have found a link between violence and trace metals. Extremely small amounts of the metals, notably copper, sodium and zinc, settle in hair shafts, and an analysis of the hair samples of violence-prone people showed two patterns of imbalances. 'Psychotic' criminals who are normal much of the time but suffer from episodes of violence had high levels of copper and low levels of zinc and sodium. 'Sociopaths,' career criminals who are constantly prone to violence, had low levels of copper, high levels of sodium and medium levels of zinc. Both the psychotics and the sociopaths also had high levels of lead and cadmium which can be toxic, and low levels of cobalt and lithium. Deficiencies of cobalt and lithium have been associated with mental problems. Some cases of improvement in violent behaviour have been reported when the chemical imbalances were corrected by diet supplements or chemical treatment.

A British researcher has asserted that a person's blood type may be a factor in his social achievement. John Beardmore, professor of genetics and head of the Genetics Department of University College, Swansea, found that people with Group 'A' blood have a 15 per cent higher probability than chance would dictate of becoming professionals or managers.

Physiologists have mapped the brain and assigned different functions to different parts of the brain, but a map of the mind is a contradiction in terms. Although scientists now view the brain as a 'unified' organ, highly interdependent and interacting rather than a set of autonomous, evolutionary-bound parts, the brain does not explain the wholeness and oneness of our consciousness. The unity of our conscious experience is not the result of a synthesis accomplished by the neuronic apparatus. The integration and unification fundamental to our consciousness admits of no spatial attributes. Man's ego, the centre of attribution and subject of all conscious activities, including all sensations, has no parts (notwithstanding the split personality of schizophrenics).

The absence of all spatial relations in man's consciousness (space is only perceived in the objects of sensation) is an indication of the inner independence of the mind from matter. Because the mind depends on the brain, not as a cause but as a condition, it is possible to influence the mind by manipulating the brain. The electromagnetic and chemical actions and reactions which account for the functions of the brain supply the inputs to the centres to whose excitation the mind responds in conformity with the ego's attention and interest. Even if we sleep, the mind fathoms the cortex but the brain may not always be active. It ceases to function in deep anaesthesia or in a coma.

Aristotle termed woman a 'misbegotten male' and considered her a lower type of human being. Such a depreciation lacks even the slightest foundation. Man and woman are limitations of human possibilities but although the sexual determination constitutes the most fundamental and extensive of all limitations, it is only one of the innumerable 'definitions' inherent in human existence. As an individual, every human being possesses only an extremely limited selection of the vast number of possible human properties. Man's body can have only certain qualities which exclude all others. A man who has blue eyes cannot have brown or grey eyes; people may dye their hair but its natural colour can only be one.

Nature -v- Nurture

As an organism, man is embedded in the biological flow of generations of human beings but he is not condemned to a fate determined by heredity. He does not inherit fixed patterns of thought, emotions, or conduct but certain dispositions. Out of the plenitude of possible human properties, man receives a certain structure of basic functions and capabilities which provide the framework for an integrated development. The individuation by hereditary factors limits the possibilities of individual formation but the development of man's properties and capabilities is not genetically determined. Within the limits of the biological inheritance, the development can be influenced by man's own choice, by education and other environmental factors. Nor does the inheritance of psychic properties mean the transmission of completely developed qualities but of dispositions that make the development in a certain direction possible but not necessary.

Man can cultivate or neglect his inherited corporeal or psychic capabilities but he cannot add new ones. He cannot transcend the possibilities founded in his inheritance. Every human being is different, but this difference does not negate the fact that every individual is in the full sense a human being.

These biological conditions are of fundamental importance for understanding the controversy which is often reduced to the formula nature *versus* nurture. Are the differences in human capabilities, for example, the differences in intelligence (as measured by intelligence tests and expressed by the IQ) due mainly to inheritance or to environment? This controversy has far-reaching implications. If an individual's mental ability is largely determined by genetic factors, the basic assumption of the egalitarian philosophy underlying many modern educational policies is wrong. It also means that the environment or society is not the decisive factor for man's mental or moral development which does not mean that the environment or society has no influence.

The word 'influence' is often connected with the assumption that the factor said to influence somebody or something is the efficient cause of the influence and that the substratum which is affected is merely a passive receptor. In case of purely mechanical influences it often happens that the object receiving the influence modifies but does not cause the effect (for example, the effect of a blow with a hammer on a stone or a bundle of straw). But in case of organisms, the effect depends on the way in which the influence is received or accepted (for example, the influence of sunlight on a plant or on the human eye). This is often referred to as reaction but the effect corresponds to the specific way in which the organism receiving the influence acts and not on the specific way of operation of the influence. Aristotle already stated the principle for which scholastic philosophy used the formula *Quidquid percipitur, per modum recipientis percipitur* (whatever is perceived, is perceived in the manner of the perceiver).

The recognition of the modality of influences is, as Oswald Spengler has emphasised, of special importance in the assessment of psychological or cultural influences. Not what the environment offers is of primary importance but what the organism accepts from the environment. Naturally, the organism can only accept what is in the environment but what is present in the environment is entirely irrelevant so long as the organism cannot receive it or, in case of psychic influences, so long as man will not accept it. That man is capable of absorbing the outside world and the mode in which he absorbs it is a preliminary condition of all environmental influences.

Man and woman are different not only in their bodies but also in their minds. This difference affects the entire mental development, the self-consciousness and emotional life of every human being. To be a man or a woman constitutes the most fundamental characteristic of man's personality. Sexuality is of elementary and all-pervasive importance in the development of the individual and has been the most influential factor in the evolution of the human race. Culture, the unmistakable product of the human mind, is only possible on account of the personal nature of man, and the diversity of the sexes has been a conspicuous factor in cultural development. The consciousness of sexuality already found expression in the wall paintings of the Stone Age.

Cultural anthropologists contended that each society was different and that man's feelings and thoughts were shaped by the way he lived. They did not believe in a fixed, hereditary human nature. Early in her career, Margaret Mead tried to show that even the notions of maleness and femaleness varied from place to place.

Differences in Natural Endowment

The assertion that man and woman have been trained for different roles by culture and society is not only unproven but basically wrong. 'No one is born a woman' was the thesis propounded by Simone de Beauvoir (who later became the companion of J.J. Sartre) in 1949 which has been the leitmotiv of feminism. One is merely born a 'female' but becomes a 'woman' through the influence of the model prevailing in a given civilisation. But the 'female' is intrinsically ordained towards womanhood and motherhood. It cannot be denied that education and society exercise a strong influence on the development of the individual but the natural inequalities of the sexes greatly transcend the obvious anatomical and biological differences (which, of course, the feminists do not deny).

There are marked peculiarities in the growth process and the capabilities of men and women, and researchers have attributed some of these variations to differences in the organisation of the brain. One of these differences is the often discussed asymmetrical arrangement of the right and left halves of the brain. According to Dr Roger Sperry of the California Institute of Technology, the left brain (in right-handed persons) houses speech and analytical skills such as reading, writing, arithmetic and logic. The right brain is the site of space and pattern perception — the recognition of faces, for example, and artistic appreciation. The localisation is not complete and there is considerable sharing and crossover. Some researchers have expressed doubts on the validity of the localisation.

The left half is more specialised in women so that they are better at oral communication, and girls learn quicker to read than boys and are more gifted in music and social studies. The right half handles space-related activities so that men have a natural advantage in the perception of spatial connections. These differences may help to explain the fact that there are relatively few women architects, engineers, X-ray technicians, painters and composers — fields in which spatial imagination constitutes a necessary condition. There may be similar differences for emotional perceptions. In women, both halves of the brain seem to participate in emotional transmissions so that women's emotional behaviour is less dissociated from rational-analytical operations. Therefore, emotional stress has a direct impact on women's motivation and interest in their work. Women are not only more intuitive than men, but are also more inclined to rely on their intuition. While feminine intuition is proverbial nobody speaks of male intuition. Women's visual and auditive perception and their sense of taste are also sharper than those of men.

Boys are poorer at everything in their early years and suffer more brain damage, foetal mortality and genetic disorders than girls. Among dyslexics, boys outnumbers girls by an estimated ratio of 4:1. According to American studies, there are marked differences in scholastic achievements. Males generally score better in mathematics, sciences, social studies and citizenship. In these fields, scholastic understanding of males and females is fairly equal at age 9 but by age 13, females have begun a decline which continues downwards through to age 17 and into adulthood. Females are more proficient in reading and literature at age 9 but fall behind males in this area by the time they are young adolescents. Females maintain a slight advantage in music at all ages. Only in writing do females consistently outperform males by a wide margin.

Some psychologists maintain that boys and girls possess equal mathematical ability as measured by standard achievement tests and that the avoidance of mathematics and technology by girls and women is 'culturally programmed'. Female dislike of mathematics has been transferred to computers. Where computers are available in the early school grades, girls are less interested in using them. Attendance at computer camps and classes showed a pattern of three to one in favour of boys for all grade levels.

American researchers found that boys who reached sexual maturity early scored better on standard intelligence and achievement tests than did late maturers. This difference did not appear in girls, but girls who matured late matched or outscored their male counterparts in mathematics. Usually, adolescent girls begin to fall behind boys in mathematic ability, and the early-maturing girls could not match the performance of boys.

By nature, woman is programmed for the birth and rearing of children and is not adapted to this task by society. Her skeleton is different from that of man. In particular, her pelvis and pubic symphysis are built for pregnancy and childbirth. Even during childhood, a large part of the bodily and psychic growth impulses of woman serve as preparation for her tasks. The need to care, to succour, to beautify and to decorate belong to woman's specific endowment.

There is no mother instinct in the same sense as a self-preservation or sex instinct but the biological and hormonal changes connected with pregnancy and birth enable the mother to bear the hardships and bring the sacrifices required by the care of the newborn. The mother switches off her instinct for self-affirmation and even her healthy egoism and devotes herself patiently to the care of a being imperiously demanding attention and crying for its mother.

The difference in body-build of man and woman shows up also in their performance in sports. The records established by women have been improving faster than those of men. Women are relatively better in long-distance running and swimming but men show a better adaptability for most events involving strength and quickness. The male arm length is greater relative to body length; when women hold their arms down with the palms facing forward, they have a larger carrying angle than men. The female body has more fat and less muscle per unit volume than the male body which imposes a tremendous handicap on woman in most aspects of physical activities relative to her male counterpart. But women have greater joint mobility and better health records against cancer, coronary heart disease, respiratory conditions, ulcers, diabetes and hardening of the arteries. Women tolerated the altitude at the Mexico City Olympics in 1968 better than men.

In lifelong development, conditions improve in favour of women. The ratio of male to female embryos after conception has been estimated at 130-150 male to 100 female, but male foetuses seem to be exposed to greater dangers than female ones during pregnancy and at birth because the ratio of live births is 104 to 107 male to 100 female. Between birth and puberty, the mortality rate is higher for boys than for girls, and with the beginning of the secretion of sex hormones, the danger becomes higher for men. Testosteron, the main male hormone, exercises a strong influence on the formation of muscles and the reproductive capacity, but it also seems responsible for an increase in male susceptibility to circulatory disorders and coronaries so that the life expectancy of women is higher than that of men. In developing countries, however, the combined rigours of childbearing, hard work, malnutrition and unsatisfactory sanitary conditions considerably reduce the life expectancy of women. There is no essential difference between the bodily strength of men and women, but men are capable of more intense momentary exertion while women have greater power of perseverance. But Pentagon studies have shown that women soldiers have only 55 per cent of the muscle strength and 67 per cent of the endurance of their male comrades.

Male Aggressiveness

According to geneticists and psychologists, the male's aggressiveness and combativeness has a hereditary foundation. The thesis of man's innate aggressiveness has been propounded by such authors as Konrad Lorenz and Robert Ardrey. The instinct of aggressiveness has been represented as superseding reason and moral convictions so that neither the individual nor society can be blamed for outbreaks of violence or war. Lorenz states that men may enjoy the feeling of absolute righteousness even when they commit atrocities and he cites an Ukrainian proverb: 'When the banner is unfurled, the reason is in the trumpet' (*Die Rückscite des Spiegels, p.302*).

While man's instinct of self-preservation can be interpreted as including aggressiveness and male initiative in sex relations belongs to his sex-specific behaviour, there is no aggressive instinct which relieves the individual of responsibility for violence or justifies mass riots. Lorenz and Ardrey adduced the ferocity of wild animals to illustrate man's innate belligerence inherited from his apelike ancestors, but the savagery of the animals is a human falsification. Field studies of primates (gorillas, chimpanzees and orang-utans) have shown that their groups are not bellicose and bloodthirsty. In the groups of primates and some other animals, the female is wooed by the males and chooses the best partner while the male seeks to mate with as many females as possible. When the mother is occupied with rearing her offspring, she does not yield to another partner because this would mean sacrificing her offspring. Ferociousness and sexual aggressiveness are not residues of man's animal past.

Sex-specific Interests

Ursula Scheu, who emphasises the influence of the social environment on sexuality, wrote a book with the title 'We are not born as girls but made thereto.' However, the studies of J. Eibl-Eibesfeldt disprove the theory that sexual orientation is the product of society. Eibl-Eibesfeldt investigated and photographed the behaviour of primitive peoples: the Bushmen of the Kalahari desert, the cave dwellers in the forests of Mindanao, the neolithic planters in the mountains of West Irian, the Yanomani Indians in the upper reaches of the Orinoko, the Himba, a people of herdsmen in South-West Africa and the Balinese. His conclusion was that children developed sex-specific interests although their upbringing was not sex-specific. Girls identified with women and boys with men, and they adopted the corresponding roles in their play. Girls tended to occupy themselves with things related to the home and showed a preponderant interest in fellow-men, games of skill and dolls. Boys manifested a marked inclination to technical pursuits, experiments and competitive and war-like games. They were less tied to the home, were more aggressive than girls and roamed further away when exploring the neighbourhood. In short, the natural sexual differentiation leads to sex-specific behaviour. Woman conducts herself as a woman because she is a woman. She plays the role assigned to woman in a particular culture because she feels it concordant with her personality.

Using biological, psychological and sociological data, some authors have tried to construe a difference between man and woman in which man is assigned a leading or superior role. This sexual typology finds a structural dominance of the male over the female. Starting with the generative act in which the male is said to be active and endowing, the female passive and receptive, these studies assert that the spheres of social activities corresponding to the sex-specific qualities of man and woman give man a position of social leadership, particularly in matters transcending the limited sphere of the immediate family, and enable man to guide the destiny of the group. There is no reason to deny the natural differences between man and woman but the axiological deductions from such premises are fallacious and based on androcentric value systems.

Biologically, there seems to be no necessity for organisms to age and die. Protists such as the amoeba are potentially immortal since they split into two when they reach a certain size, leaving no mother which could finally become a corpse. During the lifetime of a multicellular organism, its material substratum is almost entirely replaced but there is a limit to its regenerative capability which admits of wide differences between the various kinds of organisms and also varies within the same species. Cells divide and multiply, making carbon copies of themselves, but as the organism grows older, the quality of the carbon copies deteriorates. The new cells are not terribly good and the signs of aging appear. Not only aging and death, but also enemies, hunger and disease endanger the existence of the individuals so that the preservation of the species requires the production of new individuals.

Evolution and the Origin of Life

According to the theory of evolution, the preservation of the species by the substitution of individuals provides the possibility of mutations in which short-lived species have an advantage over long-lived ones because their evolution is more rapid. These conditions create selective pressure in favour of organisms with a short life span and the danger of gradual elimination of long-lived species. These assumptions of Darwinian evolutionism have been disputed by the theory of punctuated equilibrium. (See below).

Scientists have described many forms of organisms which can be interpreted as successive stages of life and they have postulated a connection between these forms referred to as descent. Actually, not only the origin of life lies completely in the dark but scientists do not even agree on what life is. Moreover, despite the many stages and so-called transitional forms, the process of the alleged descent of new (higher?) forms from preceding (lower?) forms is completely unknown. In evolutionism, the nineteenth century believed to have found the solution of the problem of the origin of life, one of Du Bois-Raymond's 'seven riddles of the universe' to which he had considered a solution possible. But until now, neither the possibility nor the mechanism of such a development has been scientifically demonstrated, and there is not a single experiment in which one species has been transformed into another.

Evolutionists describe the ascent and spread of life in relation to the major divisions of geological time but this is pure hypothesis and in no way proven scientific knowledge. The transition from one species to another has never been observed. Evolutionists contend that evolution is not a theory but a fact. However, fact is only that there existed and exist a multitude of species (what a species is remains uncertain) which appeared successively and can be arranged in a generally ascending order of complexity. But we do not know whether one species developed from another and are ignorant of the mechanism by which it could have happened. Hugo de Vries tried to show that the origin of new species came through new forms suddenly appearing which he called mutations. But experimentally, mutations have only been proven for changes within one and the same species and most of the observed mutations were deteriorations rather than improvements (for example, the famous Drosophila experiments of Hermann Joseph Muller and

Thomas Hunt Morgan). Still unclear is the role of 'transposable elements' ('jumping genes') discovered by Barbara McClintock, bits of DNA which appeared at different positions of the genetic structure. If they turned up on a specific part of the chromosome, the colour of the /next generation of kernels would be different from the parents (for example, yellow instead of red).

Many years later, a British scientist, Jim Shapiro, and a German geneticist, Peter Starlinger, discovered 'vagabonding' genes which edge in between genes and facilitate or impede the activity of genes in the neighbourhood. The insertion of gene particles produces the same effect as the 'transposable elements' of Mrs McClintock who was given the Nobel prize for medicine in 1983.

New research has pointed out other instances of the mobility of genes and gene particles. A Japanese team at the University of Kyushu studied the 'copia' elements of *Drosophila melangogaster* and showed their similarity with retroviruses, and other scientists have demonstrated that viruses can act as 'horizontal' (across the boundaries of species) transporters of genetic material picked up during their sojourn in unicellular organisms.

Scientists speculate that transposable elements could explain cell differentials, in which one particular kind of cell produces entirely different cells to form all the variegated tissues of the whole organism, particularly during the early stages of development.

With the transition to sexual reproduction, the emergence of a new species would postulate the appearance of a male and a female specimen at the same time and at the same place. So far, evolutionists have failed to furnish even a hint of the way in which this came about.

Geographic isolation and selection have been adduced as other factors of adaptation that are supposed to have led to the origin of new species, but here again the 'how' of such an adaptation lies completely in the dark.

While Darwin assumed that the work of evolution through the process of natural selection was slow, gradual and continuous, the proponents of the theory of 'punctuated equilibrium' assert that most species have evolved relatively quickly (on the scale of geological time) and have persisted virtually unchanged for millions of years. The theory largely originated from the embarrassing inability of paleontologists to find the so-called 'missing links,' the fossils of transitional forms between species. Darwin himself conceded that the fossil record was too spotty to demonstrate the gradual changes he postulated but he was confident that they would eventually be proven. However, a century of digging has failed to supply the evidence for the gradual transitions. (Darwin also called for experiments to demonstrate the formation of new species but never tried to carry out experiments himself.)

The new theory, therefore, wants to replace Darwin's 'gradualistic model' by a 'punctuational model' which can do without missing links. Natural selection in Darwin's sense is of little significance because it produces very little evolutionary change. Instead, by a mechanism not yet understood, new species appear to split off at random from existing ones. The old species may become extinct but it is also possible that both species will coexist for a long time until a major change in the environment wipes out one or both of them.

The punctuational theory stresses two phenomena. First, established species are normally very stable. Some species can be traced through layers of sand and mud with remarkable continuity for up to three million years with no change of identity. Secondly, although no significant gradual changes were taking place, many new kinds of animals were appearing all over the world. A particularly rapid expansion of mammals involving not only large species but many altogether new families occurred after the extinction of the dinosaurs about 65 million years ago.

Life from Outer Space

Recently, Sir Fred Hoyle, one of Britain's leading astronomers, told an audience of scientists at London's Royal Institution that the chemical structures of life were too complicated to have arisen through a series of accidents, as evolutionists believe. Humans depend for their functioning on 200,000 chains of amino acids which are arranged in a particular pattern. The odds against arriving at this pattern by the accidental process imagined by Darwin were enormous, similar to those against throwing five million consecutive sixes on a dice, Sir Fred asserted. Biomaterials, with their amazing measure of order, must be the outcome of intelligent design, he said. According to Sir Fred's own theory, this design was the work of a life form in the universe's remote past which, doomed by a crisis of its own environment, wanted to preserve life in another shape. Viruses and other influences carried by micro-organisms from space jolted the evolutionary process on earth forward and, as suggested by the periods of rapid change, perhaps modified its direction.

In a similar vein, Sir Francis Crick, the co-discoverer of the DNA-double helix, assumed that life was sent to earth by rockets from a distant civilisation.

The possibility of extra-terrestrial life possesses a certain fascination for scientists, but this theory just moves the problem of the origin of life back to a completely unknown cosmic intelligence and contributes nothing to the explanation of the various forms of life which, with the growing complexity of order and teleology inherent in their structure, require no less a reason than the origin of life.

In the last decades, many finds of hominid fossils have greatly added to our knowledge of prehistoric forms. Researchers are inclined to the view that the series leading to today's *homo sapiens* originated from an extinct mammal. The line exhibits advances as well as retrogressions, including extinct sidelines, such as the Neanderthal man who was a 'man' but had nothing to do with today's 'man.' The basic forms and the possible width of variation of the more than 200 single bones of today's man have been studied intensively so that the similarity or dissimilarity of each find with present man can be established, but the question which of the so-called ancestors of man can be regarded as a member of the species *homo sapiens* remains unanswered.

One of the major puzzles in the development of man is the origin of the human races. The concept of race itself is not very exact. The existence of subdivisions of the human species differentiated by a fairly distinctive combination of inherited traits can be traced through known history, but it is impossible to establish a fossil record. Intermarriage does not affect fertility so that all races undoubtedly belong to the same species, and within the limits of racial diversities, individual differences exhibit innumerable variations of the racial characteristics.

There are very few fossils of hominids the theoreticians of evolution consider the immediate predecessors of man, and there are no fossils at all for the time from eight million to four million years BP (before present). A fossil dated back eight million years belongs to a species called *Sivapithecus indicus;* this species, however, is unrelated to man's ancestry. The oldest hominid fossils found up to now were dug out in 1981 in the Awash river valley in Ethiopia in an area called the Afar Triangle. They consisted of the upper part of a left femur and seven skull fragments. Their age was estimated at four million years which makes them 400,000 years older than the fossils commonly referred to as 'Lucy' which, together with other finds, were called *Australopithecus afarensis*. According to the discoverers of the latest find, the femur belonged to a young 11-17-year-old male about 4½ feet tall and capable of walking upright. Its cranial capacity was about 400 cc., barely a fourth of the size of the brain of *homo sapiens*.

Because of the evolutionary stability of over 400,000 years, some scientists considered the find a confirmation of the view that species do not change gradually as the Darwinians contend but in relatively short periodic outbursts.

Based on a computer and statistical analysis of about 900 teeth as well as jaw and skull fragments found in China in the last few years, Charles Oxnard of the University of Southern California theorised that there is a direct link between *ramapithecus* and *homo sapiens*. *Ramapithecus,* once considered a direct ancestor of humans, was displaced from that position in favour of *Australopithecus afarensis*. Since *ramapithecus* roamed across Asia from 8 to 15 million years ago, human development, Oxnard submitted, would have taken much longer than the 4½ million years now assumed on the basis of the African connection.

Although *Australopithecus afarensis* was claimed to belong to an upright species, the present form of the human body first appears in finds dating back one million years, shortly before the transition from the late Tertiary to the Pleistocene. The oldest specimen of *homo sapiens* is an Australoid skull from the Niah Cave in Borneo dated 37,650 BP.

Our knowledge of man's fossil past will always remain fragmentary if only because skeletons or their pieces are only found in calcareous earth. In soils without calcium carbonate (chalk, limestone), the water trickling through the soil contains free carbonate acid which dissolves the bones. For this reason, conclusions regarding the geographical distribution of early man from the location of fossil finds cannot be complete.

Max Westenhöfer contended that man was the oldest of all mammals. The development of the human brain, man's most characteristic feature, must have started very early, not in the latest geological periods. The hominids formed a special branch before the apes appeared. The differences between man and all other mammals, including the anthropoid apes, are so fundamental that only man can be the ancestor of man.

In a similar vein, Edgar Dacqué turned Darwinian evolutionism on its head and asserted that man did not develop from the animals but that the animals developed from man. The various geological epochs do not contain all possible forms of life but certain forms are characteristic of certain periods. Evolution proceeds in spurts in which a certain form typical of the period is expressed in different groups and branches. But all specialised forms are variations of the same primitive form and this primitive form, Dacqué maintained, is man. Man represents the common primitive form of all animals which, in the course of evolution arose and split from the primitive form by specialisation. The principle that the higher or more complex derives from the lower or more primitive has to be reconsidered. Dacqué said, because it is an unscientific way of thinking.

2

Genesis of Sexual Differentiation

THE BASIC MEANING OF SEXUALITY is the transmission of life. Life refers to individual organisms as well as the totality of all beings of which we say that they live. Life is one of the phenomena for which philosophers have endeavoured in vain to find an appropriate definition and scientists are still unable to explain the possibility of existence.

Aristotle considered life as 'entelechy' which means something having its goal in itself. Life is distinguished by some kind of independence, something existing in itself and for itself. The pivotal concept in Aristotle's analysis of life is self-movement. The movement of something that moves itself can have neither beginning nor end so that life as such is immortal. In man, life is soul, the inner form moving man towards the full realisation of this form. But it is not clear whether Aristotle attributes an individual soul to every organism and asserts personal immortality for man. Despite the immanence of the form, matter is the foundation of individual being, and matter as such is lifeless. Death means that life which animated the body departs but life itself cannot die. Human life is inseparable from life itself.

Immortality

Personal immortality is an article of faith of many religions but a murky philosophical question. Materialism denies the existence of anything superior to matter so there is no soul as a reality different from the body and death means the complete extinction of man. On the other hand, systems teaching the transmigration of the soul maintain that after death, the soul passes from one human or animal body to another human or animal body. As taught by the Pythagorean school in antiquity and by religions such as Hinduism and Buddhism, metempsychosis assumes a two-way immortality, the pre-existence of souls before their union with a human body and infinite existence in the course of the transmigrations. The traditional Christian view interpreted death as a transient suspension of the union of body and soul in which the soul continued to exist in order to be reunited with the body at the end of time. The resurrection of the dead implied the restoration of life destroyed by death, the reestablishment of the union of body and soul, and the identity of the resurrected body with the mortal body but in a spiritualised and glorified state. The state between death and resurrection was sometimes described as sleep, but the prevalent view assumed a state of bliss for the separated souls of the just also before resurrection.

Modern anthropology stressed the unity of man and considered the soul not as an essentially independent spiritual substance but as a function of the body. Death means the biological end of man, and total death involves both body and soul. Theologians such as Hans Küng comment that total death does not mean destruction into nothingness but demise 'into the hands of God' and the promise of life everlasting. The assumption of the complete extinction of the biological existence of man seems at variance with at least some data of parapsychology.

Kant considered immortality (together with freedom and the existence of God) as a postulate of moral-practical reason. It is with regard to these three ideas that he formulated his famous dictum 'I had to eliminate knowledge, therefore, in order to get room for faith'. Immortality, according to Kant, is the continuation of our existence after our earthly existence with the moral and physical consequences appropriate to our moral behaviour continuing into eternity. Moral law demands sanctity, that is, the complete conformity of the will, but no rational being in the world of senses is capable of such perfection at any time of its existence. As a postulate of practical reason, therefore, Kant poses a 'progressus' to complete conformity with the moral law. Such an infinite 'progressus' is only possible on the premise of the existence and personality of the same rational being into infinity (which is called the immortality of the soul).

The idea of immortality and bodily resurrection implies the unanswerable problem of man's personal relations after death. Can sexuality be projected into life after death? The best-known commentary is the answer Jesus gave the Sadducees to their casuistical question whose wife a woman would be who had been married to all of seven brothers: 'For in the resurrection they neither marry nor be married, but shall be as the angels of God in heaven' (Matth. 22,30). However, in a theological discourse pronounced on 2 December, 1981, Pope John Paul II expressed the view that men and women will retain their sense of sexuality in heaven although there will be neither marriage nor procreation. The human bodies recovered and renewed together in the resurrection will maintain their masculine and feminine peculiarities and the sense of being in a masculine and feminine body will be constituted and understood differently in the other world than during the terrestrial existence. There will be spiritual rather than physical fulfilment.

In Kant's view, life is based on the inner capacity of determining oneself by one's own will. It is impossible to demonstrate the existence of the soul, the principle of life, but there can be no doubt about the existence of immaterial nature. The soul is the 'thinking self', the 'ultimate subject of thinking that cannot be thought of as the predicate of something else'.

What is Life?

Life can be characterised as self-movement, self-preservation, self-control and self-regulation. In man, the three forms of organic, sensitive and spiritual life are united to a whole in which the functions proper to these three modes of life are dependent on and related to one another. Without the organic and physiological life, neither senses nor mind can function, but organic life as such does not appear in our consciousness and cannot be consciously controlled. Nevertheless, consciousness can influence organic life and is influenced by it. Emotions can affect the operations of physiological systems and the secretion of hormones influences conscious moods. Man's experience of his own self and his self-consciousness are based on his sensitive and mental consciousness in which man apprehends himself as the 'ego' that possesses and uses his body and performs the sensitive and mental acts as his acts. In this individual consciousness, man experiences himself as growing and decreasing life subject to critical limitations, heading towards the last limitation, death.

What life actually is transcends our present knowledge, and neither philosophy nor science has been able to explain the origin of life. So far, all attempts of evolutionists to demonstrate that life derived from an organic matter have failed. Stanley Boyd Miller's famous experiment intended to show the possibility of a biotic synthesis of 'organic' matter from a simulated primitive atmosphere by electric discharges, but the experiment actually proves the impossibility of such a synthesis. The experiment produced amino acids of which proteins are composed. Proteins in themselves are not life. The amino acids produced in Miller's experiment are supposed to combine by mutual reactions to polypeptides. But, as A.E. Wilder Smith has observed, the reaction by which polypeptides would be formed is reversible. The formation of polypeptides occurs as a condensation, and condensation means the elimination of a simple molecule, such as water. In the presence of a surplus of water, however, condensation is impossible; the polypeptides would immediately be decomposed into the original amino acids. Wilder Smith, therefore, says the only place where the proteins necessary for life could not be formed were the oceans.

Another flaw in Miller's demonstration is that the amino acids formed in the experiment are a mixture of right- and left-handed amino acids whereas the amino acids present in living organisms are exclusively left-handed (that is, polarised light is deflected to the left).

Moreover, recent research seems to indicate that the earth's primitive atmosphere was quite different from the methane-ammonia-hydrogen mixture assumed in Miller's experiment. Scientists now think that it consisted of carbon dioxide, nitrogen and water vapour. They still maintain that the atmosphere provided conditions for the auto-genesis of organic matter; energised by lightning or radiation, formal-dehyde and hydrogen cyanide could have been precipitated and fallen into the ocean where life first started. So far, there is nothing to back up this hypothesis.

In connection with Miller's experiment and the discovery of the genetic code (the double helix) by J.D. Watson and F.H.C. Crick, the origin of life was explained on the basis of molecular biology with the help of cybernetics and information theory. Manfred Eigen proposed the theory of self-organisation of macro-molecules to autocatalytic hypercycles. Autocatalysis means a catalysis caused by a catalytic agent formed during reaction. Here it is used in the sense of capacity to self-reproduction. Like other evolutionary theories, Eigen's theory of self-organisation of matter tries to explain the transition from 'less' (lifeless matter) to 'more' (living organisms) without a new adequate input.

No biologist has ever observed a hypercycle and nobody has ever succeeded in creating one. Even if such an experiment were successful, it would not produce a living cell. As Ilya Prigogine (who subscribes to evolutionism) has stated, even the simplest cell involves metabolic functions consisting of thousands of related chemical reactions and presupposing a delicate mechanism for their coordination and regula-tion. The complex sequence of operations is executed in what might be called a conveyor-belt method. That such a complex system should have originated from accidental chemical reactions is not only incredible but an assertion affronting human intelligence.

Improving on the idea that life emerged from a 'primordial soup', biochemists at NASA's Ames Research Centre in California reported that clays attract the antecedents of protein and might have leached them from the sea during high tides. Clays, the researchers said, scavenge energy released by such natural processes as radioactive decay. They store the energy in the form of electrons and release it when subjected to stress. But the ability of clays to store energy and to catalyse chemical reactions leaves a long way to go to the formation of amino acids. Professor Graham Cairns-Smith of the University of Glasgow suggested that clays were 'proto-organisms' because the metals in clay lattices provided a structure able to store energy, catalyse reactions and self-replicate. This conjecture recalls attempts to metamorphose crystals into some kind of organisms.

Many biologists have expressed the opinion that no clear line separates the living from the non-living. About half a century ago, some scientists propounded the thesis that crystals represented a transitional stage between the organic and inorganic. They relied above all on the growth processes of crystals. But different from the growth of organisms which proceeds by intussusception, crystals grow by accretion and the growth phenomena can be explained by purely mechanical physicochemical operations. Viruses have been said to constitute a transitional form between living things and non-living matter. But a virus cannot reproduce by itself; it can multiply only by invading a host cell and getting the cell to manufacture more viruses.

Even more mysterious than the origin of organic life is the emergence of mind. Materialism has tried to explain mind and the spirit as a function of matter but such an explanation runs counter to the fundamental facts of self-experience. The entire development of man testifies to the flowering of the human spirit as an evolution transcending the limitations of matter. Neither the unity nor the continuity of human consciousness can exist without the self-sustained existence of the mind. Thinking and knowledge, belief and doubt are realities given in our experience, and the human mind perceives itself directly and implicitly as well as in philosophical reflection as the subject of these experiences. Just as the origin of life from the womb of the mother, so also the beginning of the mind involves a mystery not solved by philosophy and which the answer of theology does not make understandable.

One of the remarkable results of the transmission of life by sexually differentiated procreation is the combination of the maintenance of the species with a growing diversity of individuals. In asexual reproduction or in the propagation by cuttings, shoots or similar pieces, the new organism is genetically the same as the old which means that its reactions to the environment will generally be the same as those of the preceding generation. If, however, the new organism results from the union of the gametes of different parents, the new organism cannot be exactly the same as the parents. The reason for this lies in the formation of the cells required for the reproductive process.

Cell Division and Chromosomes

Apart from very few exceptions, the division of cells is accomplished by the division of the cell's nucleus. This division occurs in three different forms. In the first form, the direct method of cell division (amitosis), the cleavage of the nucleus takes place without the appearance of chromosomes. The indirect method (mitosis), which is typical for animals and plants, is accomplished in four steps or phases. The nucleus contracts into a cluster of threads and the nuclear membrane disappears. Each of these threads, the chromosomes, then starts to separate longitudinally into two parts (prophase). The bisected chromosomes arrange themselves on the equatorial plane in the middle of the cell like spikes of a wheel (metaphase). Perpendicularly to the plane a bundle of protoplasm threads in the form of a spindle appears. The longitudinal halves of the chromosomes (chromonemata) segregate and move along the threads of the spindle, one half going to the upper pole of the spindle, the other half to the lower pole (anaphase). They there form two new nuclei while the threads of the spindle form a membrane in the middle of the old cell (telophase). Each of the daughter cells, therefore, receives one of the halves of each of the original chromosomes of the mother cell.

Since the chromosomes are always present in pairs, the normal nucleus is called diploid. The number of chromosomes and their forms are the same in all cells of the organism and in all organisms of the same species. The nuclei of human cells have two complements of 23 chromosomes each; altogether, therefore, each nucleus possesses 46 chromosomes. This is an indication that, notwithstanding all external differences, all human beings belong to the same species *homo sapiens.*

Under a powerful microscope, the chromosomes appear as a thick bundle of molecules composed of numerous parts (somewhat like rolls of coins). The parts of the chromosomes (the single coins) are made up of the chromomeres, beadlike granules arranged in a linear series in each chromonema. The chromomeres contain the genes. The genes are the bearers of the characteristics of living organisms transmitted from one generation to the other. The genes consist of molecules formed by two spirals (helices) of deoxyribonucleic acid, usually referred to by the abbreviation DNA. In most cells, the helix turns right but biologists have also found left-handed helices. The DNA helices contain the 'instructions' for the activities of the cell called the 'genetic code'. In experiments, parts of the helix of one species of organisms have been cut out and inserted into the helix of another species (recombinant DNA) which thereby received the hereditary properties of the first species connected with these genes ('genetic engineering'). The advocates of genetic engineering stress the valuable organic products obtainable by this method (for example, insulin or interferon), the opponents fear that the method could result in an uncontrollable synthesis of harmful products or in diseases that cannot be overcome by the organisms.

Biologists use what I can only consider as metaphorical language when explaining the mechanism of heredity. The genetic 'instructions' contained in the DNA molecules are said to be 'coded' in a chemical 'alphabet' employing four different 'letters' to form 'three-letter words'. The four letters, also called the 'symbols' of the 'language' in which the genetic code is written are the four bases adenine, guanine, cytosine and thymine. They form the bridges keeping the two strands of the double helix together and come in pairs in which adenine is always linked to thymine and guanine to cytosine.

To my mind, information, knowledge, experience, language and similar expressions, if used in their literal sense, necessarily presuppose and imply consciousness. If they are used in an analogous, figurative or metaphorical meaning, the context should make clear just what the words signify. I do not deny that the genes actually are the means by which heredity works and that the mechanism involves the double helix, but I cannot detect the slightest indication of the meaning of the 'information' the genes are said to contain and pass on. What exactly are the 'instructions' said to be coded, transmitted, mutilated, repaired or destroyed?

A third form of cell division, called meiosis or reduction division, occurs in the formation of the sex cells. In this form, the chromosomes do not divide but half of the chromosomes move to one pole and the other half to the other pole of the spindle so that the sex cells have only half the number of chromosomes of ordinary cells (the diploid chromosome number is reduced to the haploid). In ordinary cells, one of the complements of chromosomes comes from the father and the other half from the mother. The one set of chromosomes which the sex cell receives in the reduction division is a mixture of the chromosomes derived from the father and the mother. Each sex cell, therefore, contains a set of chromosomes (and thereby hereditary properties linked to the genes) which is different from other sex cells, so that the children of the same parents are different unless they are identical twins, that is, twins developed from a single fertilised ovum.

This process also constitutes the basis of the differentiation of the offspring in male and female descendants. The two sets of chromosomes in each diploid cell are the same with the exception of the sex chromosomes, usually referred to as X and Y. In man (and in all mammals and flies), the cells of the male individual contain an XY pair of chromosomes whereas the cells of females contain an XX pair (in butterflies, fishes and birds, the cells of females contain an XY pair and those of males an XX pair). The Y chromosome is usually smaller than the X chromosome and may even be absent.

The cells of man include 22 pairs of non-sex chromosomes (called autosomes), and either a pair of XX or XY chromosomes. In the reduction division forming the sex cells, all female cells will have an X chromosome (22+X) whereas one half of the spermatozoa will have an X chromosome (22+X) and the other half a Y chromosome (22+Y). There exists, therefore, an equal probability that fertilisation will result in a zygote (the cell formed by the union of spermatozoon and ovum) with an XX pair of chromosomes (22+X + 22+X = female offspring) or in one with an XY pair of chromosomes (22+X + 22+Y = male offspring) so that on average the number of male and female descendants will be equal. A French researcher has called the female sex the basic sex and the male sex a manipulation of the female sex. For every male cell (with the exception of one half of the sex cells) contains the female X chromosome and an X chromosome is essential for life. On the other hand, the sex of a child depends on the sex chromosome in the sperma-tozoon fertilising the ovum.

A Japanese team developed a technique for separating sperms with X chromosomes from those with Y chromosomes. The process is based on the observation that X and Y chromosomes carry slightly different electrical charges. The semen is mixed in a solution, slightly centrifuged and then poured into a narrow space between two sheets of glass, one near a negative electrode, the other near a positive one. All the X-bearing sperm gather near the positive electrode while 83 per cent of the sperm near the negative electrode have Y chromosomes.

A different sperm-separation procedure is based on the discovery that sperm with Y chromosomes are somewhat better swimmers than X-bearing sperm. Albumin, a liquid protein, impedes the mobility of X-type sperm more than that of sperm with Y chromosomes. If semen is placed on top of a glass column containing albumin, the sperm remaining on top after 2½ hours are of the X type while about 80 per cent of the sperm at the bottom carry Y chromosomes. The method is said to have led to the conception of boys in 75 per cent of the cases when the sperm at the bottom was used for artificial insemination.

Besides the danger of possible birth defects, the question must be asked whether it is morally permissible to manipulate the sex of human beings.

Heredity

The nucleus of the zygote retains a full complement of (46) chromo-somes but the chromosomes (and therefore the hereditary properties) are neither identical with those of the father nor with those of the mother. Sexual propagation includes a twofold variation, first, the selection involved in the formation of the sex cells, then, the difference resulting from the union of the male and female gametes. Hereditary properties, therefore, can go back to the father as well as the mother. However, researchers found that the genetic material of the mito-chondria comes exclusively from the mother. The mitochondria are tiny rod- or ball-shaped bodies found in all plant and animal cells. They convert food energy into a form that the cell can use for movement, the production of protein, the synthesis of DNA and almost every other life function.

It should be mentioned that the genes are not the only instru-mentality of hereditary transmission. Equally important is the germ plasm, the protoplasm of the germ cells (also called idioplasm) which transmits characteristics not subject to Mendel's laws. The plasma of the zygote comes almost entirely from the ovum (which is natural since the volume of the ovum is 85,000 times larger than that of the spermatozoon) so that the non-Mendelian characteristics are based on the plasma type of the mother.

It can happen that irregularities occur in the process of the distribution of the chromosomes. Spermatozoa as well as ova can be equipped with too few or too many sex chromosomes. Sometimes, both chromosomes of a pair may go to one sex cell (nondisjunction). When two sex cells unite, there can then be not two paired chromosomes but three. Such a cell is called trisomic (for example, XXX, XXY). The unpaired chromosome may be fused to another chromosome and can then be carried through the succeeding generations. When neither chromosome of a pair goes to a germ cell, the zygote is short of a chromosome and has one chromosome impaired. This is called a monosomic anomaly (monosomy).

Individuals with three X-chromosomes have all female sexual characteristics and are often called superwomen but they are infertile. In the case of the XXY chromosome, the individual has the appearance of a man but the testes are small and do not produce spermatozoa. An XO chromosome (that is, a chromosome consisting of only one female chromosome) gives a female type in external appearance and sexual organs but such individuals do not achieve sexual maturity.

There are cases in which an extra male chromosome is found (XYY) but a chromosome structure of 44 autosomes and a pair of YY chromosomes is impossible. An X chromosome is necessary even for intrauterine life. Very rare combinations such as XXXY or XXYY are usually linked with mental deficiencies; such individuals are infertile but of abnormal sexuality. These more complex anomalies usually disrupt development so early that spontaneous abortion occurs. This happens also in the case of trisomies of all but a few small chromosomes and of all monosomies except those involving sex chromosomes.

The so-called intersexuality in which an individual possesses male as well as female sex characteristics (for example, the external sex organs of one and the sex glands of the other) can be the effects of irregularities in the sex chromosomes. These gynandromorphisms do not constitute special forms of the human being but are rare and accidental (resulting from unpredictable causes) deviations from the norm.

Man and woman are differentiated in body build, sex functions, and the unit of each living organism, the cell. The anatomy distinguishing male from female is the result of the development which starts with the origin of the embryo and gains its functional adequacy in puberty.

Embryonic Development

In the beginning of the embryonic development, there is no indication what the sex will be. The formation of the genitals begins in the seventh week but gender is not recognisable until the end of the third month. (Foetal life is usually calculated on the basis of the first day of the last menstruation which precedes the actual fertilisation by an average of two weeks but is generally the only reliable mark.) The genetic material from which the development of the sex organs and gonads of both male and female embryos starts is the same and no difference appears in the early stages of the intrauterine development.

From the inner cell mass (that is, the cells not split off for the formation of the yolk sac, amnion, allantois and umbilical cord), two undifferentiated gonads and two pairs of parallel ducts (Wolffian and Müllerian ducts) are formed. Externally, a protrusion appears where the sex organs develop and below it a groove (urethral groove). The groove is flanked by two folds (urethral folds). On either side of the genital protrusion and the grooves are two ridgelike swellings (labioscrotal swellings). Until the gonads start to differentiate into either testicles or ovaries, the material from which the sexual apparatus of the embryo evolves seems undetermined. If testes appear, they secrete two hormones, one of which causes the Müllerian duct to recede and finally to vanish almost completely. On the other hand, the Wolffian duct is formed into the vas deferens (the duct that transports the sperm from the epididymis to the penis), the epididymis (where the spermatozoa are stored), the seminal vesicle and related organs. The urethral folds grow together to form the urethral tube of the penis. The genital protrusion becomes a penis and the ridges on either side of the urethral groove are joined to the scrotal sac into which the testes descend later.

The other hormone, testosterone, plays an important role not only in the development of both internal and external sex organs, but also later. It circulates throughout the body in the bloodstream. Together with related hormones that are derived from it, it diffuses into cell nuclei where it switches on genes for masculinisation. It is involved in the appearance of the secondary sex characteristics such as facial hair and manly muscles and causes subtle differences in the chemistry of organs like the liver and the kidneys. According to recent research, the male hormones may be a factor in coronary heart disease. Women suffer far less heart disease and on average live longer than men. It has long been known that men may be relatively impotent after drinking and alcoholics are completely impotent, even after they stop drinking. The reason is that alcohol reduces the production of testosterone and thereby interferes with sperm production.

The hormones secreted by the gonads contain male as well as

female factors and sexual specificity means the prevalence of one or the other of the sexual determinations. In this sense, there is no one-hundred per cent man and no one-hundred per cent woman, and this also involves the possibility that temporarily (for example, during puberty or the menopause) features of the opposite sex may appear.

In the development of a female embryo, the Wolffian duct retrogresses while the Müllerian duct is formed into the Fallopian tubes, uterus, and part of the vagina. The clitoris evolves from the genital protrusion, and the groove below the clitoris stays open to become the vulva. The inner lips of the vulva (labia minora) are shaped from the folds alongside the groove while the ridgelike swellings grow into the large lips (labia maiora).

In the later months of female foetal life, the primary ovarian follicles develop. They are primordial sex cells encased in a capsule consisting of a single layer of ordinary cells. At birth, such follicles number several hundred thousand, and they remain dormant until puberty.

In the early stages of embryonic development, the formation of the head overshadows the growth of the other parts of the body which differentiate in dependence from the head and create the preconditions for man's erect walk in mutual interaction. This kind of dominance of the development of the brain is not found in animals.

An important aspect of the embryonic development of man and the genesis of all other organisms is the holistic integration of the growth processes. Many scientists and philosophers have denounced such an approach as 'unscientific' and 'anthropomorphic', but the fact that the development constitutes a unified process in which all parts grow in conformity with one another and with the whole cannot be denied. There is no reason whatever for such a conformity in the single physical or chemical processes and the assertion that no reason is needed amounts to the negation of its intelligibility. Biologists who regard the genes as the bearers of hereditary properties speak of 'instructions' contained in the 'genetic code' of the DNA helices directing cell activity. This, of course, is also a highly anthropomorphic expression because nobody has ever seen such 'instructions' under the microscope, and that certain processes 'transmit' such instructions is a metaphorical interpretation.

In 1859, Ernst Haeckel proclaimed his 'fundamental biogenetic law' as a principle of his morphology. This 'law' asserted that ontogenesis (the development of the individual organism) is an abbreviated phylogenesis (development of a type or kind of organism). This proposition had already been refuted by Karl Ernst von Baer, the founder of modern embryology, and Dr E. Blechschmidt has called the fundamental biogenetic law one of the most glaring errors of biology. Man's ontogenesis is an integrated advance in differentiation, and there is no hiatus up to which it would be impossible to regard the embryo as something else than a human embryo.

The attempts at a mechanistic interpretation completely disregard the character of the cell as a holistic system. The development is not controlled by the 'genetic information' contained in the genes. The genes only react to the stimulation of the plasma, the extragenetic substance of the cell. The cell always operates as a unit, and the genes are only of significance within the totality of the cell. For the process of differentiation, the genes constitute a necessary condition but not the sufficient reason. Differentiation is only possible if the 'genetic information' is incorporated into the autonomous phenogenetic process of differentiation of the cell.

The two blastomeres resulting from the first cleavage of the fertilised ovum are different in their metabolism which means that they 'read' the genetic instructions differently. The differentiation is largely controlled by influences not contained in the genetic substance of the ovum. It is directed by the peculiar biodynamic properties of the cell by which the genes are subject to different influences depending on the difference of position. The cells of the primary germ layers of the embryoblast, for example, do not have predetermined, limited capabilities. These germ layers have developmental potencies that exceed the formations that actually derive from them. They constitute assembly grounds from which the component parts of the embryo emerge in a process which is not completely determined by the antecedent conditions nor by environmental factors. Biological processes are always more than just mechanical phenomena. Already the simple fact that symmetrical as well as asymmetrical arrangements are found and that these arrangements fit into the holistic structure of the organisms indicates that the processes are not mere accidental happenings.

Teleology

The direction of the life processes in accordance with the requirements of the organism as a whole is not limited to the embryonic and foetal development. Processes such as breathing and digestion take place independently of consciousness. Man can breathe more or less rapidly but what happens in breathing (supply of oxygen and removal of the carbon dioxide resulting from the oxidisation process) or digestion cannot be regulated by man's will (naturally, interference by drugs and so forth is possible). Human life would be impossible if these processes would require conscious control. The same, of course, holds true for other organisms. Ordinary and extraordinary growth processes (for example, the healing of a wound) take place in accordance with norms inherent in the organism and are directed so as to meet the needs of the entire organism. Many of the processes essential to procreation, such as the production of sperm and ova, the woman's monthly cycle and the secretion of hormones, are spontaneous, that is, independent of conscious control (here again, arbitrary influence, such as by drugs, is possible). These processes are inherently directed to the generation of offspring which means that the teleology characteristic of every organism extends not only to the development and functioning of the individual but also to the conservation of the species.

Mechanism

The majority of today's biologists and writers on the philosophy of nature reject teleological considerations and regard the use of the concept of 'purpose' for describing biological processes as an anthropomorphism although they cannot avoid using 'purposeful' or similar expressions in their own elucubrations. The phenomenon of inherent teleological ordainment of all organisms is incontestable and the dispute concerns the explanation of the phenomenon. Mechanism holds that organisms are nothing more than complicated machines; that the whole is the sum of its parts, and that the activities of the parts can be reduced to purely physico-chemical laws. The advances in molecular biology will be able to explain the arrangement of the parts which are moved by an internal energy source in accordance with a built-in programme of purposeful action.

As against mechanism, vitalism maintained the view that an immanent factor — often called the vital principle — constituted the foundation of the unity, wholeness and purposefulness of all organisms. Organisms are subject to the laws of organic life but every organism constitutes a supramechanical whole in which the single mechanical, physical and chemical processes are ordained toward the whole in a 'prospective tendency'. In order to explain the 'obstinate' development towards the goal of a final form not determined by the initial situation and environmental conditions, Hans Driesch, the founder of neo-vitalism, repudiated the mechanistic creed of his teacher Haeckel and postulated an immaterial teleological factor which, following Aristotle, he called entelechy. Only such a factor, Driesch thought, could account for the harmonious cooperation of all chemical and physical phenomena in organisms as well as the origin and reproduction of integral structures. The relative indetermination of the germ plasm, for example, in experiments with eggs of frogs, tritons and sea urchins, was one of the points of departure for Driesch. He called attention to the teleological phenomena in the restitution and regeneration of organisms (hydroid polyps such as the Tubularia and the Clavellina) and what he termed equipotential and totipotential systems. Driesch stressed the harmony in the composition and function of organisms; for example, subsystems such as eyes or ears develop relatively independently but come out in the right places and proportionate to the entire system; functions such as blood circulation and digestion work independently but are regulated so as to correspond to one another. These phenomena, Driesch maintained, defy an explanation by purely mechanistic theories.

Biologists have rejected Driesch's entelechy mainly because such a factor cannot be proven independently of the phenomena that it seeks to explain. But teleology is a reality. Aristotle's doctrine of entelechy does not mean the adaptation of a means to a consciously chosen purpose but the immanent ontological ordainment of a being towards its specific goal. Vitalism has been pronounced dead but the problems it tried to solve remain unanswered. Some biologists retain the basic idea that organisms must be seen as functioning wholes which cannot be understood by means of physics and chemistry alone. This point of view has been called organicism. The unifiedness and wholeness of the activities of every organism demand an explanation which is not given by the theory that organisms are complicated mechanical systems operating within the parameters of molecular biology. The levels of organisation with the biological ends of maintenance and reproduction cannot be reduced to the modes of action of lower unities.

It is true, as Kant has said, that purposes cannot be observed in nature and that natural purposefulness is an interpretation. But the wholeness of the organism, its integrated structure and function can be observed and the assertion that such an organism is the result of purely mechanical causes is irrational. The structural and functional integration is something basically different from the sum of the parts and the accumulation of physical and chemical processes. Evolutionists maintain that adaptation, usefulness or purposefulness is merely the result of a selective process by which the useless, inefficient and disadvantageous was eliminated. In retrospect, it appears as if the 'survival of the fittest' had been intended, but it is merely the outcome of a random development in which there have also been useless and faulty forms.

Accident, the 'antipode of intelligence', is insufficient to explain order in the technical sphere and neither accident nor 'natural selection' provides a rationale to the origin of order in the organic world. Without 'know-how' (information, idea, 'logos'), matter cannot produce order. It is strange that scientists who claim that organisms (which they regard as complex machines) have been produced by accident, have been unable to find even a primitive mechanical contraption produced by accident in the millions of years of the world's existence. A purely mechanistic explanation leaves the intelligibility of nature and man unexplained. Today's biologists use the term 'teleonomy' (introduced 1958 by Colin S. Pittendrigh) to designate apparently purposeful phenomena in organisms which, they think, can be explained entirely by purely mechanistic efficient causality. Teleonomy, therefore, simply registers the fact of actual teleology and, denying metaphysical teleology, considers it as an accidental result in an ateleogical cosmos. Order, the most essential aspect of the structure and function of all organisms, transcends the explanatory capabilities of molecular biology.

A consideration related to entirely different phenomena but also requiring the integrated wholeness of the organism is the unity of consciousness in man and at least in the higher animals.

Fulguration

The impasse of evolutionism results from the certitude that somewhere in the evolutionary process something new must have appeared but that we do not know how. Konrad Lorenz tried to solve this problem by his theory of 'fulguration'. If two independent systems are combined, entirely new properties may appear, properties that the independent systems did not posses, not even rudimentarily. In the same way, if a linear chain of causality closes to form a circle, a system can arise in which the functional properties are not only gradually but fundamentally and essentially different from the subsystems.

Progress in the organic evolution has almost always resulted from the integration of a number of independently functioning pre-existing systems to a unity of a higher order and in the course of this integration, changes appeared that adapted the subsystems to cooperation in the higher integrated system. In the course of the subsequent evolution, the new system is often simplified by the specialisation of the subsystems to a particular function whereas in the new division of labour, functions which the subsystems used to perform are taken over by other parts of the total.

The system of higher integration cannot be deduced from the subsystems which remain as elements in the higher system, and the construction of the higher system is a 'fulguration', a unique and purely accidental event.

The theory of fulguration is a typical *petitio principii* (begging the question). Undoubtedly, the combination of two independent systems to an integrated higher system can produce entirely new functions, but what caused the combination? Accident, says Lorenz. But the combination is a meaningful, teleological formation for which an adequate reason is necessary — accident is the negation of reason. The fulguration theory assumes that such a combination is possible and that the systems are compatible and complementary — a completely unproven and gratuitous assumption. Lorenz thinks that the combination just 'happens', but the problem exactly is how it could happen.

A completely different problem from the inherent teleology of living things is the order in the universe, the basis of all natural laws.

Just as scientists have taken the position that the order in organisms is a mere fact and that there is nothing to explain, old and modern philosophers have maintained that human understanding can only register the phenomenon of universal order and that the question 'why' is inapplicable and irrelevant. This is intellectual nihilism. Plato linked the phenomenal universe to the realm of eternal ideas by having the demiurg, the artificer of the world, shape the cosmos in view of the ideas, particularly the highest idea, the good. But he also assumed a world soul as the inner principle of the orderly movement of the universe. Stoicism supplanted the teleological views of Plato and Aristotle by attributing the order of the universe to the activity of world reason, a rational force operating purely as an efficient cause.

Influenced by theology, Saint Augustine and the Scholastic philosophers of the Middle Ages elaborated the Christian doctrine of creation in which Plato's ideas became the prototypes of all possible participations of God's being in finite beings. These ideas, eternally present in the divine mind, are the exemplary cause of the order in the universe created by God's omnipotence which constitutes the basis of the teleological argument for God's existence. The concepts of exemplary cause and final cause used by Scholastic philosophy do not provide an explanation but indicate phenomena requiring a reason for their intelligibility.

A factor to be considered in the development of all organisms is the interaction with the environment. The form into which man (and the same, of course, holds true for animals and plants) develops, results from the hereditary properties peculiar to the organism and its reaction to the influences of the environment. The hereditary potentialities include the capacity to respond differently to different conditions. In some organisms, this plasticity is very great which enables them to adapt to a wide range of environmental conditions. Dandelions possess an enormous ability of modification and can adapt to large differences in climate while orchids succumb even to slight changes in the environment. Man can expand his hereditary ability of adaptation because, as a cultural being, he can modify his environmental conditions. But man is not the product of his environment. Even the best environment cannot produce something good if the hereditary potential is bad. In man, the somatic aspects of his growth are subject to the conditions of his inherited nature, man's conscious activities, however, are influenced but not determined by his inheritance and man must form his personality himself.

3

Development of Sexuality

AT BIRTH, BOYS AND GIRLS POSSESS the entire neurophysiological equipment, but the reproductive system is inoperative and the development to sexual maturity proceeds in several unequal stages.

Hormones

Of enormous significance for the specific development of the two sexes are the hormones, above all the characteristic sex hormones, testosterone in the male and estrogen and progesterone in the female. The influence of hormones on growth as well as behaviour has been studied more thoroughly in animals than in man but some results seem to have general application. Hormones initiate structural changes in the brain, for example, changes at the junctions between nerve cells, affecting the 'messages' that can pass from one nerve to another, as well as changes in the gross volume of different groups of brain cells. Sex hormones also activate specific responses in the brain later in life. Testosterone induces copulatory behaviour in the males of many species, and estrogen and progesterone have an equivalent effect on females. In animals, hormones are involved in the recognition of a suitable mate and in the subsequent courtship patterns; they also influence the roles of the two sexes in rearing the young and are connected with feeding preferences, male aggression, learning ability, habits of play and responses to brain damage.

The influence of sex hormones on human behaviour is more difficult to examine. This is partly because of the comparative ease of experimenting with animals but it also reflects the concentration of effects of sex hormones in instinctive parts of the brain (such as the amygdala and hypothalamus). Man's greatly enlarged neocortex, or thinking brain, is able to override these instinctive parts of the brain. So the effects of nature are harder to separate from those of upbringing and culture.

After birth and until puberty, the testicles and ovaries produce relatively few hormones, and little boys and girls are much alike in size and appearance. At puberty, however, these organs begin to produce hormones in greater abundance, with dramatic results. The androgens secreted in boys cause changes in body-build, greater muscular development, body and facial hair, and voice change. In girls, the estrogens stimulate breast development, menstruation, and feminine body-build. A boy castrated before puberty does not develop masculine physical characteristics and possesses in adult life more of a feminine body-build, lacks masculine body and facial hair, has small genitalia and less muscular strength and retains a high voice. The growth of a girl who has her ovaries removed before puberty is less markedly affected but her body-build remains childlike, she does not develop breasts and never menstruates. Castrated individuals or persons producing insufficient amounts of hormones can be helped by the administration of appropriate hormones.

Some behavioural effects of hormones have been observed among girls suffering from a genetic defect resulting in an excess of male hormones from foetal life onward. Such girls develop male genitals, and even if this condition is corrected shortly after birth, the girls tend to exhibit tomboyish behaviour. They like intense outdoor activities but have little interest in playing with dolls or looking after babies. They do not, however, show the aggressive behaviour typical of boys and have normal heterosexual inclinations when they grow up.

High levels of testosterone have been linked to violence, particularly aggressive sexual behaviour. Treatment with drugs has reduced the erotic behaviour and subdued the disturbing sexual fantasies often experienced by such patients. On the other hand, men with congenitically low levels of testosterone seem to be comparatively unaggressive and have weak sexual appetites. In some of these men, treatment with testosterone has increased their sexual drive.

The reproductive glands are not the only tissues that release sex hormones. The placenta, through which all exchanges between foetus and mother take place, itself produces tremendous amounts of female hormones together with some male hormones which are secreted by the mother during pregnancy. As a rule, these hormones are produced too late to do any harm to the foetus, but not always. The female foetus is fairly immune because additional female hormones merely cause a child to be more feminine than usual at an early age. Male embryos, however, may be more seriously affected if the female hormone influences their development at an early stage. Boy babies may be born that are really males but under the impact of the feminising hormones appear superficially to be females and are raised as such. Even when they grow older, they usually have more or less sterile, undescended testes and an imperfect penis. The breasts are well developed, they have an unbroken voice and no beard. Such cases occur at a rate of about one in a thousand male births and may account for some of the sex changes. If the children are less severely affected, their hidden testes begin to secrete male hormones in abundance upon reaching puberty. The false female characteristics are suppressed and the male pattern asserts itself in breasts, beard, voice and sexual orientation. What were thought to be girls in their youth change into the men they were intended to be.

There are, however, also cases in which infants who seemed to be boys actually were girls. Recently, a woman who had been raised as a boy in the first four years of her life gave birth to a healthy son, 21 years after undergoing sex change operations. The baby had been damaged by a male sex hormone, methyltesterone, given to her mother during pregnancy. The child had normal female chromosomes, a womb, Fallopian tubes and ovaries which, however, were not visible while the drug had resulted in the development of a tiny penis.

Doctors recommended a change to the female sex because the penis was so small that a normal sex life in the male role seemed most unlikely whereas a fertile female sex life was possible. The woman had to undergo an operation to clear blocked Fallopian tubes in 1980 and conceived in 1984.

Infants' Development

Some authors have distinguished five phases in the development of infants: the oral phase from birth until the end of the first year (experience of pleasure from the region of the mouth); the anal phase in the second and third year (experience of pleasure from the anal region); the oedipal phase in the second and third year (characterised by the relation to the parent of the opposite sex); the phallic phase which starts in the fourth year (growing interest in genitals); and the genital phase which forms the last stage of sexual development (interest in the opposite sex).

This scheme which is strongly influenced by Freudian theories suffers from a one-sided emphasis on sexuality. There is no proof that sexuality, above all the Oedipus and Electra complexes, plays the role asserted by psychoanalysis in every human being or that the five-stage sequence constitutes the typical form of human development. One of the basic assumptions of Freud's pansexualism is the unconscious mechanism of man's instincts and the repression of sexuality. According to Freud, the sex instinct becomes active with the start of man's growth. Immediately after birth, the infant is without relation to the world and centred on himself. Freud calls this autoerotic: the infant knows only himself. The infant's sucking of the mother's breast is a lustful oral-sexual act, and the emotional relation between mother and child a camouflaged sexual relationship.

At the age of three, the little boy discovers his penis and feels the desire to copulate with his mother. This incestuous urge is the basis of Freud's theory of the Oedipus complex. The boy's father constitutes the main obstacle to the fulfilment of his longing for his mother which creates the dark impulse of killing his rival. At the same time, the boy fears that the father would retaliate against the attempt on his life by cutting off the boy's penis (Freud's so-called castration complex). The boy is already aware that women and girls have no penises and he surmises that they have been castrated because they wanted to possess their mothers. When examining their sex organs, girls discover that they lack a penis. The penis envy which Freud invented as a counterpart to the boys' fear of castration forms the centre of a lifelong inferiority complex. (Freud's psychoanalysis seems primarily a psychology of the male and the extension to the female, particularly the Electra complex, makes the impression of an afterthought.)

Freud called the period in the infant's development in which Oedipus complex and penis envy arise the phallic phase. The infant's defacation is a source of sexual pleasure which is threatened by overstrict toilet training. Freud found a connection between sado-masochism and the anal phase of infantile sexuality.

In Freud's view, sexual pleasure constitutes the basic purpose of human existence and the repression of the sex instinct is the cause of neuroses, sexual dysfunctions and perversions. Religious or moral restraints push the unfulfilled sexual desires into the subconscious, and the frustrations that produce neuroses and perversions start in earliest infancy. Freud believed that neuroses would disappear if the suppressed sexual desires were brought out of the unconscious into the light of consciousness — the basic concern of psychoanalysis.

While psychoanalysis has attained the status of a dogma in the United States, China's Communist Party warned against the seeping of Freudian theories into Chinese ideology and branded the assertion that the sex impulse is the most important basis of human behaviour as erroneous. 'According to the principles of historical materialism', the Red Flag magazine wrote, 'the material conditions of social life are the most important basis determining human behaviour'.

On account of Freud's materialistic philosophy, he failed to under-stand the most crucial factor in his field, the human psyche. The degradation of the human spirit to sexual instinct is the basic flaw of Freud's theories. Man's interaction with his environment starts with his birth, and the relations with other human beings constitute the most important experiences of the outside world. At an early stage, these experiences involve not only the senses but also the mind. The biolo-gical aspects of human development are much less important than the influences which provide the occasions for the unfolding of man's hereditary potential and the learning process by which social norms and values are assimilated.

Freud's theory of infantile sexuality was already repudiated by Carl Gustav Jung, Freud's erstwhile follower, and Alfred Adler, another of Freud's disciples who turned against the master, discredited the Oedipus complex by showing that Freud had not only grossly mis-understood the Oedipus myth but had also based his theory on his own sexual hang-ups, his infatuation with his mother and his jealousy of his father. Adler himself considered man primarily as a social being who acquires his basic qualities through socialisation in early childhood.

The theory that man is attracted by the breasts of women because, as a child, he received nourishment, warmth and security from his mother's breast of which he was then deprived is equally unconvincing. It is true that in a society in which women usually do not bare their bosom, a woman's breasts, possibly the most sensuous feature of the female form, constitute an erogenous zone, often more exciting than the pudenda, the buttocks or the thighs. Touching or kissing the breasts, particularly the nipples, is a customary part of the foreplay and a means of sexual stimulation. In view of the biological modalities, the role of the breasts as symbols of feminine sexuality is just as obvious as that of the penis as a masculine sex symbol, and it is unnecessary to go back to subconscious reminiscences of infantile sexuality. Needless to say, the role of the woman's breasts as a sex emblem is perfectly compatible with their role as a symbol of motherhood, but the rationale of these roles is different.

Puberty

In the overall development of human sexuality, puberty constitutes an extremely important phase. This period is initiated by the release of a chemical called lutinising hormone release factor (LHRF) from a part of the brain known as hypothalamus. The hypothalamus is the brain's control centre for many chemicals that influence behaviour. The LHRF discharged by the hypothalamus stimulates the pituitary gland to secrete hormones called gonadotropines which, in turn, induce the production of the specific male and female hormones (testosterone and estrogen) that bring on puberty.

Puberty is characterised by accelerated growth. At the culmination of the growth period, the increase in the height of the body would correspond to a rate of 10.5 cm a year for boys and 9.0 cm for girls. Actually, this tempo is not maintained during a full year. In the six months preceding and the six months following the fastest spurt, the addition to bodily height comes to 7-12 cm for boys and 6-11 cm for girls. Head, brain and lymphatic tissues achieve the relatively most rapid growth in the first six years of life whereas the sex organs complete their development during puberty. In boys, the accelerated growth of the sex organs starts with the testes and the scrotum; the skin of the scrotal pouch becomes reddish and wrinkled. A little later, pubic hair begins to appear. About a year after the fastest bodily growth and the accelerated growth of the scrotum, the penis becomes larger, and under the influence of the same stimuli, the seminal vesicle, the prostrate gland and the bulbourethral (Cowper's) gland, which all contribute to the spermatic fluid also grow. But ripe spermatozoa are not produced before the age of 15. About a year after the growth of the penis, the first ejaculation takes place. Axillary hair appears about two years after the first growth of pubic hair, and about the same time, beard and moustache begin to sprout. The other body hair (chest, arms and legs) comes considerably later than puberty.

Growth depends on a chemical produced by the hypothalamus known as growth hormone release factor (GRF) which stimulates the pituitary gland to make growth hormone. A GRF deficiency results in stunted growth. Midgets — persons who are extremely short but normally proportioned — often lack sufficient quantities of this key chemical. In 1982, researchers at the Salk Institute isolated GRF and produced synthetic copies of it in the laboratory. Recently, doctors tested synthetic GRF on two boys, aged 8 and 10 both of whom were 1 metre tall. They inserted pumps under the boys' skin which released bursts of GRF once every three hours, just as the hypothalamus does. The older boy who had been growing at a rate of less than 2.5 cm a year grew by the equivalent of about 14 cm a year during the treatment.

A boy's voice breaks and becomes harsh relatively late in the pubescent period. The change in voice results from the enlargement of the larynx, the elongation of the vocal chords under the influence of testosterone on the laryngeal cartilege, and the stronger resonance of the cavities over the larynx, such as mouth, nose and sinuses.

In boys and girls, the sebaceous glands develop, particularly in the armpits and the genital and anal regions. They cause the distinctive smell which is stronger in men than in women. The pores at the root of the nose enlarge and acne appears, especially in the face. Boys suffer more from acne than girls as an effect of hormonal secretions.

The chest shows some changes of which some are temporary and others permanent. Prior to puberty, the size of the areolae of boys and girls is the same but the areolae of girls become larger at puberty. Some boys experience a swelling of the breasts which, however, recedes later.

In girls, puberty starts with the enlargement of the breasts but in one-third of the girls, the appearance of pubic hair comes first. Together with the breasts, uterus, vagina, labia and clitoris also grow. The time from the first signs of puberty to complete sexual maturity differs greatly, from 18 months to six years. In girls, the average time from the enlargement of the breasts to the first menstruation is two-and-a-half years; but it may be as short as six months and as long as five-and-a-half years. On the basis of breast development, girls pass through puberty in a five-year period which may occur as early as the term from 8 to 13 or as late as the span from 13 to 18. Menstruation starts late in this period, between 10 and 16½, depending on the beginning of puberty. At that time, the ovaries do not yet produce ripe eggs, and although the uterus is sufficiently developed, girls have not reached sexual maturity and are not ready for a normal pregnancy. The first periods are often irregular and sometimes cause discomfort; frequently, no ovulation takes place. The beginning of menstruation is not seldom followed by an infertile period which may last up to one-and-a-half years but this is not certain in individual cases.

Girls' bodily growth during puberty is faster than that of boys but their sexual development is slower. Boys experience sexual excitement and the desire for sexual satisfaction earlier than girls but socially are not ready for marriage. In women, sexual desire reaches its climax in the middle of the twenties or in the thirties.

An American study conducted in 1981 found that 60 per cent of the boys experienced their first ejaculation at the age of 13, and 91 per cent had made this experience by age 15; on the other hand, 58 per cent of the girls had their first menstruation at age 12 and all girls had had menstruations by the age of 15. Also, by age 15, 38 per cent of boys and girls had had their first date. Of the girls, 30 per cent had indulged in petting by the age of 19 and 17 per cent had had intercourse.

Circumcision

Circumcision, the removal of part of the foreskin, is practised as a religious rite by Jews and Muslims but is also found among non-Muslim Arabs, Australian aborigines, Kaffirs and Papuans. It is often performed in infancy for sanitary reasons and may become necessary for medical grounds. Circumcision is not found in Eastern Asia although on account of genetic differences in the size of the foreskin, men may appear to be circumcised. In Japan, in particular, the prepuce naturally restracts at puberty leaving the gland exposed in most cases.

A special problem is the circumcision of girls which is very painful but widely practised in Africa and the Middle East. In its simplest form, the rite nicks the clitoris but in a more radical form, the entire clitoris and the labia are removed, apparently to enforce chastity by depriving women of sexual pleasure. A hardly less barbaric method is infibulation which assures virginity and thus enables the father to sell the girl at a higher price.

At the world conference of the United Nations Decade for Women in 1980, the delegation from Upper Volta (now Burkina Faso) left the conference hall when a resolution condemning sexual mutilation was debated, and other African delegates demanded that the deliberations should be confined to problems such as illiteracy, hunger and disease.

Officials of the World Health Organisation estimate that as many as 75 million women have been subjected to this rite. Recently President Daniel Arap Moi of Kenya banned the custom after 14 girls had died as a result of the excision. In France, police arrested a migrant sanitation worker from Mali who had removed his three-month-old daughter's clitoris with a pocket knife. Doctors saved the baby's life who had been bleeding intermittingly for two days before her parents brought her to an emergency hospital.

Legislation prohibiting excision has been passed in Norway, Sweden and Denmark after hospital workers had reported the effects of crude, amateur surgery. But there is no law against this operation in Britain and private doctors acknowledge that they perform clitoridectomies for immigrant women at fees as high as $1,700 although the Royal College of Obstetricians has called the procedure 'barbaric, futile and illogical'. A public outcry against the mutilation of girls in Britain seems to have prompted Arabs to shift their patronage from British to German clinics. A Malian labourers' group demanded that the French government guarantee their rights to live according to their customs, and the defence attorney of the father on trial for the mutilation of his daughter urged the judge to declare that no western law applied to the case. Some experts warned that prohibition of the practice would drive it further underground.

Adolescence

After their first menstruation, girls grow by about 6 cm, but their height can increase by twice as much. Although the basic form of the body is already fixed during the intrauterine development, the later growth is not without significance. Girls have a larger pelvis than boys already at birth which, of course, is related to the function of motherhood. But the pelvis enlarges further at puberty and due to the influence of estrogen on the hip bones, the hips become larger. This has nothing to do with pregnancy but makes women sexually more attractive to males.

Little is known with regard to the impact of emotions on puberty although emotional instability seems characteristic of the period. A noteworthy result of the interaction between environment and inheritance is the long-term tendency of an increase in height. Compared with the former generation, children now grow more quickly, they are stronger and healthier, and menstruation starts earlier. This development can be attributed to better environmental conditions, better food and healthier living conditions, better medical care and less illness, more sports and less heavy work.

Mentally and emotionally, young people want to be their own masters, to make their own decisions and to shape their own lives. On the other hand, they are not only materially dependent on their families but are also psychologically immature, unable to cope with their difficulties and to direct their own activities. One of the most difficult tasks of adolescents is to come to terms with their own sexual development, to understand the bodily changes and to grasp the meaning of the impulses they feel. Very often, young people are ashamed or even frightened by the manifestations of sexual maturation. In the People's Republic of China, some adolescent girls felt embarrassed when their breasts started to become larger. They bound them up tightly so that many young women are found with small, flat and concave breasts causing problems later in nursing their babies. Boys often feel ashamed when nocturnal emissions soil their night clothes or sheets. Mothers usually counsel their daughters when menstruation starts but boys are often left to their own devices. Telling them what to do (or not to do) would spare them much anguish and should be an integral part of sex education.

Adolescence may bring emotional disturbances which sometimes develop into psychoses requiring medical treament.

Maturity requires more than biological growth; man must also develop spiritually. Only when the growth of the body is accompanied by a corresponding cultivation of the mind can man become a fully-fledged member of society. Human growth must encompass both sides, the maturity as an individual and the preparation for his role in society, particularly his role in the propagation of the human race. Until puberty, man depends on the family into which he was born, and the adjustment to an independent role constitutes the special difficulty of adolescence.

For man, sexual maturity manifests itself in the erection of the penis and nocturnal emissions, but for the young woman, it brings the beginning of the cycle of preparation for and exclusion of pregnancy which gives a special character to the life of woman for many years. The propagation of the human race imposes tasks on man and woman, but the enlistment of the woman's body for this purpose makes much greater demands on woman than on man, and these demands become most exacting in motherhood which requires the maximum in physiological and psychological exertions. Woman, therefore, experiences human life in a particular way as feminine life, because her body and mind are singularly exposed to the natural changes connected with her sexual destiny. This may be one of the reasons for the greater adaptability of women.

Pre-menstrual Syndrome

In recent years, the so-called pre-menstrual syndrome has found much attention. It results from hormonal imbalances and causes psychic disorders in about 10 per cent of all women. The symptoms include physical complaints such as headaches, hot flushes, pelvic pain, breast pain or tenderness, oedema, abdominal swelling, change in bowel habits and thirst as well as psychological disorders such as irritability, tension, anxiety, aggression, depression, lethargy, insomnia, crying, change in appetite and sexual desire, loss of concentration and poor coordination. The condition may last anywhere from a day to two weeks before menstruation.

Pre-menstrual syndrome symptoms usually appear during the second part of the menstrual cycle and end when the bleeding begins. But some women have symptoms before and around the time the egg is released, then feel fine until just before the menstrual flow starts. Treatment is difficult because the cause is unknown and different women show different symptoms. The appearance of symptoms at different times in the cycle, the variation in response to medications and ambiguous results may indicate that there are more than one factor. Some doctors think brain chemicals are responsible, others believe hormonal abnormalities are to blame. One of the brain chemicals apparently connected with pre-menstrual syndrome is beta-endorphin, an opiate-like hormone. Scientists reported that in the beginning of the menstrual cycle, women with and without pre-menstrual syndrome had comparable levels of endorphin in their blood but that 20 days later, the levels were much lower in women suffering from pre-menstrual syndrome.

An American doctor found that a drug used in treating high blood pressure was effective in helping women suffering from pre-menstrual syndrome. The drug, *spironolactone,* stimulates the elimination of salt and water by suppressing aldosterone, a hormone that reabsorbs or retrieves salt in the kidneys. Researchers at Vanderbilt University in Nashville, Tennessee, distinguished two groups of sufferers. In one group, the progesterone levels never went as high as those in normal women and dropped off more steeply; in another, small group, women had higher than normal levels of an ingredient of another hormone, androgen. Treatment with progesterone worked for about 85 per cent of the first group, while anti-androgen therapy helped 50 per cent to 60 per cent of the latter group. Sometimes, doctors prescribe lithium, diuretics or anti-depressant medication before or during the pre-menstrual period.

In addition to medication and diet control, reducing stress by lessening the demands made on the woman seems to help. In some cases of child abuse or murder, courts have held that severe pre-menstrual syndrome diminishes responsibility.

The menstrual cycle implies not only physiological and psychological burdens, it may also disrupt ordinary living patterns. It requires special hygienic care, and the toxic shock syndrome connected with the use of tampons has even resulted in deaths.

Just as the rise of sexuality involves more marked changes in woman than in man, its downward curve also has a stronger impact on her. The menopause which usually occurs between the ages of 45 and

50, brings the gradual dismantling of the generative system. The retro-gradation of the sex glands affects the entire endocrine system and not only woman's physiological but also her psychic life. Whereas a woman in her late forties is no longer capable of childbirth (although there are considerable differences in the onset of the menopause), a man remains able to engender offspring until a relatively advanced age. This differ-ence, together with the other effects of aging on woman, is not without influence on marital relations and may be one of the reasons for repudiating the first wife and marrying a younger woman.

Sex Instinct

The anatomical features of sexuality indicate only the static part of man's sexual equipment. Essential to the functioning of sex are the impulses called sex instinct which originate in the central nervous system, particularly in the diencephalon. Two aspects of the sex instinct can be distinguished: the impulse to sexual activity arising from within and the receptivity to sexual stimulation. Sexual stimulation can come from external sense perception but also from imagination. There is some reflex sexual response which is not controlled by the brain. Stimulation of the genital and perineal region can cause the 'genital reflex': erection and ejacultion in the male, vaginal changes and lubrication in the female. But these reactions can be superseded and suppressed by voluntary decisions. The various systems of stimulation are not separated but are subject to different influences in the course of their development and their disorientation can derail man's sex life.

The sex instinct is one of the instincts found in man as well as animals. It impels to its satisfaction by the activation of the sex organs and is thereby directed to copulation. There are similarities and differences between the sexual behaviour of man and other primates, but what other primates do or do not do is entirely irrelevant to man.

Sometimes, instincts are distinguished from impulses. Instincts are inborn inclinations to a certain behaviour while impulses can be innate as well as acquired. The concept of instinct has often been criticised but instincts are basic mechanisms related to the preservation of the indivi-dual and the species (the quest for food, fear of danger, orientation, sex). There seems to be a sharp difference between the two basic instincts, the instinct of self-preservation ordained to conserve the life of the individual and the sex instinct linked to the continuation of the species. The instinct of self-preservation impels to actions directly related to its purpose while the satisfaction of the sex urge may serve purely individual and arbitrary desires. The manifestations of the sex instinct disappear when bodily strength is sapped by the lack of protein, undernourishment or consumptive diseases.

It is true that we know very little about the manner in which instincts operate. But the fact of instinctive actions is beyond doubt. The sucking of newborns cannot be explained by imitation or some other learning process (this is apparently not the case for the feeding of the infant by the mother). Instinctive actions are inherently teleological and even complex processes show great precision, but instincts are of little plasticity. Instincts cause tensions which impel to actions for their relief. The feeling of hunger, for example, arises at regular intervals on account of inner changes in the nerves and muscles of the stomach lining, but it can also be released or increased by external stimuli.

Characteristic of instincts is their orientation to their specific objects. The satisfaction of the instinct is achieved in a two-fold way, either positively by enjoying the pleasure connected with its gratification or negatively by relieving the discomfort arising from its disregard. The instinct impels to satisfaction without regard to other circumstances. If a dog is thirsty, it laps water wherever it finds it. If man allays his hunger or quenches his thirst or gratifies other wants, he considers many circumstances and does not simply follow the thrust of the instinct. To call this a restriction of human freedom reveals a misunderstanding of freedom and the nature of man. Freedom is not the same as licence. Freedom in its negative (freedom from) as well as its positive meaning (freedom to) includes responsibility, and responsible behaviour must recognise the order, values and norms given with human nature. Instinctive reflexes do not force man to act; they merely nudge him in a certain direction. Man can and must control the response to the instinctive impulses and cannot act by relying merely on his senses. He must decide by his reason whether and how to do what he is impelled to do by instinct and how to handle instinctive reflexes. Instinct does not dispense man from personal and social obligations.

The powerful urge of the sex instinct is one of the prominent phenomena of puberty and this experience often leads to masturbation. Children become aware of the pleasure associated with the activation of the sex organs long before puberty. In boys, playing with the genitals often becomes a habit and pre-schoolboys and girls already rub their genitals against tables or chairs. Masturbation is less common among girls than among boys. About 10 years ago a French study claimed that 81 per cent of all women had never masturbated but this certainly does not apply to the United States. Shere Hite found that masturbation was a regular feature of the sex life of both men and women. Girls start to masturbate earlier than boys, between five and ten, while boys begin between seven and twelve. Boys tell one another about masturbation but girls seldom speak to other girls about it. Boys also practise masturbation together (possibly because they also urinate together) which does not necessarily involve homosexual acts. According to Kinsey and some other researchers, children, both boys and girls, possess a greater capacity of experiencing multiple orgasms before puberty than thereafter, and this capability declines gradually with age.

It has sometimes been asserted that women do not feel sexual desires but this is certainly erroneous. The More Report† states that 96 per cent of the women covered in its second survey felt sexual lust. Age, sexual experience or marital status make little difference although, the same as in men, there are variations in intensity and susceptibility depending on, for example, health, mood and fatigue. The excitation of the sex instinct is the same as for males. Besides inner tension, stimulation by erotic representations or descriptions, talk or bodily contact, and encounter with or imagination of a sexually attractive person lead to sexual arousal. In males as well as females, the ultimate objective of sexual lust is orgasm, but there is a certain difference in the intermediate stage. In men, sexual stimulation centres on the erection of the penis but in women, it is not confined to the clitoris but extends also to the vagina and the nipples. Women who have had intercourse desire the insertion of the penis but also women without such an experience may stimulate the vagina by inserting their fingers or some other object.

An American sexologist, Dr Theresia Crenshaw, maintained that women have the equivalent of a prostrate and that the gland is the highly erogenous area called G Spot by some researchers. Autopsies, she said, indicated the existence of glandular tissue in the front wall of the vagina, between the bladder and the urethra. It contained acid phosphate, a substance not usually found in the female body but characteristically produced by the male prostrate. Her conclusion: 'There is another special erotic zone in women that some find sexually pleasurable and capable of producing orgasm'. The G Spot, a bean-sized area, is named after Dr Ernst Gräfenberg, a German gynaecologist who in 1944, first described a 'zone of erogenous feeling' in the vagina.

Women experience more intense sexual desire in connection with menstruation; the release of the ovum is connected with a stronger sexual urge. Women's experience of sexual lust accords with the finding of the More Report that 92 per cent of the women masturbate or have masturbated at one time or another, with the majority starting between the ages of eleven and fifteen.

Adolescent Sexuality

Traditional western morality expected that men and women did not have sexual intercourse before marriage. In recent decades, pre-marital sex has become almost commonplace in 'developed' countries and partners who had no sexual experience have apparently become exceptions. Moreover, the first sexual intercourse which used to occur in the

†The More Report comprises two surveys on female sexuality undertaken by the Japanese magazine *More*, published by Shûeisha in 1983.

beginning of the twenties may now happen in the early teens. This has resulted in a sharp increase in pregnancies among girls aged between 14 and 19.

Boys very often press their girlfriends into sexual relations while girls usually are reluctant to go all the way. They consent because they fear that their boyfriends will look for somebody else if they do not agree to intercourse, or they are afraid that they will be disliked if they refuse.

The present pattern of adolescent sexuality has, created an ambiguous attitude among girls with regard to 'virginity' (in the purely physical sense of an intact hymen). Many girls still consider virginity as something they should preserve until marriage but others want to lose their virginity as soon as possible so as to become a 'woman'. Some girls 'make a present of their virginity' as a sign of special affection and in the expectation of a lasting relationship but others feel that boys want to deflower as many girls as possible and then expect to marry a virgin. It happens that girls lose all restraints once they start having sex relations. A girl who gave up her virginity when she was 18 had affairs with ten different men within a year.

During the early nineteen seventies, students both male and female were loathe to admit that they had no sexual experience and girls were eager to lose their virginity in order to become 'women'. Now, virginity is considered very normal and nothing to be ashamed of.

Most youthful sexual experiences have nothing to do with true heterosexual love. In many cases, the motive is curiosity. Boys are often under strong peer pressure to prove themselves as men by seducing girls into sexual intercourse. These 'conquests' give them a feeling of superiority and boasting of sexual exploits is a favourite topic of 'masculine' conversation. It even happens that fathers or other relatives arrange for an adolescent boy to have intercourse with a prostitute in order to initiate him into sex life.

It is possible to distinguish man's physiological and psychological capabilities and processes but these capabilities do not exist or function separately. They belong to the unit man consisting of body and soul. The sex instinct, therefore, should not be treated as if it were the only manifestation of man's sexuality. The reason why man is a sexual being lies in the ordainment of sex towards the propagation of the human race. Sexuality exists because man is a reproducible being, and because reproduction is accomplished by the union of the two sexes, sexuality has a superindividual meaning. In and by itself, the sex instinct does not ensure the preservation of the human race because human offspring requires many years of care and training in order to become adult (biologically speaking, sexually mature) individuals. Man's sexuality, therefore, includes an element that leads to the socialisation of the sexual relations necessary for the rearing of children. This element has often been called 'erotic instinct'.

The sex instinct as the tendency to activate the sex organs has no continuity and is without social connotation. The sex act as the satisfaction of the sex instinct is an intermittent ephemeral event. It is only as a person that man feels the need for an emotional complement. The desire to love and be loved, to give oneself and to possess the other is necessarily involved in man's instinctive urge of wanting the physiological complement of his own sexuality. The lust for bodily union is made human only by the yearning for personal union. 'Sexus' must be joined by 'eros' in order to approach the partner not only as a sex object but as a person complementing and delighting one's own personality.

The connection of sensual sexuality with man's spiritual destiny determines the special nature of man's sexual potentiality which creates the depth and strength, the warmth and tenderness of a relation reflecting the freedom of man and the dignity of the human person.

4

Man's Body

IN THE HISTORY OF THOUGHT, the evaluation of man has been influenced by the denial of the spirit as well as by the denigration of the body. Materialism maintains that, basically, all being is material being so that the human spirit does not represent a special kind of being and man's living body essentially is not different from a heap of chemical substances. Man, in this view, is the product of a linear development in which every stage in the growing diversity of forms is deducible from the conditions prevailing at the preceding stage. This means that the transition from vegetative and sensitive life to the mind and spiritual consciousness does not involve any difference in kind from the being subject to and explainable by physico-chemical laws.

Spirit and Matter

On the other hand, the conflict between spirit and matter is a widely held way of thinking. A certain opposition between spirit and matter is already apparent in the doctrine of Zoroaster (Zarathrustra; around 500 BC). Zoroaster taught some kind of monotheistic religion. The supreme god, Ahura Mazda ('Wise Lord') is the creator of heaven and earth, the material and the spiritual world, the highest lawgiver, the originator of the moral order and the judge of the whole world. But Zoroaster's cosmogony involves two spirits whose free decisions lead to a good and an evil principle and to the struggle between the realm of justice and truth and the realm of falsehood and evil. Zoroaster's doctrine was transformed into an absolute dualism in which the good and creative spirit Spenta Mainyu, the offspring of Ahura Mazda, contends with Angra Mainyu (also called Ahrima), the evil spirit. The opposition between good and evil, however, is not the same as that between spirit and matter, although Zoroastrian ritual stressed purity in the sense of avoiding defilement by death or contact with dead matter. By his moral decision, man is drawn into the cosmic conflict of the good with the evil which will end with the triumph of the good and the glorifying transformation of the world.

Manichaeism

Many religions somehow seek the deliverance from the body. The more or less pessimistic religions consider the body by which man is fettered to the material world as a painful burden and the source of all evil.

The most sweeping devaluation of the body was propounded by Manichaeism. Mani (born 216 AD, death 274, 276 or 277) taught a rigorous dualism represented by two antagonistic substances, the absolute good and the radical evil. Spirit and matter, good and evil, light and darkness are irreconcilable opposites. Man's soul is a part of God that is imprisoned in bodily darkness. Salvation consists in man becoming aware of the divine origin of his soul and escaping the impurity of the flesh by renouncing copulation, procreation, possessing material goods, the eating of meat and the drinking of wine.

In the Manichean communities, only the 'elect' who hoped to be admitted to paradise upon death were bound to chastity, poverty and abstinence from meat and wine. The 'hearers,' who postponed the hope of redemption to later rebirths, supported the elect by works and alms. They lived in the world, could marry or have a mistress, produce children, drink wine and eat meat. With the exception of those who practice absolute continence, the shameful imprisonment in bodily darkness forced upon the luminous soul will cease only at the end of time when the absolute separation of light and darkness will be definitely reestablished.

Manichaeism expanded widely from Iran to Mesopotamia, Egypt, and North Africa where Saint Augustine for some time belonged to the sect which he later attacked. The Manicheans had adherents not only in all parts of the Roman Empire but as far as China. In the eighth century, Manichaeism became the official religion of Uighur, a realm in the northern part of Mongolia which extended from the Ili River in the West to the Huang Ho, the Yellow River, in the East. Manichean communities existed in Fukien province and on Taiwan. In the West, Manichean ideas reappeared in several movements, particularly in Catharism. In southern France, where the Cathari were commonly referred to as Albigensians (after Albi, their main centre), they lasted until the fourteenth century, and in Italy, Catharism was alive in the fifteenth century.

Mani considered himself as the last of a long line of heavenly messengers or prophets who began with Adam and included Zoroaster, Buddha and Jesus. A form of Zoroastrianism was the official religion of the Sassanids, and Mani came into contact with Jewish and Christian doctrines through the sect of the Elkhasites (followers of the prophet Elkhasai, about 100 AD). He encountered Buddhism in Beluchistan. Basically, however, Manichaeism was a form of gnosticism.

Gnosticism

Gnosticism, which goes back to Chaldean astrology, achieved its largest expansion in the Hellenistic world. In the first Christian centuries, the gnosis combined ideas of the Semitic and Iranian Orient with late Hellenistic philosophy and the Christian expectation of salvation. Gnosticism taught a fundamental dualism of spirit and matter which equated spirit with good and matter with evil. Through gnosis (interior illumination), the soul can be delivered from the body and regain the unity with God. The Christian gnostic sects which retained the dualism of spirit and matter taught that the world had not been created by the supreme god but by the demiurge (a borrowing from Plato). Christ was one of the numerous "aeons" who emanated from God and descended to earth but he only seemed to have a human body (Docetism) so as not to be enmeshed in sinful matter. Liberation from sin and matter is accomplished by ascetism and mystical rites through which the eternal union with God is obtained.

Classical Indian Yoga attributed the involvement in the unbearable odyssey of the cycle of reincarnations to the entanglement of the spirit (*purusha*) in nature (*prakrti*). For Buddhism, too, the existence in thebody is totally painful; it must be overcome by the suppression and destruction of bodily existence. Buddhism's twelvefold concatenation of causes explains that all suffering is attributable to the thirst for living and ignorance, and individual life with its passion and delusion is extinguished by the entrance into nirvana. The monistic Vedanta philosophy regarded the body as part of the phenomenal world, the maya, which must be destroyed to reach true reality.

Some kind of dualism is also discernible in Schelling's philosophy. Human freedom, Schelling maintains, is founded on two principles, active in every living being: one a dark primal foundation that manifests itself in carnal desire and impulse, the other a spiritual tendency whose function is to govern as a formative power. But man has placed the dark stratum of impulse which was meant only to serve the intellect as a source of power above the intellect and has thus subordinated his intellect to the impulses which now rule over him. This reversal of the right order is described in the Bible as the fall of the first parents through which evil came into the world. This perversion of man has been reversed by God who became man in Christ and re-established the original order.

Body and Soul

Basically, the body is not the adversary of the spirit and the spirit is not the antagonist of the body. Ethics considers the body as an instrument of moral behaviour because man's external actions are necessarily carried out by the body. There can be no dichotomy because man, the subject of all actions, essentially comprises body and soul. Man's duties against himself include duties against the body which are part of the duty of self-preservation. (This field involves numerous problems such as suicide, euthanasia, hunger strike and self-mutilation.) But it cannot be denied that the body puts man into a peculiarly ambiguous position. This ambivalence arises from man's nature as a sensitive being. While physiological processes as such do not enter man's consciousness, sense perceptions occupy a broad spectrum in human consciousness. The senses lie between the spirit and the body, and in western languages, the words derived from the Latin *sensus* (sense) can oscillate in their meaning from the neutral designation of sense phenomena to immorality.

The interplay of body and soul is one of the unique features of man. Laughter and tears, rejoicing and lamentation, jubilation and wailing exemplify the reflection of man's consciousness in the behaviour of his body. Man's voice is not the only instrument of expressing and conveying his feelings, sentiments and emotions, his reactions to outside impressions as well as his own inspirations. Nothing equals the expressiveness of the human face, and pantomime represents an art form of universal intelligibility. Music articulates and evokes the whole gamut of human emotions and the rhythmic move-ments of the dance may stir the passions of dancers and viewers alike. The gestures of the orator heighten his own conviction and carry his message to his audience. Not only art but man's entire life involves the interaction of spirit and matter.

Evaluation of Sexuality

Man's sexuality is essentially related to his body and is experienced through the senses. Although sexual excitement can arise from internal factors (endocrine secretions), many sexual impulses are received through the external senses, particularly vision and touch, as well as through the imagination. The reaction of the sex instinct to sensual stimulation is subject to conscious control only to a limited extent because the instinct as such naturally responds to its proper object. The behaviour of the sex instinct, therefore, appears independent of reason and therewith independent of moral norms, commandments and prohi-bitions which man recognises by his reason but which are without direct influence on the sex instinct.

The theoretical and practical evaluation of sexuality constitutes one of the most confused areas in the history of thought in which the extremes seem to have found more proponents than balanced views.

For many thinkers, the sex instinct has been a stumbling block because it appeared unprincipled, disorderly, obscuring reason and inimical to the spirit. The independence of the sex instinct from reason has been regarded as a consequence of original sin. The sex instinct, therefore, becomes concupiscence, the 'evil' concupiscence in which the blind urge obfuscates reason and the flesh revolts against the spirit. Sexual lust as carnal lust is identified with sensuous lust, sensitivity becomes sensuousness and as sensuality is perceived as a demoniacal, seductive power negating the spirit. Although the struggle between the spirit and the flesh described in the eighth chapter of Saint Paul's epistle to the Romans is not confined to the sphere of sexuality, the turbulence of sexual passion is certainly included.

In line with his pessimistic assessment of human existence, Schopenhauer rejected sexual love as the supreme and most pernicious manifestation of what he called 'blind will.' Human will aspires after self-preservation but this purpose is bad because life is identical with suffering. Since the result of the blind will can only be suffering, man is faced with the alternative of the affirmation of suffering from birth to death or the negation of the will which means the renunciation of satisfying one's impulses, above all sexual desires.

Nakedness

The association of sexuality with sin is not confined to dualistic systems, and this connection has often resulted in a devaluation of the body. The biblical account of the fall of Adam and Eve suggests the triad 'nakedness, sexuality, sin' ('And the eyes of them both were opened, and they perceived themselves to be naked' Gen 3,7). Nakedness is somehow regarded as shameful. The association of nakedness with sexual stimulation may have resulted from the use of clothing. Although the human body is not believed to be 'sinful' in itself, western culture generally thinks it 'indecent' to appear naked before others. Modern nudism, which spread above all in the form of nude bathing, advocates 'dignified common nudity on appropriate occasions and with the participation of both sexes.' Nudists often form associations which offer facilities for their members. The nudist movement has found adherents mainly in Western Europe and the United States, but nudist camps are also permitted in Communist countries such as Romania, Bulgaria, Yugoslavia, East Germany and Hungary. In many countries, nude bathing is allowed or tolerated also on public beaches.

The state of New York enacted a law prohibiting nudity in public places. The law inhibits nudists from disrobing at public beaches and some nudists protesting against the law were cited for 'public lewdness.'

In a marvellous mixture of traditional prudishness and the sexualisation of advertising, the Christian Democratic majority on the local council of Tropea, a small town in Calabria, passed an ordinance forbidding people to go naked on the town's beaches except 'beautiful naked women — young women in a position to exalt the attractiveness and femininity of their bodies.' This ordinance and other measures of local authorities led to a great debate on nudity on Italian beaches which even reached Parliament. The Tropea ordinance was soon rescinded.

Nakedness, in particular naked movement, is felt as a kind of liberation by people who usually wear clothes. Some time ago, on a Sunday afternoon, people thronging the street in front of Meiji Shrine in Tokyo, were startled when a young woman of about 22 suddenly shed her clothes and began running about in the nude. After a chase of about 500 metres, police caught up with her. 'I had drunk a bottle of beer and got irritated when I saw so many people. I felt the urge to free myself,' she declared. The feeling of liberation explains some of the attractiveness of the nudist movement.

To man, his own body can be a source of joy which need not necessarily be sexual. Many people only pay attention to their bodies when they get sick, but there is also a positive feeling of well-being which includes sensitive-corporeal factors as well as psychic elements. The joy in one's body is at least partially a joy in movement which may be the original motivation of dancing, playing and sports. In modern dance and sports, success may often be the main or even the only goal, but outside of professionalism, the joy in movement survives.

In many places in the western world, people have become accustomed to representations of the naked human body so that actual nudity is no longer regarded as shocking and people undress in public without self-consciousness. A National Nudist Day is celebrated in the United States on Cape Cod. In the summer of 1982, nudism was practised on about 200 French beaches, and sunbathing in the nude was officially allowed in some German cities and tolerated in others. People became accustomed to seeing their neighbours in the buff. In Munich, nudists flowed over from the parks and promenaded in the streets. Nevertheless, a young woman caused astonishment when she boarded a streetcar with only a handbag. So many Germans took off all their clothes at public beaches and parks that the picture magazine *Quick* dubbed 1983 the 'nakedest summer.' At La Tropez, most of the sunbathing women were topless and at least half of the women on Spanish beaches and a large percentage of those sunbathing at Madrid's outdoor swimming pools followed the same 'skin fashion.' Bikinis, the Spanish daily *ABC* lamented, were so skimpy that they accentuated what they were supposed to hide.

On the other hand, India's Supreme Court rejected the demand of a 22-year-old member of a Hindu sect that does not wear clothes to appear naked in court. 'The sky is my garment,' she proclaimed and argued that wearing clothes would cause her mental harm. In British Columbia, a 63-year-old woman sat naked with only a scarf covering her head through her two-day trial for arson. She was a member of the Doukhobor sect and refused to wear clothes for religious reasons. (The Doukhobors, originally a Russian sect, believe in the supremacy of the inner voice. They were persecuted, mainly for refusing military service. Tolstoy organised a relief fund for them and many emigrated to Canada.)

In a Harris survey covering 1,000 French adults, 86 per cent of those polled said that nudism should be allowed on French beaches but 73 per cent wanted to have it restricted to certain beaches. Only 19 per cent found topless sunbathing shocking. The sight of nude women on the beaches was not embarrassing to 68 per cent of the men while only 54 per cent of the women said the same of male nudism.

Nakedness was common in ancient Greece. Athletes needed no sportswear but practised and competed in the nude. In Sparta, boys and girls joined in military training which was conducted naked. At home, Greek women often wore rather transparent clothing which was easily discarded if the mood was right. In Rome, on the contrary, human nakedness was considered indecent and sports unmanly; only military exercises were stressed. But nakednesss was recognised in arts and some of the representations unearthed in Pompeii and Herculanum are highly erotic.

Bathing

In the western world, the attitude towards nakedness greatly influenced the practices of bathing. For bathing, people shed their clothes, and if nakedness becomes taboo, bathing will also be affected. Moreover, bathing has been associated with sexual pleasure almost everywhere in the world. In ancient Greece, sexual relations with boys were the norm in public and private baths. Mixed bathing became the custom in Rome at the time of Aggripa (62-12 B.C.) and with it prostitution. Cesar reports that mixed bathing was customary among the Germans. The anchorites dispensed with all washing and there have been times when even solitary naked bathing in a tub was considered sinful or at least as an occasion of sin. The custom of wearing something when bathing started in the sixteenth century. On the other hand, the Nicene Council found it necessary to prohibit clerics to bathe together with women, and through the crusades, the western world rediscovered the bathing pleasures of the Orient.

From the castles of the knights where, as in the Greece of Homer, the daughter, wife or maid of the host washed and massaged the guests, bathing spread to the cities and towns. Everywhere, bath-houses were established and, as in ancient Rome, attendants, both male and female, got involved in prostitution. Bath-houses became hotbeds of homosexual even more than heterosexual prostitution. In 1486, the city of

Breslau ordered the bath-house owners to have only male attendants assist women bathers in order to stop lesbianism. As a rule, bathers and attendants were naked although women sometimes wore necklaces or a small apron to cover the genitals. Unmarried men and women squatted together in large or small wooden tubs. Bath-houses became amusement centres. Idlers strolled between the tubs and threw flowers to the bathing women, musicians entertained the crowds and naked female bath attendants served food and drink, bantered with guests and onlookers and retaliated saucily as required.

The syphilis and plague epidemics put an end to the bathing culture and even after the plague had died out, Europe remained allergic to cleanliness. In the seventeenth century, physicians declared bathing not only in the open but also at home a health threat and soap was replaced by perfume. The elegance of the eighteenth century was accompanied by an unbelievable lack of personal hygiene, foul smells and infestation with vermin. When the Finns introduced the sauna to Russia, mixed bathing became so widespread that Catherine II prohibited the use of saunas. Bathing survived in some Balkan countries. Until the twentieth century, gypsy girls (known as 'Hindu girls') worked as bath attendants and prostitutes. In many hotels, guests who wanted a bath were asked: 'With or without?'

Shame

A much-discussed question is whether there is an instinctive feeling of shame at being naked. In the West, the use of clothing has been attributed to a specific impulse to cover the genitals. Ethnologists and sociologists have pointed out that this function of clothing is unknown in many cultures. In tropical regions of South America, Africa and Melanesia, habitual nakedness was common. In many cases, men as well as women went naked, in some cases, only the men, in others, only the women did not wear clothes. Even outside the tropics, for example, in North America and Australia, nakedness was common and sometimes the only protection against the cold was a skin thrown over the shoulders. In the Arctic and in Greenland, men and women discarded clothes inside the dwellings because the lamps used for heating made the room very warm.

Children are not self-conscious and are not embarrassed when seen naked by strangers. In societies in which public nakedness is taboo, disrobement is tolerated at certain occasions (such as medical examination, common washing in the military, sports, or coal mines) and common naked bathing of both sexes is not rare. There are groups in which clothing does not cover the genitals or only some kind of ornament or emblem is worn. It happens that the removal of the adornment triggers a feeling of shame. To be naked or clothed is a matter of habit and custom and thereby of conformity to the social norms defining good manners. What is termed indecent does not necessarily offend against moral norms but in the sphere of sexuality much of what is regarded immoral is also socially unacceptable so that the boundary line between 'immoral' and 'indecent' is somewhat fluid. The feeling of shame, therefore, is culturally conditioned and cannot be ascribed to an innate or natural feeling of morality.

There are considerable differences in what individuals consider as decent or indecent. While posing in the nude seems to have become as commonplace as applying lipstick, a contestant in the 1982 Miss World contest refused to pose for photographers wearing a new-style 'revealing' swimsuit in the swimsuit parade.

Clothing

The use of clothing is one of the most remarkable differences in the behaviour of men and of animals. It has enabled man to populate nearly all regions of the globe whereas animals are confined to the regions where their skin or fur allows them to stay. Clothing is a product of cultural development which, however, does not necessarily reflect the views of society on the human body or sexuality. In many cultures, clothing serves the double purpose of protection and embellishment. In its protective function, clothing involves the concealment of sexuality whereas in its role as adornment, clothing often emphasises and exhibits sex. The codpiece common in men's clothing in fifteenth and sixteenth century Europe as well as the custom of some papuan tribes to insert the penis into a kind of cucumber points to the exhibitionist nature of some forms of clothing. In the history of clothing, the tendency of both sexes to please and to attract the attention of the opposite sex is unmistakable. Clothing and ornaments serve for displaying rank and success, and the origin of the awarding of decorations to the victors in battle or in sports is not free of exhibitionist elements.

Among the many aberrations of old and modern rulers are the attempts to regulate clothing. In the past, the so-called sumptuary laws which controlled personal expenditures, especially those on food and dress, often perpetuated class distinctions. In many cases, such regulations sought to ban fashions judged offensive on moral or religious grounds. The veiling of Muslim women is based on the Qur'an: 'Oh Prophet, speak to your wives and your daughters and the wives of your faithful that they should veil themselves in their cloaks. In this way, they will sooner be recognised (as decent women) and not be violated' (Sura 33,59). Totalitarian regimes are particularly prone to resort to such regimentation. In Mao's China the uniform-like clothing reflected the egalitarian creed of the party ideology; in Khomeini's Iran, women have to wear the chador to conform to the Ayatollah's hatred of the West, and in Pakistan, women were forbidden to wear the sari, women's dress in arch-enemy India.

On the other hand, uniforms not only serve to distinguish friend and foe but also enhance the esprit de corps and are indispensable as badges and credentials of public professions.

Although it is impossible to speak of an instinctive feeling of shame as an innate moral reaction, we experience antecedent as well as subsequent shame as a protective tendency against the impairment of our personality. The inclination to hide real or imagined defects from the eyes of others is some kind of social shame. We are afraid of being compromised and try to prevent faults, shortcomings or defeats from becoming known. If personal deficiencies or mistakes are revealed, we are distressed and often want to wipe out our failures by some kind of success or accomplishment. This tendency obtains not only in a social, but also in a moral context. A similar propensity appears in our endeavour to maintain our dignity and have our worth and achievements recognised by others. If this desire lacks a corresponding objective foundation, we call it vanity.

Shame is felt as an accompaniment of man's animal functions such as the processes of metabolism and sexual activities. This shame protects man against being absorbed completely by his instinctive forces. With regard to sexual impulses, man may feel shame for the lustful excitement in his own body (what Max Scheler called libidinous movements) or in the approach to a heterosexual partner. In this sense, shame fulfils a biological, protective role by moderating the urge to sexual advances. For man, sexuality is attractive and repulsive, and this ambivalence of sex constitutes a distinctive feature of human sexuality. Sexual shamelessness often is a sign of degeneration.

Konrad Lorenz thinks that shame is the result of cultural ritualisation. Unritualised conduct, above all unritualised instinctive acts, are socially proscribed. 'Comfort behaviour,' such as scratching, stretching, or picking one's nose are just as taboo as excretion and copulation. Shame is the direct consequence of comprehensive cultural ritualisation.

The feeling of shame functions as a protective shield for man's inner life and a guard against the denudement of his inmost personality. This feeling is often explained as fear combined with habit and education, but the desire to protect one's personality may well be related to the instinct of self-preservation. The cultivation of the feeling of shame is one of the tasks of sexual education but it is equally important not to nurture false ideas of shame. The educator, therefore, must know of what man should be or should not be ashamed.

Beauty and the Representation of Nakedness

The human body, and especially the naked human body, plays an important role in the representation of beauty. The beautiful man evokes a positive response. Human beauty has been described as the harmonious configuration of bodily form and movement. The imitation of antiquity which gained currency in Europe towards the end of the eighteenth century frequently resulted in a conflict with the moral views of this epoch. Of a bas-relief model of the young Flaxman (John Flaxman, 1755-1826), whose sculptures were apostrophised as 'too noble, too antique and too naked,' Josiah Wedgwood, the developer of the Wedgwood ware, once said: 'To clothe the figures would not only mean much additional work, but would also require an experienced master, and moreover, the pieces would no longer be true imitations of antiques. I know it would be possible to blot out the respective spots with leaves. But the unclothed figure is so widespread with the Greeks that it is difficult to do without it.' The frankness in the representation not only of the human body but also of sexual activities can be found in other countries, too, in India and wide parts of Asia.

The living body is the form in which the spiritual-sensual nature of man finds its most eloquent expression and the full scale of man's emotions can become manifest. In the antique ideal of *kalokagathia,* goodness belongs to the perfection of beauty. But the beautiful man is only one of the possible representations of the human body, and the portrayal of man in pain, suffering and despair can touch the deepest recesses of the human heart.

Beauty, above all female beauty, has hardly been less important in the history of the human mind than ideas such as happiness and freedom. For Plato, beauty is the scintillation of the idea in the sensuous. His inquiry into the beautiful probes the ultimate destiny of man. In his *Symposium,* Plato propounds his doctrine of the unity of love, beauty, and human happiness. Mortal man is carried near to the immortal gods by eros, the love of the beautiful, by begetting in beauty with body and soul. Beauty leads to generation, and generation is a divine undertaking, the saving of the mortal from extinction. Generation of children in a beautiful body fulfils the desire for perpetuation by offspring, and the generation of works of the spirit in the beautiful soul fulfils the desire for perpetuation by fame. Beyond this, however, man must become similar to the immortal gods by ascending step by step to the idea of beauty and to form the true man.

Stressing the primacy of the spirit over nature, Hegel propounded the thesis of the supremacy of the beauty created by art. In his antagonism to the traditional triad of the true, the good and the beautiful, Nietzsche identified beauty with aesthetics, goodness with the ought, and truth with reality in the sense of the scientifically demonstrable material being apprehended by sense perception. Beautiful is what carries man into a life-enhancing frenzy. Beautiful art is the affirmation of the sensual, the will to appearances. The denial of the true, the good and the beautiful as the metaphysical attributes of all being and the formal objects of man's faculties in his contact with reality fractured the inner harmony of being and cognition. Empirical psychology reduces the beautiful to psychic experiences in which the excitation of the nervous system creates emotional conditions; for technology, the beautiful constitutes an aesthetic object characterised by calculable arrangements of order.

But the beautiful cannot be extenuated to what is created by art or what can become the object of man's cognitive faculties. That there are unbridgeable differences between what individuals find beautiful does not mean that things are beautiful because we experience them as beautiful. Beauty is said to be in the eyes of the beholder but beauty is not something we attribute to an object; there must be something in the object that impresses us. It may be a certain quality that strikes us as beautiful, colour, form, rhythm or a combination of traits, but something different from perfect, agreeable, or useful. But as far as we know, only man can respond with a specific reaction to what we call beautiful, and the joy or pleasure given by the beautiful is not a sensation but a spiritual experience which can also come from something beautiful not represented to us by the senses. Man's capacity of an emotional response to the beautiful is analogous to his capability of knowing the truth and his inclination to pursue the good.

The metaphysics of beauty may sound abstract but beauty is of immense practical importance. And, pace the feminists, beauty is the most wonderful asset a woman can have and something most women are anxious to preserve. Not only for beauty contests and professions such as acting and modelling, but also in the quest of a marriage partner and for a woman's self-esteem, there is no substitute for beauty. Beauty culture has become a multi-billion dollar business and the list of things a woman should or should not do in order to enhance or protect her beauty is endless. But despite the saying that beauty is only skin-deep, the beauty of the human body can be the beauty of the human person and, as Vergil wrote: 'Even virtue is more pleasing when it comes in a beautiful body.'

5

Women's Liberation
Institution -v- Identity

BEING A COMMUNITY, the family must face the fundamental problems involved in every social entity, the relation between the whole and its parts, that is, the collectivity and the individual, and, from a somewhat different point of view, the polarity of permanency and change, that is, stability and progress. As an institution, marriage means stability, but in their personal growth, the partners bound in and by matrimony experience not only biological but even more psychological changes. Marriage is a process of exploration, conflict and compromise in which the two partners live, grow and mature or wither and decay together. Ideally, this process should not be an undertaking in which each of the two individuals tries to gain an advantage for himself by exploiting the other. The life in common is based on the possibility of mutual understanding and demands not only tolerance and sympathy but readiness to fulfil together the common task of overcoming the natural closeness of the individual and live in the confidence of touching the depth of each other's soul so as to make the life of another heart one's own. It requires the unreserved trust in the pureness of each other's intentions and the mutual surrender for a life no longer attributable to the individual 'I's' of the partners but to the common 'We' of the spouses. The marital community of life implies that the union of man and wife is greater and higher than the life of its components.

The Ideal Marriage

It is evident that the realisation of such an ideal is exceedingly difficult. The leopard does not change its spots. Man cannot alter his character, his disposition and inclinations, but his views, value judgements and emotions can change. Growth means 'becoming' and thus involves the antinomy which led Heraclitus to the view that all things are in a state of eternal flux: *panta rhei* (all things flow); we cannot descend twice into the same river (we are not the same and the river is not the same). Man remains the same and yet is not the same. No man can foresee what kind of man he will be the next day, let alone in twenty or thirty years. In marriage, the problem is doubled because two people cannot be sure that they will not develop away from each other. It seems almost certain that the 'beautiful time of first love' will not stay and that everyday life can become an almost unbearable burden.

At a time when instability seems to have become the universal life-style, it may not be surprising that people feel reluctant to bind themselves beyond the today for an indefinite future. People hesitate to trust their own reliability and are afraid to engage themselves in an open-ended undertaking; how can they have sufficient faith to confide themselves to another for the rest of their lives?

However, the recent debates on the appropriateness of marriage concerned not so much the possibility of a divergent transformation of the marriage partners but rather the conflict between the restraints imposed by marriage as an institution and the right of every individual to develop his or her own personality or, as it is usually expressed, the right to self-fulfilment, the right to personal identity. The human being has the right to be who he/she is, but in marriage, the human being is bound to another human being, grafted into a certain social system and condemned to play a role fixed by social rules and conventions.

As an institution, marriage undoubtedly involves the problem of constraint and social power, including the possible misuse of power. A one-sided emphasis on the institutional meaning of marriage can lead to the neglect of its personal aspects. Marriage and the family may cause an irrational cumulation of personal and interpersonal power which may wax into the misuse of physical force, sexual brutality and the repression of the rights of women and children. But today's emphasis on identity is not directed against abuses in the institution but against the institution itself and rejects any kind of bond that cannot be solved at the will of each of the partners if he or she finds it incompatible with the right to self-fulfilment.

This idea of self-determination and self-realisation denies all natural and social restraints and ends up by the reversal of all values and the dissolution of all institutions. The attacks on male chauvinism have distorted the image of man into the bugbear or an enemy of woman, and monogamy into a trap imprisoning woman and making her the property of the male. Actually, the anarchical desire of liberation leads either to chaos or to the despotism of doctrinaires. The assumption that human life is possible without any kind of obligation, that there is happiness without duty which can be consumed like a refreshment completely misinterprets human nature and the inner ordainment of human personality. The identification of self-fulfilment with an unconstrained and limitless feeling of happiness creates the craving for a permanent escalation and an intensification which can finally only be sustained by drugs and intoxication. The last step in this kind of self-realisation of the lonely individual is death.

Self-realisation

Self-realisation was the creed of the upside-down world which the

West's 'cultural revolution' dreamed of in the sixties. Its emphasis was on sexual and personal freedom and the ethics of self-fulfilment. But the emancipation from all restraints in a world without obligation and dependence is a dangerous illusion and can only lead to atomised egoism. The right to satisfy every individual 'need' or 'desire' is a moral and social absurdity. It offers no way of choosing between all the personal impulses, no way of distinguishing what is personally and socially meaningful and what is destructive, no way of living up to our commitments to others which we need just as much as we need our own fulfilment.

Partly as a result of the scare of herpes and the threat of AIDS, the American sex scene has changed radically from the torrid sex revolution of the nineteen sixties and seventies. Casual relationships and one-night stands are out and marriage is in. The lovelorns who place ads in *New York Magazine's* 'Strictly Personals' are 'absolutely looking for serious relationships,' a spokeswoman for the publication said. People are looking for partners in life and are very serious about finding a mate.

The situation of complete independence and emancipation from domination, the illusion of total freedom leads to an inhuman competitive pressure of egoistic self-realisation which makes a life in common unbearable and necessarily creates oppression, violence, terror and tyranny.

The realisation of the freedom and happiness of the individual is linked to the freedom and happiness of others. In the family, happiness can only come from the fulfilment of the tasks of the common life which demand sacrifice and self-denial. Freedom can only exist in a framework of order in which life is lived in conformity with this order. A free society is only possible if it recognises the freedom of its institutions, including the freedom of the family.

The antinomy between marriage as an institution and the identity of the marriage partners has been one of the themes ventilated by feminist groups. The emotional components of social bonds are undoubtedly more intense in women than in men. Evolutionism maintains that just as man's body and brain have been formed by evolution, so has his primitive behaviour. Because the offspring of the primates could not survive without their mothers, they developed a strong bond with them which resulted in an emotional attachment of great intensity. It seems somewhat odd to explain the mother's behaviour by the conduct of the children because long before the child can do anything it needs the help of the mother and her readiness to sacrifice herself for her offspring. This supposes a powerful emotional involvement on the part of the mother which can at most be reinforced later by the affection of the child. Negatively, the mental strain resulting from the dissolution of affectionate relations is much greater for women than for men. The separation of a young woman from the parental home, the

departure of grown-up children when they get married or become independent, the shock of divorce or the death of the husband perturb the
feelings of a woman more sharply that analogous experiences of a man.
It is ridiculous to reduce this to the century-long submission of woman
to a system that denied her an independent personal value. For man as
well as woman, self-realisation is only possible within the framework
of social bonds appropriate to the prevailing culture and a sphere of
action corresponding to the individual's capabilities.

For a woman, the emotional stability and the confidence secured
by marriage and the family constitute an important factor contributing
to her mental health, and the sphere of activity given with her role as
wife, mother and mistress of the house can be no less satisfying than a
professional career. The intense attachment to man in the woman's
emotional make-up is no denial of her own personality because she can
find her true identity in her self-surrender. A survey on the mental
health of mothers in the German Federal Republic in 1975 found that 75
per cent of all mothers considered themselves 'happy' or 'very happy.'

Rejection of Marriage

One of the early advocates of women's liberation was Wilhelm Reich,
an Austrian psychoanalyst and disciple of Freud. He fought against the
suppression of sexuality by society and condemned the double moral
standard for men and women. He propounded the view that in a male-
dominated world, woman is degraded to the status of an instrument for
the preservation of the family in the interest of the state. For economic
reasons, woman is forced to fulfil the role of bearing children for the
state and to manage the household without remuneration. Marriage is
an institution that protects woman but, at the same time, exploits her.
Marriage makes a woman economically dependent on man and forces
her to be satisfied with less sex by denying her extramarital relations.

Feminist theory regards the denial of the role of mother as the
most effective instrument of achieving equality with man. The French
feminist Elizabeth Badinter, the first woman professor at the Paris
University of Science and Technology, rejects the view that motherhood is a woman's fulfilment, Maternal instinct, she writes in her book
L'amour en plus, is a myth created by Rousseau and Freudian
psychology and she stresses that many women find full-time child care
boring and distressing.

In the ten years from 1970 to 1980, the percentage of single
households rose from 6 per cent to 30 per cent in West Germany. In
Japan, this percentage reached a high of 19.6 per cent in 1981 but was
down to 18.8 per cent in 1982 which was not much different from the
18.5 per cent in 1970. In the large cities, however, the percentage of
single households is much higher. According to a government survey,

people living single constituted 35.8 per cent of the population of Tokyo, 26.8 per cent in Osaka and 22.6 per cent in Yokohama (for comparison: New York 30.3 per cent, Paris 47 per cent). Of the men in the Japanese survey, 52 per cent were satisfied with living alone, 48 per cent were not. In the last category were widowers, male divorcees and employees forced to live apart from their families because of their work. Among the women living alone were widows, divorcees, career women and young women living apart from their families because of their jobs or their studies. Of the women, 72 per cent were satisfied with living alone, 28 per cent were not.

In a poll conducted by the Japanese government in May 1984, 24 per cent of all women and 34 per cent of the single women said that they would live single if they could support themselves economically. The Hakuhodo Institute of Life and Living found that a larger percentage of women living alone owned consumer durables than single men although they remained below the level of general households: 89.2 per cent of the single women possessed refrigerators (single men 77.2 per cent, general households 99.8 per cent), 66.1 per cent washing machines (single men 39.2 per cent, general households 99.4 per cent), 81.5 per cent colour TV sets (single men 78.8 per cent, general households 99.1 per cent), 30.3 per cent air conditioners (single men 29.5 per cent, general households 47.3 per cent), 24.1 per cent passenger cars (single men 23.2 per cent, general households 61.5 per cent).

Although voluntary or enforced singleness may afford opportunities for self-examination and self-affirmation, it does not seem desirable as a long-term life-style. Most singles hope that their solitary life will some time be ended by a (new) partnership.

The feminist movement reflected the discrepancies characteristic of western culture in our generation. The major inconsistencies were the formal equality of rights and responsibilities of men and women and the actual participation and influence of women in public life; the political and economic contributions demanded of and made by women and the constant attempts to relegate women to kitchen and children; the high expectations with which women entered marriage and the low esteem in which society held domestic work.

The goal to which the protagonists of the emancipation of women and the perfect equality of the sexes in the sixties aspired was the professionally successful, independent and self-assured woman who was sexually free and unconstrained, aggressive if she wished to be so and undeterred if she was rebuffed. In its extreme form, the sexual revolution implied that every woman should be free to go to bed with everyone she wanted. For the emancipated woman, marriage was only meaningful if it did not involve any kind of personal restriction. (It should be stressed that the sexual revolution and women's lib are two different phenomena.)

In his book *America Now*, anthropologist Marvin Harris attributed the rise of the feminist movement to the transformation of the production economy into a service economy. The conversion from production to services meant that corporations needed a large pool of docile, literate workers willing to accept boring jobs at low pay. Women became the 'new coolies' of the service economy because living costs had gone up (for which Professor Harris blames the shoddiness of the products of the production economy) and families needed more money. Mothers with children under 18 began entering the labour market which shut the door in the face of black and Hispanic men while undermining the 'marital and procreative imperative.' With the decline of the male-dominated breadwinner family, the idea that women should stay home, have babies and let men run the world collapsed. Sex was no longer considered mainly for procreation, making homosexuality a legitimate form of sexual conduct. Hence, Professor Harris argues, women's liberation did not create the working woman but rather the working woman — especially the working housewife — created women's liberation.

While it is true that the growth of the service economy opened many jobs to women, the basic tenet of feminism is not founded on economic considerations. Because feminists deny a 'natural ordainment' of woman to be wife and mother and assert her right to an independent life, they uphold her right to choose a business career.

Marriage Male-oriented?

Dr Jessie Bernard, an American sociologist, who has studied marriage particularly from the point of view of its effects on mental health, thinks that the traditional marriage has been the male's marriage, making the male healthier, wealthier, less suicidal and less prone to crime than his unmarried brethren. But far too often, marriage has been destructive of women. Dr Bernard contends that, statistically, marriage has militated against the woman's health and happiness. Wives are much more likely to have mental problems, more apt to commit crimes than their unmarried sisters and they are less protected than their husbands from suicidal tendencies. The factors mainly responsible for the destructive effects of marriage on the distaff side are isolation, tedium, and the lower status of housework and childbearing. Even schoolage children, especially those in the 6 to 14 age group, seem to have a depressing influence on the married wife. Among the strains are the negative feelings from the low level of companionship, low satisfaction with children, and the exhausting demands made on her. The husband is usually devoting himself to his profession.

In Dr Bernard's view, research on marriage and women has been dominated by an all-pervasive male bias. Sociology has documented the dependence of wives but failed to ask how to overcome it. Today, women are finding that they can be independent but they do not necessarily choose freedom. There are, however, a number of factors that will change the position of women, among them, the women's lib movement, the concept of no-fault divorce, the relaxation of the laws on abortion, the spread of contraceptive information, available also to unmarried women and adolescents, the four-day working week, the proliferation of communes, greater tolerance of homosexuality and the acceleration of the so-called youth culture. Although the institution of marriage will remain, it will be less rigid and include such options as limited-term marriage, group marriage, mate swapping and *ménage à trois*.

Some of the movements from which Dr Bernard expected a correction of the male-oriented form of marriage and the family turned out to have been rather ephemeral phenomena. Although it is undeniable that a one-sided tendency stressing the position of man has influenced the social appreciation of marriage, its legal regulation and actual practice, the traditional view of marriage does not necessarily include such a one-sidedness. It is certainly true that there are women who find their identity in self-surrender. To them, the intimate attachment to a man is the content of their lives; their man is their haven. On the other hand, there are men who have not the slightest inner relationship with their wives. Their wife is merely the figurehead of their ship of successs, one of the possessions they can display for flaunting their wealth.

A Chinese feminist, Yu Luojing, rejects women's liberation groups as self-indulgent and the official women's organisations as stodgy. Her creed is that women have the right and power to change their lives and she considers it her mission in life to write about love and her own unfortunate experiences which she has detailed in a novel entitled *A Springtime Fairy Tale*. She has a child from her first husband who, she says, raped her on their wedding night, but she does not want to have anything to do with her child. She walked out on her second husband with whom she lived for four dreary years without love and had a love affair with a married, elderly editor. After several other sexual involvements, she married a third time. She is still searching for the meaning of love which, she says, is so complex and ever changing. 'Many young women in China today think sex is everything and seek sexual liberation because of their unhappy sex lives,' she was quoted as saying.

Greater emphasis on the personal meaning of marriage does not necessarily involve rejection of its institutional character. Marriage as an institution connoting a social structure with legal restrictions and obligations is by no means identical with marriage as a living com-

munity of a twosome making human life their common task, but does
not deny it. The commonness of marriage is not lived in order to
comply with legal norms, but because it is the meaning and contents of
a common experience, common happiness and common suffering,
common triumphs and common difficulties. A marriage without
duties, common duties as well as reciprocal duties, is just as impossible
as marriage without sacrifice.

In an address to the International Conference on Human Values
held at Tsukuba University (Japan) in October 1980, Betty Friedan, the
well-known champion of women's rights, stated that mankind was
moving towards a great change in the twenty-first century. The time
was coming when woman would exist not as a sex object or an
appendage of man, an instrument for bearing children in order to
preserve the race, or as a provider of services for the household, but as a
human being. Woman should live in her capacity as a human being and
be active in various fields on the basis of her social experience rather
than because of her biological characteristics. Ms Friedan proclaimed
that the women's movement had entered on a second stage at which it
had to change into a mainstream movement. Men have to change, too.
People must give up the stereotype image of the home, but women
should not try to become superwomen. The important thing was to
overcome the polarity of the traditional roles of man and wife. The
problem was not simply to exchange the roles of men and women. A
just allocation of sexual roles should create a humane female as well as a
humane male. Men as well as women should be free to be themselves,
not bound by old clichés of masculinity or femininity. Excessive
competition for money and position was not the goal of man's life. The
dehumanisation of labour, the priority of economic efficiency turns
man into a slave. Women's liberation had to become human liberation,
a movement for a new emancipation of man.

Marital Commonness

The polarity of individual and society is essential for each human
group. A one-sided emphasis on one or the other of the poles invites
the destruction of the group. As a community of life, marriage implies
that life is no longer an individual, but a common task, embracing not
only one or the other aspect of human life but its entire fullness. The
commonness comprehends external conduct as well as inner attitudes,
the bodily relations and economic situation of the partners and their
intellectual, moral and emotional life. If man and wife share such an
understanding of marriage, they can find a solution of the difficulties
that arise when both have a job they want to retain in marriage. The
problem cannot be settled on the basis of economic prudence but must
be approached in the spirit of identification with the beloved and the

priority of the common life. Each of the partners pursuing a career should think of it not as 'his' or 'her' career but 'our' career. Husband and wife will be able to work together as a team only in very few cases when they are engaged in the same profession or occupation, but even if their actual work is separate, each can have a genuine interest in the work of the other, not only showing understanding, but also making sacrifices for helping and furthering each other's activities.

Whether two people of whom each has a job should continue working after marriage may be a difficult problem. From the point of view of the woman's identity, there is no principle demanding that a woman should quit working after marriage. It is a question that the spouses must face together and to which no universally valid answer can be given.

The Catholic Church considers a marriage to which consent is conditioned on avoiding children invalid, but it cannot be said that a marriage in which the partners renounce having children either temporarily or permanently is completely meaningless — even the Church recognises marriages in which conception is impossible if coitus can be performed. In the same way, a marriage cannot be regarded as strange because the wife does not make the role of housewife her full-time job. On the other hand, the role of the wife who does not hold an outside job deserves more recognition, not only socially but also in tax legislation and social security arrangements. The economic and social value of a woman's activities as housewife, mother and educator cannot be measured by the categories of a just wage but they are basically irreplaceable and in this sense unremunerable.

Traditional Sex Roles

The attempts to fix the roles of man and woman in such a way that each shoulders a 'fair share' of all family matters such as household chores and child care indicates a tendency to a sterile egalitarianism which assumes that everything can be reduced to a common quantitative denominator, disregarding the basic differences between man and woman and their functions. The endeavour to obliterate the diversity of the sexes fails to understand the importance of the peculiarities of man and woman not only for the personality of each individual but also for family and society. The old Chinese contrasting differentiation between Yang and Ying indicates that the attitudes of man and woman differ. Man wants to possess, woman wants to be loved. Man's will to possess is the real stumbling block of feminism but this desire is so deeply rooted in man's psyche that it is almost identical with his sexuality.

A British survey (1983) found that today's brides and grooms share many of their parents' traditional views on marriage. With regard to household responsibility, 78 per cent of the brides expected to do most of the cooking, 87 per cent were prepared to do the ironing, and 91 per cent were ready to do the washing. Only 3 per cent of the bridegrooms volunteered to take over the kitchen, 4 per cent the ironing, and 1 per cent the washing.

In West Germany, only 8 per cent of the married men (and men living together with a woman) helped with the housework. Even if the wife had a full-time job, only one husband out of five pitched in with the household chores. Mothers should remain home was the opinion of 83 per cent of the men and 43 per cent thought that it would be better for the success of the marriage if the wife did not work outside.

In individual cases, husband and wife may change their roles and both may be happy with the arrangement. There are men who loathe going out to work but like to keep house and are excellent cooks and very efficient at all household chores. Moreover, men may be better educators; they do not get excited and keep more of a cool head when handling the children. (This, again, is one of the generalisations criticised by feminists.) On the other hand, there are women who had an interesting and successful career before marriage and who feel frustrated when they are confined to the routine of house-keeping.

A German study found that men who quit their jobs to become 'housemen' had been dissatisfied with their work. They had no ambition to succeed and their job had not provided opportunities for advancement. Women who became the breadwinners of their families often had higher incomes than their husbands; they had a strong engagement in their work, were adept in making social contacts and eager to improve themselves and to advance. Some couples were able to find part-time jobs so that the husband worked in the morning and the wife in the afternoon. In this way, both were able to devote themselves to the education of their children.

Men who took over the role of housekeeper confirmed the general feeling of women that household chores are monotonous but they also found that planning and organising made housekeeping much easier.

While many men do not object to married women having a job, one third of the husbands of working wives refuse even to lift a finger at home and the help given by the remaining two-thirds is usually sporadic and desultory.

A poll conducted by the Allensbach Institute of Opinion Research asked women what they thought of the change in roles when the husband took care of the household and the wife went out to work. The younger generation of women considered this an acceptable arrangement but older women found it absurd. They clung to the idea that a woman's place was in the home.

Despite the emphasis on equality and the widespread employment of women in the Soviet Union, the old role attribution of man and woman is strongly maintained. Writing in the trade union newspaper

Trud, a Leningrad child psychologist, V. Garbuzov, reminded parents that boys and girls were meant to be different. Women must teach traditional feminine behaviour, raising daughters who play with dolls, do housework and 'respect the stronger sex.' 'The true strength of a woman lies not in her physical strength but in the weakness of her sex,' the article said. 'By her tenderness, her pure female tact, her delicacy, she first wins the heart of her father, then that of her husband,' — 'Giving a girl an apron as a present before she is given a Sunday dress instils in her the skill of housekeeping . . . the skill and taste for this eternal female cause.'

The author expressed alarm at a survey that showed that Soviet women did not respect their men and placed the blame squarely on the women. 'There is yet another thing that daughters must be taught,' the article admonished. 'To respect the stronger sex . . . in the form of a specific boy, youth or man for his personal qualities.'

Feminism has failed to change the image of man. For a time it seemed as if soft manliness would replace the macho type. But the 'houseman' who took the place of the housewife when she opted for an outside job has become a psychiatric patient and the machismo of the untamed, unsentimental male seems to have made a comeback. The affluent society of the seventies with its economic prosperity, its social turbulence and its freedom from anxiety enabled men to metamorphose to the companion-type marriage partner doing the dishes, hanging up the laundry and changing the baby's nappies. But the sensibility in tune with feminism seems to have evaporated and the statistics of battered wives and abused children are sufficient evidence that male brutality is still with us. And the women trained in fitness centres, exuding the charme of a strong and beautiful body, demands as counterpart the athletic outdoor man — who should not necessarily be the chauvinist of yesteryears.

Mrs Germaine Greer, who fought for female equality in the 1970s, has stressed the serious aspects of sex. 'We've now become increasingly preoccupied with sex to a point where it dominates our very culture,' she says, 'but recreational sex ignores the real issues involved in sex.' In her book *Sex and Destiny,* in which she discusses colonialism, the breakdown of family life, sexual techniques, the value of chastity, the moral degeneracy of the West and population control, she contends that the chemical and mechanical birth control methods with which the West tries to prevent the population explosion in the Third World can actually be dangerous and that abstinence is an effective and much safer form of birth control. She still insists that women should be free to make their sexual choices but she says that real sexual freedom is to be able to say 'yes' or 'no' to anyone without feeling any pressure. She argues in favour of chastity, family life and sexual self-control.

WOS1-F

Reaffirmation of Family

In her book *The Second Stage,* Betty Friedan swings resolutely to the defence of the family. She thinks that feminists who disparage the family are woefully out of step with most of their sisters. 'Virtually all women,' she writes, 'share a basic core of commitment to the family and to their equality within and beyond it, as long as the family and equality are not seen to be in conflict.' The abolition of the family is not what women want but a form that suits the aspirations of the modern woman. 'Today the problem that has no name is how to juggle work, love, home and children.' Women should not be expected to renounce children. Having children is still a dream of many women when they get married. What feminists should demand are changes necessary to make the two-career family work: day-care centres and flexi-time for working mothers and fathers in business and the professions. The interests of men and women begin to converge: women are moving out into the labour market, men no longer identify themselves solely in terms of their jobs and seek more fulfilment in the home.

The reaffirmation of the family is upheld by Erica Jong: 'I have always agreed with Friedan that many feminists were beating their heads against a wall by trying to deny the importance to most women of nurturing, childbearing and warm familial relationships. Denying women's needs will get us nowhere but deeper into the trouble we are now in.' Equality for women, therefore, cannot be restricted to the role of woman in public life and the labour market but must also extend to her function as mother and housekeeper. The problem is to find out what that means.

Women's liberalisation has contributed to the dissatisfaction of women who were stuck, or considered themselves stuck, with house-hold chores they detested, or little children they hadn't wanted. They convinced themselves that it was terrible to be cornered in this way and because they felt they could do nothing about it, they kicked the dog or the cat or hit their children. The negation of the values and ideals of motherhood by emancipated women has had a devastating effect on the emotional security of their children.

Many publications give the impression that the fight for women's emancipation has led to scepticism against the movement. Woman has proven that she can replace man. She can work like a man, can tend a machine day and night, and sits beside men in auditoriums, councils and board meetings (where, of course, she is in a minority). She writes, paints and composes poems like man — or almost like man. It is this symmetrical competition with man, in the same occupations, with the same success and the same attitudes, that has caused scepticism about emancipation. 'If woman seized power to become a man, exactly the same as those whom she has replaced, the whole thing is worthless'

(Simone de Beauvoir).

Then, the question arises what women should strive for. Femininity as opposed to masculinity should not be interpreted as a symmetrical negation. It is not a question of two poles (despite the frequent use of the word 'polarity' in discussing sexual relations) or the reverse of a mirror. The quest for the determination of femininity has been seen as a quest for the lacunae left in the dominating male culture, its order and purposeful rationality. Femininity, it has been said, means the asymmetrical negation of the present cultural structures, the completely different beyond the ingrained patterns of thought and perception.

Sexist Language

Hélène Cixous has criticised that up to now, the male, notwithstanding his particularity, has too often been used to represent the totality of the human being. In other words, 'man' meant the 'human being.' What the human sciences of the eighteenth and nineteenth centuries defined as 'human' and for which they claimed universal validity reflected a certain historical understanding of human nature in which human was identified with the masculine. But Hélène Cixous also distinguishes between 'man' and 'masculine' as well as between 'woman' and 'feminine.' There are men who do not suppress their femininity and women who stress their masculinity.

As far as the English language is concerned, the term 'man' has always had the two basic meanings of an 'adult male person' and a 'human being,' and in the latter sense, it is used as a synonym for the 'human race.' The latest edition of Roget's Thesaurus, the reference book on which writers rely for finding the right word, has gone overboard in removing sexual bias. To consider 'mankind' as a sexist term is outright silly.

More than 'some linguistic discomfort' was created by the lectionary compiled by a committee of the National Council of Churches which purged the Biblical texts of all 'male-oriented' language. It avoids masculine pronouns for God, replaces 'Lord' by the 'Sovereign One,' 'Son' of God by 'Child' of God, and 'son of man' by the 'human one.' One of the most startling and arbitrary innovations is the bisexualisation of the deity. The word 'Father' has been expanded to '(God) my Father (and Mother).' An androgynous conception of the deity is not uncommon and has been asserted for the Old Testament on the basis of Gen 1,27 ('And God created man in his own image; in the image of God he created him. Male and female he created them'). But Christian tradition has always denied that sexuality can be predicated of God. The expression 'God, Father and Mother' confuses the trinitarian terminology. The terms 'Father' and 'Son' are used because this is the terminology of the New Testament on which most Christian churches rely for their doctrine of the Trinity. The name 'Father' is applied to God with priority as a personal name because, as St Thomas explains, 'this name "Father," whereby paternity is signified, is the proper name of the person of the Father' (S. theol., 1, q. 33, a. 2), whereas 'Father' can signify the relation of God to creatures by way of a certain likeness. It is proper to the Father to be unbegotten, without principle and the principle of the 'only begotten Son.' While the Father is Father of the Son from eternity, God is Father of the creature in time. Because Creator and creature have not the same nature, it is possible to call the Creator 'Father and Mother.' But Father and Mother cannot be used as the personal name of the first person because this would require to call the second person 'Son and Daughter' which is incompatible with the hypostatic union, the union of two distinct natures, God and man, in the one person of Jesus Christ.

Less absurd than the work of the National Council of Churches is a revision of the Jerusalem Bible by an English Benedictine, Dom Henry Wansbrough, who spent seven years expurgating sexist language from the text. He doesn't think it necessary to avoid the word father and pray to 'Our Parent in heaven,' but still replaces 'man' and 'men' by human being, person, people or humanity.

Feminist theology is one of the expressions of the new self-understanding of women. It is connected with the ordination of women to the priesthood (discussed below in Ch.6), the reform of the religious organisations of women after the Second Vatican Council and the debates on the role of women in the Church. In West Germany, 35.1 per cent of all theology students are women. Female theologians are at work in almost all Christian denominations and their common characteristic is the examination of the tenets and methods of classical theology in the light of their consciousness as women. They contend that male attitudes and prejudices have shaped the traditional positions and want to correct the male bias in the doctrine, discipline and activities of the churches.

The femininity discussion has prompted the question whether there is something that can be called 'feminine' literature and whether there is a feminine language, feminine style or feminine aesthetics. Two points ought to be stressed in this connection. First, that men and women are human beings. That the common human nature can exist as reality only in the form of man or woman does not eliminate the fact that both are human beings. The late Indira Gandhi once remarked: 'Aren't we women human beings, too? Aren't we from the same species? Why should we be viewed differently?' That a man thinks differently from a woman presupposes that both think, and there is no criterion to discern the thought of a man from that of a woman. The second point is that the difference between men and women is inseparable from the difference between individuals. As an individual, a human being is necessarily either a man or a woman. The same biological heritage that makes a human being a man or a woman also gives him or her the original characteristics of an individual. Just as there exists no human being 'as such,' there exists no 'man as such' or 'woman as such.' The thinking, feeling and conduct of a human being are necessarily the thinking, feeling and conduct of a person who is a man or woman. Masculinity and femininity appear only in the infinite variations of male or female persons.

If understood in the sense of 'egality,' 'equality' between men and women would cease to be an appropriate goal because it would imply the sameness of disparates. Men and women are the same as human beings but this refers only to the abstract idea or metaphysical essence of man and not to the human individual. A woman wants to be recognised as a human being in her own right, entitled to independence and a lifestyle based on independence if she so desires. Her position should not be determined by a comparison with man. This way of thinking should also be applied to the economic system. The problem is not to make economic conditions such as employment, wages, hours of work, etc., the same for men and women but to create an economic system in which every human being can earn a living and advance in accordance with his or her abilities and efforts.

The emancipation movement has retreated from some untenable positions and reordered its priorities. Its marching orders for the eighties are reproductive freedom, democratisation of the family, more recognition of the work done in the home and comparable pay for the work done outside. While the last two goals can claim general support, the first two require considerable differentiation and refinement to free them from sweeping ideological generalisations and adapt them to the requirements of reality.

Equal Rights Amendment

In the United States, a ten-year battle came to an end when, on 30 June, 1982, the proposed Equal Rights Amendment to the Constitution fell three states short of the required ratification by 38 states. The broad language of the amendment ('Equality of rights under the law shall not be denied or abridged by the United States or by any state on account of sex') had aroused fears of endless litigation to determine the exact meaning of the words 'equality' and 'denied or abridged.' Genuine concern about the extension of the draft to wives and daughters were mixed with the fear of ERA's impact on employment and the ridiculous fantasies of unisex toilets.

The Equal Rights Amendment was resubmitted to Congress in December 1982 but failed to obtain the required two-thirds majority when it was put to a vote in the House of Representatives in November 1983 (the vote was 278 to 147, six votes short of the necessary 284).

Opinions on the importance of ERA are greatly divided. George Will, for example, thinks that ERA is a nullity that adds nothing to the equal protection, due process and other guarantees for all 'persons' already in the Constitution and that it would hardly secure substantial advantages for women if adopted.

President Reagan, who is personally opposed to ERA, maintained that women could be better protected by changing federal and state laws discriminating against women. But in a scathing attack written for · the Washington Post, Ms Barbara Honegger called the project a sham and charged that the President had reneged on his commitment to women. The gender changes in 100 laws proposed by Senator Robert Dole, (Republican, Kansas)), were 'non-controversial' and would not make a major difference, she said.

Although the women activists lost the battle, their campaign has had far-reaching results. Women have become aware of what counts in public life; they know that there is no substitute for power. Politics on all levels will no longer be left to men. The era of women auxiliaries in which women did the humdrum work to support men is over. With their heightened political consciousness, women have made organisational progress and built organisations of women, by women, for women. With its own political machine, the women's movement will no longer depend on the good graces of men. Women will make their influence felt in all fields, not only in the problems involved in sex, marriage, motherhood and education, but wherever man's sexuality calls for advertence to the difference of man and woman, the adjustment of their roles and the accommodation of their interests. Women did rather poorly in the American elections in November 1982, but in the long run, women will change not only the political but also the economic landscape and build an order just to both sexes.

Women legislators were pushing the Economic Equity Act which, divided into five bills, would bar sex discrimination in insurance, reform pension laws, and grant tax breaks for housewives and parents who have to rely on day-care facilities. On average, women live longer, have fewer motor accidents but higher medical costs — at least until the age of 55. Insurance companies are opposed to unisex insurance and argue that there is nothing discriminatory in charging women lower rates for life insurance (for which they receive smaller annuities) and higher rates for health coverage. Critics claim that actuarial tables do not take into account other factors that influence mortality rates, such as race or religion, and that nondiscrimination is more important than actuarial arithmetic.

UN Decade for Women

To mark the end of the United Nations Decade for Women, a conference was convened in Nairobi. The official conference which was to last from 15-26 July, 1985 (it actually extended into Saturday, the 27 July), was attended by 2,100 delegates from 140 countries. The same as in Copenhagen in 1980, the official conference was preceded by a forum of non-governmental organisations with an eclectic agenda for 14,000 participants. There was much exchange and confrontation between women from different regions. Emotional issues such as apartheid and the status of Palestinians, migrant workers and refugees were hardly conducive to a harmonious exchange of ideas and it was difficult to find common concerns. While women from the western world stressed equality, those from the Third World cared more about development and the representatives of the socialist industrial countries focused on peace.

Repeating the clash at the end of the 1975 conference in Mexico City, the final documents of the Copenhagen conference had condemned Israel and equated Zionism with racism so that the United States, Canada, Australia and Israel had refused to sign the documents. In order to preclude a similar outcome, the US delegation, led by Maureen Reagan, President Reagan's daughter, demanded that all resolutions be adopted by 'consensus' (meaning unanimous approval) which would give any country a veto. But the western bloc compromised by agreeing to fall back to a majority decision if no agreement could be reached.

The United States had strenuously lobbied against the injection of political issues but became involved in political skirmishing by proposing the condemnation of terrorism in the final document. Leticia Shahani, the Filipina secretary-general of the conference, remarked: 'Politics affect the lives of women. One is not living in the real world if one does not see the linkage.' The conference nearly broke up over the call for a new international order and the reordering of the world economy. Political altercations on the situation of black women living under South Africa's apartheid system, conditions in Namibia and in Israeli-occupied Arab lands split the delegates into the traditional political camps of West, East, and the Third World. The squabbling in the last three days of the conference showed that women's issues are inextricably intertwined with what Maureen Reagan called 'the boys' games.'

In the official statements read by the delegates, women's conditions were generally described as oppressed and problematic the world over with the exception of the country at the podium where enormous progress had been made — or problems that admittedly existed were blamed on outside forces.

In the original draft, the title of the statement issued at the conclusion of the conference was couched in authentic bureaucratise: 'Forward-Looking Strategies of Implementation for the Advancement of Women and Concrete Measures to Overcome Obstacles to the Achievement of the Goals and Objectives of the United Nations Decade for Women for the Period 1986 to the Year 2000: Equality, Development, Peace.' The compromise formula condemned racism in all its forms and advocated women's equality in education, politics and health care.

A United Nations report on the state of the world's women noted that 90 per cent of all nations have official bodies charged with the advancement of women, half of them established since the beginning of the UN Decade for Women. In most countries, constitutional or legal provisions guarantee equality between women and men and 65 countries have acceded to the Convention on the Elimination of all Forms of Discrimination Against Women. Despite equal-pay-for-equal-work legislation in 90 countries, the average earnings of women working in manufacturing in 1982 were 73 per cent of the average earnings of men.

Women and Politics

Women who represent one-half of the world's population perform nearly two-thirds of all working hours but, in 1980, received only one-tenth of the world's income and owned less than one per cent of world property. In 12 countries, women must still obtain their husbands' approval for taking a job. Boys still outnumber girls in schools and women account for 60 per cent of the world's illiterates. But in 1985, girls made up 41 per cent of the secondary school population in developing countries. Half of the women of the world have access to contraceptives but women's participation in politics has made little progress during the decade. In developing countries such as India, Kenya and Venezuela, women occupy only 6 per cent of places in government.

The heightened political awareness of women has made them critical of the direction of national and international politics, the way political decisions are reached and political objectives pursued. In the male-dominated world of politics, the quest for power, status, fame and riches overrides morality, decency, truth and compassion. The cynical disregard of the risk of war, the entirely irrational expansion of armaments and the immense military expenditure while millions of human beings starve and die of hunger demonstrate the absurdity of the policies followed by the politicians now in charge. A change can only occur if the male dominance in politics is broken and women gain a decisive influence on the formulation and execution of politics.

The women's movement has undoubtedly achieved considerable

practical success. It has greatly fertilised thinking about the characteristics of men and women and their roles in family and society and promoted the recognition of women's rights. Women's organisations have worked for the solution of problems confronting women in private life as well as in the labour market. One of these organisations is the International Feminist Network (IFN) which specialises in fighting 'crimes against women.' It claims to have intervened in more than 50 cases involving the rights of women all over the world. One of these cases was that of Noreen Winchester, an Irish girl sentenced at the age of 20 to seven years' imprisonment for killing her father. Noreen had been sexually abused by her father ever since her mother's death when she was 13 and her father had threatened to kill her brothers and sisters if she dared speak. After getting raped once again one spring evening in 1976, Noreen drove a knife into her father's neck. The judge who tried her case found that Noreen had been a 'willing partner' for years and pronounced her guilty. One of the publications related to IFN, the Isis International Bulletin, took up her case. A Noreen Winchester Committee created as a result of the publicity put pressure on the authorities in Northern Ireland which eventually led to the young woman's release. According to the Committee, the case brought to light the occurrence of incest in 20 to 40 per cent of Belfast families.

Women everywhere are no longer willing to suffer the sexual aberrations of men silently. In Autofagasta in Chile, a group of women karate experts got hold of men cheating on their wives, undressed them and told them to be better husbands. They also punished men known to have raped women but not caught by the police.

When the French government refused to make an officially proclaimed 'Women's Day' (8 March, 1982) a national holiday, the French Women's Liberation Movement (MLF) called on all women to go on strike. The strike was also to advertise the movement's other demands which included pay for housework and free nursery schools. The last examples of direct action or overstated claims show that the women's movement is still experiencing growing pains but they also confirm the seriousness of the women's resolve to get a better deal for women.

An Asian women's group, the Japan-based Asian Women's Association, has attacked the cosmetics industry for 'pressing on women a uniform ideal of beauty in order to make money.' The cosmetics manufacturers, the group alleges, have implanted into women's consciousness the idea that 'beauty is make-up' and induced women who cannot even afford the necessities of life to spend money on cosmetics. The firms start by holding beauty classes on high school campuses, distributing free samples and advertising heavily in the mass media, particularly on TV. Since the Japanese market is saturated, the manufacturers have begun overseas selling campaigns, aiming at markets in East Asia and the Middle East in addition to Europe and

America.

It is meaningless to consider individual dispositions such as charm, sweetness or patience as universal attributes of femininity although certain human traits may be more pronounced in one sex than in the other. As all generalisations, the 'typical' woman does not exist in reality; nevertheless, some women may be closer to what men (or women) regard as feminine, and certain generalisations may be valid.

One of the woman's most outstanding qualities, for example, is her capacity for suffering and sacrifice. Man, too, can sacrifice himself, and the identification of manliness with courage, heroism and risking one's own life for a cause or a person is not without foundation. But the silent and suffering heroism of woman has saved innumerable families, and woman's self-sacrificing work in schools, hospitals, orphanages, old-people's homes and institutions for all kinds of people in need of help, care, warmth and love deserves more recognition than the assertion that this involves a degrading role attribution. This does not mean that the traditional role model of woman was right but that it was not completely wrong and included much that was based on what women are and have shown themselves to be throughout history. It is ridiculous to ascribe woman's capacity for self-sacrifice to a century-old role attribution by society.

The 'civilising' influence of woman has prompted the prison authorities in Calgary, Canada, to house seven women prisoners in the same jail with 97 male convicts. Living quarters are separate but men and women spend much of their work and recreation time together. Says prison director Ed Vandal who hopes that the experiment will have a humanising influence: 'Men in any kind of setting tend to behave at a higher standard when women are present.'

The traditional qualification of woman as the 'softer' or 'weaker' sex is only a half-truth at best. In most countries, women live longer than men, they are more enduring than men and recover quicker from damage to blood vessels and stress. In many cases, aspirin helps to prevent the recurrence of strokes in male patients but has no such effect on women, possibly because women's inner immunity is already stronger.

6

Woman's Social Position

THE FEMINIST MOVEMENT has led to a heated debate on woman's role in society in which attention has largely focused on the question of discrimination. At times, however, the discussions became rather emotional and often meandered into quite peripheral issues.

Role Attributions

The fundamental principle to be stressed in the consideration of woman's role in society must be that the well-being of society demands the recognition of the value and capacity of woman as a human being and her sexual distinctiveness. As a human being, woman can claim unimpeded access to education and all spheres of private and public life. Women's emancipation is not a question of making or treating women like men but of recognising women as equal though different human beings. Women have zero desire to act like or be treated as men. They want to be accepted as individuals, in their personal as well as their business life. A woman must be able to display her talents and abilities in whatever field she chooses and engage in any pursuit for which she can qualify. This does not mean that every woman should want to become president of a company. The respect due to women as human beings precedes and transcends any role attribution but does not negate the distinctiveness of many roles nor make it superfluous. Society needs women who can gracefully accept and competently fill the roles of wives and mothers without hating themselves for taking on these roles. No woman should be forced to accept any role on account of her sex, but it is obvious that there are functions that only women can perform and without which society cannot exist.

In the role attribution, a distinction must be made between sex-related functions and those unrelated to sex. There may be activities or occupations more suitable to one or the other of the sexes, but apart from some practices such as the couvade (ritualistic imitation of pregnancy and labour by the father), the functions related to sex are circumscribed by biological conditions. There is an enormous variety in the attribution of functions and occupations to the two sexes in different societies or at different ages and in different classes of the same society. The tendency to regard certain occupations as typically male or female goes together with the nearly equal participation of men and women in other fields.

Generally speaking, there is more interchange in functions and activities than is commonly assumed. Under circumstances in which groups are composed exclusively or almost exclusively of men, functions 'normally' fulfilled by women are discharged by men. The predominance of chefs in restaurants and hotels shows that the preparation of food is not a typically female concern. Household chores such as the washing or mending of clothes may be performed professionally by men and are done by men in the army, on expeditions or journeys, on ships or hunting trips, by gold miners or trappers or in similar situations.

Japanese Women

In most societies, women's role is still determined by tradition. In a comparative international survey conducted in 1982, Japanese women showed a considerable awareness of the discrimination against women in Japanese society but a strong adherence to the traditional sex roles. Separate roles for men and women were supported by 71 per cent of the women, 72 per cent gave priority to husband and family and 89 per cent said that housework was the woman's responsibility. While 73 per cent wanted their sons to graduate from college, only 27.7 per cent expressed the same ambition for their daughters.

Japanese women know that men are privileged in home life, employment, education, politics, legal status and social customs. Only in leisure activities is there anything approaching sexual equality. But there is little support for a feminist movement.

Chie Nakane, who is one of Japan's best-known sociologists (Professor at Tokyo University), maintains that, in Japan, status precedes age and sex, and that Japanese women are nearly always ranked inferior not because of their sex but because women seldom hold higher social status. It is certainly true that, as far as we know, Japanese women were never relegated to the abject conditions found in other societies. The veneration of Amaterasu-ô-mikami as the highest deity and ancestress of the Imperial house, the frequent succession of women to the throne and the possibility of women succeeding to the headship of a house show that the female sex was no obstacle to status. The recognition given to the writings of Murasaki Shikibu and Sei Shônagon (tenth century) prove that women were not regarded as inherently unqualified for cultural achievements. Nevertheless, Japanese society was and is a male-dominated and, to a large extent, male-oriented society in which women have very little influence on public life.

In the old Japanese 'house,' the wife was subservient not only to her husband but also to the husband's entire household. According to

Japan's moral code, a man had to put his obligations to his parents (*kô, kôkô*) first. These obligations existed irrespective of feelings or pleasure. Therefore, the parent's needs and wishes preceded those of his wife or children. As daughter-in-law, the wife was practically a servant of her mother-in-law and her consolation was that, one day, it would be her turn at this role.

Frequently, divorce resulted from dissatisfaction with the wife's behaviour on the part of the husband's parents rather than the husband himself. But even in feudal times, the wife was responsible for the inner working of the household and particularly for the upbringing of the children although her mother-in-law had a decisive voice in both. Because the master of the house was cast into the role of an absolute ruler, the children's affectionate ties were almost entirely with their mother which laid the foundation for the ascendancy of the mother in the next generation. Hence, the dichotomy of power in the Japanese family, the outward dominance of the male and the inward rule of the mother as the actual head of the household.

Japanese women bore much of the burden of the country's industrialisation. In the Meiji era, girls, largely recruited from rural areas, worked in the spinning mills, often under appalling conditions (tuberculosis, for example, claimed many victims). Textiles were Japan's first mass production industry and became one of the country's main export products.

During the Second World War, women, including schoolgirls, constituted a large part of the work force in the munitions industry, and in the era of rapid economic growth, large numbers of girls worked in industries such as electric appliances and precision machinery (such as cameras).

In the post-war years, physical survival depended greatly on the ability of the housewife to make ends meet and to find the necessary food. The housing shortage in the large cities, partly resulting from the war-time destruction and partly from the enormous influx of people from the country into the cities, has been an important factor in the rapid transition to the nuclear family. This effectively stopped the influence of in-laws on young couples and, at least in the cities, to live separately from parents became the dominant pattern.

The post-war development resulted in accentuating the sharp contrast between the position of the woman in private and in public. An English novelist, Angela Carter, wrote: 'I have met some perfectly splendid women in Japan, women of all kinds. Many women, however, are so happy with the present situation — in which they have unlimited power, within the home — and they can't see their position in the home as degrading. And they don't want to change it, not basically. Besides, I'd rather be a Japanese housewife than a company man. Anyone in their sense would' (*The Japan Experience,* ed. by

Ronald Bell, p.32f).

According to Suzanne Vogel of Harvard University, in her role as housewife, a Japanese woman is largely independent of her husband and has real power in this sphere. She is the boss and manager of the home, organising her work according to her judgement. She does the budgeting, the shopping, the banking and saving and allots an allowance to her husband for his daily expenses. She makes most decisions about child-rearing on her own. The customary speeches at wedding receptions — mostly by men of the older generation — voice the traditional clichés on the roles of husband and wife. The actual situation in Japan is reflected in the reaction of a Japanese woman to the United Nations Conference on Women in Copenhagen in July 1980: 'Women hold power at home and they are neither oppressed nor weak.'

Recent marketing research has stressed the influence of women on purchasing decisions. The old distinction between 'typically male' and 'typically female' products has become invalid which causes serious miscalculations in marketing strategy. Women are at least involved, even if they do not decide, purchases from alcoholic beverages to cameras, electronic entertainment equipment and automobiles. They often buy what the husband wears and have a strong voice in financial investment.

An international survey, commissioned by the Japanese government, included the question: 'Who makes the final decision on living expenses?' The answers (in per cent) are given below.

	Husband	Wife	Husband and Wife
Japan	5.2	79.4	11.8
United States	14.6	36.5	45.5
Federal Republic of Germany	15.4	11.5	70.4
Britain	32.7	32.6	33.6

Formerly, the wife, trudging a few steps behind her husband carrying bundles or the baby while her lord and master strutted ahead unburdened, was a familiar sight. Nowadays, it is more common to see the wife at the wheel of a car driving her husband to the railway station, taking the children to school, to kindergarten or to a piano lesson, or going shopping. The National Police Agency reported that the number of women holding a driver's licence amounted to over 16.7 million in August 1984, equivalent to a third of the total (50.1 million). About 60 per cent of women between the ages of 20 and 39 have a driver's licence. The number of women drivers increased 2.7 times in the past ten years. Many young women acquire a driver's licence before getting married. A driver's licence is more important for a bride than the tea ceremony or flower arrangement, and a number of women use their car for part-time work.

For personal service, the Japanese man depends entirely on his wife; without his wife, he is completely helpless. It is that way not because the Japanese male wants it but because the Japanese housewife arranges it. The assertion of male superiority is completely out of line with Japanese reality but male chauvinism reigns unabated.

Social Environment and the Position of Women

Generally speaking, the upper classes tended to protect women and children despite strong discriminatory treatment of women; among the lower classes, it was largely taken for granted that women and children had to work and women had to learn to take care of themselves. Prior to the industrial revolution, women were involved in the production process because many of the things needed in the household were produced at home (such as clothing). Products manufactured by industrial production methods replaced many of the hand-made products and diminished the importance of women's work. In agriculture, the work of women was often replaced by machines, limiting women's activities to the household. These developments reinforced the image of woman as the 'weaker vessel' who needed to be protected by the male.

There remain enormous differences in the position of women and the fields of activity open to them depending on the social climate of each country. Sheik Abdel-Aziz Bin Baz, general chairman of the administration of Iftaa (Koranic interpretation) contended that allowing women to drive cars would be 'fraught with a lot of depravity, including being alone with strangers, and running the risk of falling into incalculable sin.' In many societies, the roles and activities of women differ according to social classes. In the middle and higher classes, the activities of women may be more restricted than in lower classes, and in urban areas more than in rural societies.

In ancient China, woman's position was determined by the three obediences imposed by Confucianism — obedience to father, husband and son. Women were property and trained to be subordinate and subservient. A husband could divorce his wife on seven grounds while a wife had no grounds for divorce. At the same time, however, Chinese history is full of examples of the influence of empresses and imperial concubines and empress dowagers have ruled China from the first empress dowager Lü of the Han dynasty to the last empress dowager Tz'u Hsi who died in 1908.

In modern China, too, women have played prominent roles, so the three Soong sisters of whom Madame Chiang Kai-shek (Soong Mei-ling) and Madame Sun Yat-sen (Soong Ching-ling) were best known (Soong Ai-ling was married to Kung Hsiang-Hsi, a Kuomingtang politician). In recent years, Jiang Qing, the wife of Mao Zedong, and Ye Qun, the wife of Marshal Lin Biao, achieved fame (or notoriety). Equality of the sexes is still an explosive issue in today's China. Discrimination against women persists in job assignments and pay although China is training women pilots to fly the Boeing 747 jumbo jets of the National Airline together with women navigators and radio operators. China's birth control policy allowing only one child per family has created a new problem and a situation highly inimical to the position of women. Parents want a boy to carry on the family and women blame themselves when they have a baby girl.

Compared with the Chinese mainland, the ethnic Chinese women in South-East Asia have attained a much greater degree of freedom, equality and independence although women pursuing careers outside the family still form a very small minority.

Mustafa Kemal Pasha Atatürk, who wanted to convert what was left of the old Ottoman empire into a modern state, abolished Islam as state religion. The Civil Code contains some provisions protecting the status of women. Although the wife is obliged to live at the domicile chosen by the husband, she can handle legal transactions related to the household and pay household expenses. But the religious courts remained in control of family matters and everyday life conformed to the tenets of Islam. The wife was subject to her husband who could punish her and deny her support if she neglected her duties. These included the education of the children and the management of the household. But she could not conclude contracts without her husband's consent and go out without serious reason. Formerly, she was not supposed to do the shopping which was considered the husband's business.

In the Turkish communites abroad, such as those who form part of the *Gastarbeiter* in Germany, young women have often repudiated the restraints of the home country and adopted the pattern of the host country in dress, conduct and occupation.

In many African societies, political independence has changed little in the social position of women. Most women in subsahelian Africa are still bought by their husbands for a bride price. The price usually consists of cattle, goats, sheep or cash and may be as high as $800.

Economic change may add new forms of female harassment to the unequal treatment of women based on traditional custom. In Burkina Faso (the former Upper Volta), only about 14 per cent of the girls are enrolled in primary schools and they are brought up on the premise that they are made for cooking, cleaning, collecting the firewood, having babies and being submissive to men. In the cities, the country's president, Captain Thomas Sankara charged, a woman often is obliged to go and give herself to a man, a boss, before she can get a job.

Customary law, a mix of unwritten law and statutes usually inter-preted by tribal courts, requires women to seek permission from their guardian, generally the father or husband, to leave their homes, look for jobs, open a bank account, go to night school, or even sell their own second-hand clothes. Women are traditionally relegated to the roles of mother, housekeeper, brewer of corn beer and field worker. The wife gets up in the morning without awakening her husband. Before going to bed at night after a 16-hour day, she will have prepared breakfast for her family, worked the family's vegetable patch, gathered firewood, pounded sun-dried corn for meal, fetched water from the communal pump, cooked the family supper and washed the dishes. On the African continent, 55 per cent of illiterates are women and women do 70 per cent of the farm work. Many women, discouraged from ordinary jobs by men, are forced into prostitution.

In many developing countries, the lack of sanitary facilities imposes a particularly heavy burden on women. The universal failure to introduce toilets into rural and poor urban areas forces women to relieve themselves before dawn or after sunset. They have to look for isolated spots — just the places that leave them open to rape and molestation. The lack of water is another condition resulting in severe hardships for women. In areas where purdah (seclusion of women) is observed such as in the villages of Bangladesh, women are not even allowed to collect water during the day. The lack of water is one of the major reasons for the high incidence of diarrheal diseases which kill about six million children every year in the Third World. It is not only a question of pure drinking water but also of sufficient water to keep hands clean when undertaking household chores such as cooking and serving food and handling children.

Equality of Women

The efforts to secure equality for women go back many centuries. In the West, Christianity asserted the basic equality of men and women as human beings and children of God, but this had little influence on the political, social, legal and economic position of women. The major historical religions have not always been fair to women which may have something to do with the fact that they were founded by men (some sects, however, were started by women). In the Jewish temple, women were only admitted to the Court of Women, and in the synagogues, women were mute, darkly veiled participants from behind the non-transparent barriers of the side of women, the left-hand section of the worship service area. In the Christian congregations, women came forth with speaking in tongues, hymns, prayer calls and prophecies, but St Paul returned to the synagogal principle: 'Women should keep silence in the Church' (1 Cor 14,34). Religious enthusiasm inspired prophetesses in the times of the Old and the New Testament, and there may be more charismatic women than men among the saints venerated by the Church.

St Paul stressed the irrelevance of sex to faith and salvation rather than the equality of men and women and unequivocally asserted the

WOS1-G

supremacy of man over woman (1 Cor 11, 7-10; Eph 5,22-24; Col 3,18; 1 Tim 2,11). The role attributed to Eve in the Biblical account of man's fall (Gen 3,6; 1 Tim 2,14) occasioned many adverse comments on the female sex. The great Origen who castrated himself was one of many authors vituperating woman as a sensuous and base seductress.

The ambivalent valuation of woman found its most explicit expression in western society as it developed in the Middle Ages. The cult of the Virgin Mary became a dominant feature of Catholicism. Women gained influence on public life and shaped the course of history but the belief in witchcraft claimed thousands of innocent victims. Women were sheltered in monasteries to be symbols of mankind's desire for holiness and perfection, and women were kept in whorehouses to satisfy male lust.

The first woman to obtain a doctorate from a European university, Elena Lucrezia Cornaro Piscopia, wanted to become a doctor of theology but the chancellor of the faculty of theology at the university of Padua vetoed her promotion. Despite the opposition of some professors, she was promoted to doctor of philosophy on 25 June, 1678, in the presence of numerous scholars and dignataries from all over Europe. The new *Magistra et Doctrix* who could read the Bible in the original Hebrew and Greek wrote many learned dissertations on philosophy, theology and natural sciences and became a member of many European academics.

Ordination of Women

A controversy which is of little practical interest to the ordinary woman but which shows the scope of the women's struggle for equality is the ordination of women in the Christian churches. The Catholic Church has repeatedly declared her opposition to the ordination of women although many theologians are of the opinion that there is no dogmatic foundation for this position and that it is purely a problem of Church discipline. In 1980, the British Catholic laity held a National Pastoral Conference and asked the Church to consider women for the priesthood. For good measure, the Conference also urged a reconsideration of the ban on birth control and divorce. It seems not altogether impossible that the disastrous decrease in vocations may force a change in the Church's position.

The new code of Canon Law states the principle of equality of man and woman and reduced the number of canons discriminating against women from 30 to two. Of the remaining discriminatory provisions, one excludes women from acting as ecclesiastical judges and the other retains the restriction of holy orders to men. The Church hierarchy, therefore, remains exclusively male so that women have no direct influence on the direction of the Church.

When the Second Vatican Council convened in 1962, not a single woman was present at the assembly which prompted the Belgian Cardinal Leo Suenens to ask where 'the other half of the Church' had been left. For the following session, 16 women, eight religious and eight lay representatives of large Catholic organisations, were allowed to observe the work of the council. But the position of women in the Church was not debated and the Vatican has opposed any attempt to have the problem of the ordination of women taken up by any ecclesiastical forum.

The question of women priests is only one of the issues on which the male chauvinism of the Vatican has created feminine opposition. Problems involving the position and work of women in the Church were behind the exodus of 250,000 women, about 60,000 of them in the United States, from the convents and religious communities in the last 20 years. In the United States, many of the orders and religious congregations of women have traditionally been engaged in educational and charitable work under the close supervision of the clergy — the nuns' management of the parish school under the direction of the parish priest was a typical example. But a wave of enthusiasm and religious fervour led many religious to political and social activism and they took up work related to the conditions of modern society. Some of these activities were frowned upon by the Church authorities. There is considerable discomfort among the 'new nuns' with the disregard of feminine concerns by the Roman prelates and their assertion that the views of the American nuns on the mission of women are incompatible with the Catholic tradition of the women's humble service for the Church.

The revolt against the Vatican's disregard of women's issues is less pronounced in Europe but many Catholic women are no longer willing to submit to the moral dictates of the Church. Pope John Paul II seems personally convinced that, unless she becomes a nun, the woman's mission is to bear children and to take care of the household. His personal views on sex may explain his insistence on the traditional sexual morality and discipline of the Church. But as a Dutch organisation put it, 'one can hardly expect blind obedience from people who are neither slaves nor children.'

The denomination with the largest number of ordained women in pastoral roles is the United Methodist Church. In 1983, 1,500 of its 36,500 ministers (about four per cent) were women, and one of the church's 45 active bishops was a woman. The Southern Baptists, the largest Protestant denomination in the United States, had 200 women among their 33,000 ministers, most in chaplancies, institutions or some kind of denominational work with relatively few in the pastorate, some as co-pastors with their husbands. Nationwide, the Episcopal Church had ordained 333 female priests and 164 female deacons. Opposition was strong, not only from rank-and-file church members but also from church leaders. In the Dallas diocese, only 33 per cent of the Episcopalians were in favour of the ordination of women. Nevertheless, a growing number of women were entering the divinity schools. Between one-third and one-half of the theology students at Yale, Princeton and the University of Chicago's theology school were women.

The first Anglican woman priest was the Reverend Florence Li Tim Oi who was ordained by the bishop of Hong Kong in 1944. Two years later, she was ordered to resign by the Anglican leadership but she regained her status in 1971 when local missions were allowed to ordain women. Since then, about 700 women have been ordained Anglican priests in Hong Kong, Kenya, Canada, New Zealand and the United States. The General Synod of the Church of England had agreed in 1975 that there were no fundamental theological objections to the ordination of women but did not sanction the admission of women to the priesthood. In 1983, the synod decided to admit women (who were already accepted as lay deacons) to the clerical order of deacons on the same basis as men. In November 1984, the synod voted, 307 to 183, to allow women to become priests. The change in Canon Law will have to be approved by the majority of the dioceses, sanctioned again by two-thirds of the general synod and approved by both houses of parliament.

The London *Daily Mail* reported an unbelievable outburst of opposition to the ordination of women. In a letter to his parishioners, the Reverend Andrew Reakes-Williams, vicar of Holy Trinity Church in Oswestry, wrote: 'If you take the argument for the ordination of women to its logical conclusion, you have to agree to the ordination of chimpanzees to act as chaplains to the animals.' This statement not only shows that the Reverend misunderstood the reasons for the ordination of women but it also suggests that his views on man and the ministry may be more than muddled. The atrociousness of his imbecile assertion: '. . . if you ordain a woman, you may as well ordain a chimpanzee,' is by no means mitigated by his disclaimer: 'I'm not anti-women but I want women to have the chance to be first-class Christians and not second-class men. Women should not be ordained to a male function.' That is exactly what the whole controversy is about: is the priesthood a male function?

In 1982, the Evangelical Church in Germany (Evangelische Kirche in Deutschland) had 1,302 women pastors, eight per cent of the total number of pastors. In 1964, their number had been 282, two per cent of all pastors.

After years of discussion, the Rabbinical Assembly, the professional organisation of Conservative Judaism, voted to ordain women as rabbis. Of the four branches of modern Judaism (Orthodox,

Conservative, Reform and Reconstructionist), only the Orthodox branch does not admit women as rabbis.

Women's Emancipation

The movements for the emancipation of women were particularly strong in Britain and in the United States. Following the 'Declaration of the Rights of Men' by the French revolutionists in 1789, the Frenchwoman Olympe de Gouge composed a 'Declaration of the Rights of Women.' 'Woman is born free,' she asserted, 'and has the same rights as man: freedom, progress, security and the right to resist oppression. The state is based on the community of man and woman, and legislation must be the expression of this cooperation. All citizenesses, the same as all citizens, must participate in legislation either personally or through their elected representatives. All citizenesses and all citizens must have the same access to public positions, honours and professions. 'A woman who has the right to be executed must also have the right to become a minister.' This declaration had no practical effect and, appositely with her macabre observation, de Gouge herself was executed.

In 1790, the Marquis de Condorcet, one of the leaders of the French enlightenment, wrote 'The Admission of Women to Full Citizenship,' and two years later, in 1792, Mary Wollstonecraft published her *Vindication of the Rights of Women*. John Stuart Mill who, while a member of Parliament, introduced a motion for women's suffrage, expounded his views on emancipation in his *On the Subjection of Women* (1869).

In the nineteenth century, women's societies were formed in Britain, France, Germany and the United States. These societies may roughly be divided into three types. 1. Educational women's movements claiming equal educational opportunities for women with access to all schools and institutions of learning. 2. Social women's movements asserting the right of women to influence public life and demanding improvement of the conditions of women working in industry or doing piece work at home, protection of mothers and abolition of licensed prostitution. 3. Political women's movements revindicating the legal equality of women and their participation in politics. In the latter struggle, the suffragettes caused considerable stir by their uproarious methods which included hunger strikes and vandalism. In Britain, Emmeline Pankhurt founded the Women's Social and Political Union in 1903 and in 1906 launched a militant campaign during which she was several times imprisoned.

Women obtained the suffrage in Finland in 1906, in the Soviet Union in 1917, in Germany in 1918, in the United States in 1920, in Great Britain in 1928, in France in 1944, and in Japan in 1946. In the

Soviet Union, women have theoretically had complete equality since the revolution. They have equal access to almost all kinds of work but not to political, economic and scientific leadership.

The United States is most advanced in real equality but despite all the recent legislation against discrimination, it is said that there are still some 800 federal laws that treat women and men differently, plus hundreds of laws at other levels. Some states have laws differentiating between men and women in matters such as inheritance, credit and property ownership. The Equal Rights Amendment failed to get the necessary ratification by three-quarters of the states. In the United Kingdom, the Equal Pay Act of 1970 and the Sex Discrimination Act of 1975 guarantee women equality in pay, employment, education, job training and access to housing, goods, facilities and services. Actually, women's pay reached a peak of 75.5 per cent of men's pay in 1977 but was down to 73.9 per cent in 1979.

The legal enforcement of equality is being turned against women and minorities for whose benefit the laws were often enacted. The California Supreme Court ruled that bars offering 'ladies' nights' and other businesses that give discounts specifically for women are violating the state's civil rights law. State law banning discrimination based on sex forbids the granting of special prices to women, the court decided.

In Britain, women have been in the forefront of the peace movement. Among Britain's disarmers, the women who maintained the camp of protesters at Greenham Common from September 1981 to 1984 have been the most distinctly feminist group. They have shown a typically feminine patient perseverance, remaining through three winters, living in makeshift shelters of plastic sheets and warmed only by an open fire. Distrust of men was deep-seated. No men were allowed to join them. They have no organisation, no leaders, no spokeswoman — formal organisations are the inventions of men, as are wars and politics. 'Take the toys from the boys' was their motto for disarmament. They believed in non-violent direct action, and their protest was founded on emotion rather than intellect. They were not concerned with the rationale or effectiveness of their action but only with its function as an expression of their feelings.

As elsewhere, legislation has not ended male chauvinism in Britain. Under the sex equality laws, women have the same rights as men in bars, except in private clubs where a males-only policy can be retained. On the first day of the new laws, Maggie Brittain, head of the equal rights committee of the National Union of Journalists, went to the El Vino bar, a Fleet Street watering spot known for its policy of serving ladies only at tables. She held out a five-pound note and ordered a round of drinks at the bar for the group of women journalists who had come with her. Paul Bracken, the manager, told them that the 96-year-old tradition of men only at the bar would be continued and refused.

'This is a ludicrous, pathetic and pitiful exhibition of mindless prejudice,' said Mrs Brittain. 'The rule that women must sit down was introduced for purely chivalrous reasons,' commented owner Christopher Mitchell. 'When ladies were ladies, they would never dream of standing at a bar by themselves and drinking.' Mrs Brittain went to court to force El Vino bar go give up its policy of serving ladies only at tables and not at the bar. The High Court turned down the application but three appeal court judges unanimously set aside the judgement. When the two women turned up at the bar to enjoy their triumph, the bar's management refused to serve them, citing a provision in the drinking laws that allows barmen to turn away 'troublemakers'.

Women in Public Life

In a nationwide plebiscite, Switzerland introduced female suffrage at the federal level in 1971. Women have also been given the right to vote in cantonal and communal elections in all but two cantons of the Swiss confederation. Typical of the remaining male autocracy was the decision of the all-male Landsgemeinde (popular assembly) of Appenzell-Innerrhoden, the smaller part of the canton Appenzell, in April 1982 to continue denying women the vote in town and cantonal elections.

In neighbouring Liechtenstein, women lost a court battle for the right to vote. In April 1982, the five male judges of the supreme court of the principality ruled that voting rights for men only was compatible with the clause in the constitution that 'all citizens are equal before the law.' In referendums in 1971 and 1973, Liechtenstein men rejected the idea of giving women the vote, but thanks largely to the strong support of the prince, women were given the franchise in 1984.

Everywhere, politics is still dominated by men although public consciousness has changed. A poll of the Allensbacher Institute of Opinion Research found that the majority of both men and women rejected the statement that 'politics is something for men.' In 1966, only 51 per cent of the women had taken exception to this view; in November 1984, the percentage had risen to 76 per cent. Only 42 per cent of the men interviewed in 1966 held a different opinion; they were 67 per cent in 1984. Male thinking about women's participation in politics surfaced in the remarks by White House chief of staff Donald Regan that women did not understand arms control and the political issues involved in the Geneva meeting of President Ronald Reagan and Secretary General Mikhail Gorbachev and would be more interested in the tea party for Nancy Reagan and Raisa Gorbachev. Said Irene Natividad of the National Women's Political Caucus: 'It's a rather typical statement from the men of this administration so I'm not surprised by it. This is an administration that is led by men whose minds are frozen in the 50s.'

Women have the right to vote but men still predominate in parties, representative assemblies and governments. In the West German parties, women constituted 25 per cent of the membership of the Christian Democratic Party (CDU), 24.5 per cent of the members of the Socialists (SPD) and 24 per cent of those of the Free Democratic Party (FDP). But the proportion of women in the parties' executives was much lower, 6.3 per cent for the CDU, 17.5 per cent for the SPD and 12 per cent for the FDP. Equally disproportionate was the percentage of women representatives in parliament (Bundestag), CDU 7.6, SPD 9.8 and FDP 8.6 per cent. Only one woman was in Chancellor Helmut Kohl's cabinet. Things were different in the Green Party. Women constituted between 35 and 40 per cent of its membership, 30 per cent of its executives and, in 1984, 40 per cent of its parliamentarians (because the party rotates its representatives, the percentage dropped to 25 per cent in 1985). For a year, the executive of the parliamentary party was made up entirely of women, and they worked more effectively, smoothly and harmoniously than the executives of other parties.

Political parties use (or misuse) women largely to demonstrate their concern for equality. Women politicians serve as fig leaves for men's clubs but despite their 'alibi functions,' women must have greater qualifications than men to succeed in politics. They must bear heavier pressure and must conceal their competence under a feminine appearance.

Icelandic women staged a 24-hour strike to protest against male privileges. Women constitute over half of Iceland's population of 240,000 and over 80 per cent of the women are working. A walkout by Icelandair's 160 stewardesses grounded the national carrier and President Vigdis Finnbogadottir initially refused to sign urgent legislation ordering air hostesses back to work in order to show solidarity with her sisters, but she backed down under government pressure. Although a woman is president, women mostly hold low-paying jobs in schools, medical facilities and fish-packing plants and seldom rise to managerial posts. Women complained that their men behaved worse than those of other western countries and virtually keep them out from posts of financial and economic power.

In the long run, education may enable more women to advance in public life as well as business. Today's generation of young women in West Germany has a much higher standard of education than their parents. While 61 per cent of their fathers and 71 per cent of their mothers had only gone to elementary school 67 per cent of the daughters have had some kind of secondary education. Some 33 per cent of the girls have graduated from high school (Oberschule or

Gymnasium), as against 15 per cent of their fathers and 5 per cent of their mothers. In 1983, 44,857 young women (in West Germany) finished their training as apprentices and started to work as 'journeymen' in professions such as butchers, bakers, confectioners, cabinet-makers, joiners, painters, electricians, auto mechanics, printers and stonemasons.

In the People's Republic of China, only a third of the girls go to school because of traditional discrimination. Girls started to attend school only at the turn of the century, and since the Communists came to power in 1949, they have promoted equal education for both sexes. But many Chinese parents think that educated women are quarrelsome and that it is difficult to find husbands for them.

Vietnam's war-time efforts to rely on women in running the country have not been followed through in peace-time. Despite 30 years of government campaigns to promote women's rights, Confucian thinking which honours men and despises women has not been eradicated. Communism has done away with the more debasing aspects of Cunfucianism such as arranged marriages, polygamy and concubinage and a law promulgated in 1960 gave women the right to choose their husbands and remarry without losing claim to either children or property. In Vietnam's national tradition, women are recognised as the protagonists of anti-Chinese resistance. In the first century AD, the Trung sisters, the two daughters of a local aristocrat, led an unsuccessful revolt against Chinese rule, and a legendary third-century Amazon, Lady Trieu, rode into battle against the Chinese on an elephant. During the war with the United States, women took the place of men in fields, factories and administration; they learned to plough, drive tractors and fire anti-aircraft guns. But with the end of the war, women have been pushed back into their traditional roles and now have much less influence than during the war. Many women have to carry the double burden of outside employment and household chores. Government policy emphasises the customary female occupations of child care, nursing and low-level education, and the jobs most often filled by women are in agriculture, light industry and handicrafts. The sex imbalance created by the war has furthered a return to polygamy in the form of second wives or girl-friends, while party and government have relapsed into the pattern of male ascendancy usual in communist regimes.

Women in Muslim Countries

Actual developments in Muslim countries are hardly favourable for women. Initially, Muslim women leaders supported the Islamisation movement. In Algeria, the veil became a means of protest against the French and in Iran, young women, above all women students, covered themselves with chador and shawl and even wore sunglasses and dark gloves to demonstrate their opposition to the Shah. In Egypt, too, the chador was a sign of social protest. But Islamisation has failed to give women their rightful place in society and in Iran, many of the victims of the Khomeini dictatorship are women, while all women have been reduced to the status of second-class citizens.

The literal enforcement of Koranic law has curtailed women's freedom in all walks of life and the restrictions imposed in the name of religion have made women the servants of their menfolk. Thousands of women were chased out of official posts, offices and factories. Women are no longer allowed to be judges or lawyers. Higher careers are closed to women and advancement to management positions is unthinkable. Most of the women who had been teaching in higher institutions were dismissed when the universities reopened. By decree, the percentage of women students was reduced to 10 per cent. In order to avoid contact with male students, women must sit in the last rows of classrooms. Sometimes, a curtain partitions an auditorium into sections for men and women. If a woman student wants to ask a question, she must do so in writing — the professor might be aroused by the sound of a female voice. Coeducational schools were abolished soon after the revolution. To shake hands with a man is forbidden, dancing has been outlawed as immoral, and women are banned from almost all sports.

Marriage laws have been changed to conform to the Qur'an. Men are encouraged to take up to four wives; they have the right to divorce their wives almost at will and retain automatic custody of any children. Women have been deprived of the right to divorce and family courts have been abolished. The testimony of a woman is worth only half that of a man and counts only if confirmed by that of a man. A woman's testimony is inadmissable in murder cases.

No woman now dares appear in public without a full head covering and many women are seen in the chador which envelopes them from head to foot. 'Death to the unveiled' was a favourite chant at revolutionary parades and men who found a woman's clothing not modest enough could freely abuse her not only verbally but strike and spit on her. Armed revolutionary guards now enforce the observance of clothing regulations. Offenders are lucky if they are let off with insults, the written promise not to repeat the infraction and the statement that in case of recidivism, they are willing to accept the punishment for prostitution — death by firing squad, stoning or hanging.

Not all women get away with a signature. Many are detained and have to undergo a week of moral reeducation. A girl recently committed suicide after being released from detention. In her last letter she wrote that she had been raped seven times while being detained. Young women who are imprisoned and can be visited by their parents implore them to procure them birth control pills. Especially girls condemned to death are sexually abused by their guards.

Brothels were closed after the revolution and many prostitutes executed. In the meantime, however, a different form of prostitution has been introduced. In addition to regular marriages, the law recognises temporary marriages which may be concluded for periods from one hour to 99 years. Houses in which single women live together have been established, particularly in larger cities, and the guardian has power to conclude temporary marriages for the inmates, many of whom are young war widows or orphans. The nubility of girls applying for marriage licences is tested by touching their breasts.

Different from Islamic orthodoxy, Bahaism teaches the unity of all races and the equality of the sexes. But the main reason for the persecution of the Bahaists in Iran may be their claim that Baha'i is the universal religion of the future which will create a peaceful world society with a world government.

There have been reports of discriminatory actions in Pakistan. The fundamentalist mullahs on the Islamic Ideology Council are trying to impose strict Islamic values on society and are re-writing Pakistan's laws. They want to repeal the Family Law Ordinance which is the only protection for women. It makes the registration of marriage compulsory and requires the husband to obtain the first wife's permission before taking a second wife. Islamic rules favour the male, but women have a pre-emptive right to family assets, alimony and the right to custody of their children.

The Pakistani government denies any changes in the status of women. Universal suffrage has been in existence since the establishment of Pakistan in 1947. The elected local councils have a certain number of women councillors and women hold high-level positions in the administration. Women can engage in careers and there are women doctors, teachers, scientists, journalists, lawyers, bankers and business women. Mrs Buttho and her daughter have played important roles in politics.

But critics charge that the government intends to segregate sexes in education and plans to establish separate universities for women. Only 33 per cent of the girls go to school, and women's literacy rate is 11.6 per cent. Women have been banned from participating in spectator sports except in front of all-female audiences and women were not permitted to compete in the Asian games in New Delhi in September 1982. Civil servants, teachers and schoolgirls are required to wear the Pakistani version of the chador, and women appearing in public with bare heads or arms are harassed.

In the summer of 1982, a fundamentalist preacher and member of the Council of Islamic Ideology asserted on state television that a woman's place is in the kitchen. 'In Islam, the actual field of movement for a woman remains within four walls,' he declared. Women should wear the chador because otherwise, they would be responsible for sex crimes. The laws drafted by the council include increased flogging of women convicted of adultery and lower legal protection of women. The compensation to be paid to a family for the death of a woman should be fixed at half of that of a man, the family of a crime victim could ask for the death penalty only if the victim were a man, and the evidence of a male witness should count as much as that of two women.

Fundamentalist mullahs called the women who participated in a demonstration against one of the government's discriminatory bills (which was brutally broken up by police wielding clubs and using tear gas) 'traitors to Islam' and threatened to declare any demonstrating woman an apostate which would prevent her from marrying a Muslim.

Women are generally disadvantaged in access to education. In North Yemen, the country with the highest illiteracy rate in the world (1981), 82 per cent of the men and 99 per cent of the women were unable to read or write. There are, however, Muslim countries where the education of women has made progress. In Saudi Arabia, education is compulsory through secondary school. In 1982, female students receiving secondary education accounted for nearly 39 per cent of total enrolment. In 1983, Crown Prince Abdullah, on behalf of King Fahd, announced that effective with the school year starting in September, Saudi Arabian women would no longer be allowed to enrol in colleges and universities outside the kingdom. The needs for higher education could be met by existing institutions in the country. There are eleven colleges for women (some of which serve primarily as teacher training institutions) with 14,000 students. Women are also eligible for segregated programmes at five of the country's seven universities in which nearly 80,000 students of both sexes are enrolled. Female students are separated from male professors and video screens are used for communication.

Women are not allowed to drive cars and young boys ferrying their mothers or sisters are blamed for many of the traffic accidents. A company, the Saudi Cable Co., plans to set up a 'women only' factory and in order to circumvent the labour law prohibiting men and women from sharing the same work area, the male supervisors and the female workers will communicate by video screen.

In Oman, education is separate for boys and girls but married women can work together with men. Even policewomen wear ankle-length skirts but women can drive cars and are not necessarily veiled.

An institution not strictly related to education but indicating the progress made by women in Islamic countries is the Museum of Islamic Art built up by Sheik Nasser Sabah al-Ahmad al-Sabah, a businessman who belongs to Kuwait's royal family and his wife. Sheika Hussa, a mother of four and also a member of Kuwaiti royalty, the daughter of a former emir, was the driving force behind the project. The couple started collecting works of Islamic art in 1975 for themselves but when the treasures piled up, they asked Dr Marilyn Jenkins of New York's Metropolitan Museum of Art to make the collection into a museum. She recruited nine women for her museum-creating team and assembled sections on each great Muslim dynasty. Sheika Hussa is the permanent director of the museum; she runs its conservation department and its educational programme and supervises its 40,000-volume library.

Despite half a century of feminism, Egyptian women have to shoulder two roles, the traditional role of housewife and mother and the modern role of a working woman. Thousands of young women graduate from Egyptian universities each year and most of them join the work force. Work has become a financial necessity for a woman and may even help her to find a husband. It is common for a young man to marry a woman who can contribute to the family budget although he still expects to be lord and master at home. Good nurseries are too expensive for most families so many children are deposited with the grandparents in the morning and collected again in the afternoon.

Under Egyptian law, men and women must be paid equally if they do the same job. The law bans employers from assigning hard physical work or late night work to women and allows women a fully paid 40-day leave of absence after childbirth and up to four years of unpaid maternity leave. But these benefits often prove an obstacle to the employment of women.

Women's Movements in Japan

In Japan, the movement for women's rights began in the nineteenth century, partly on a theoretical level with writers such as Kôka Doi (*Bunmeiron Onna Daigaku*) and Yukichi Fukuzawa (*Nihon Fujinron*), and partly in connection with the People's Rights Movement. In the beginning of the Meiji era, problems related to women included equal rights of men and women, equality of husband and wife, women's education and the abolition of concubines and licensed prostitution. Encouraged by the People's Rights Movement in the 1880s, Hideko Kageyama (Fukuda) and Toshiko Kishida propounded sexual equality. The World Conference for the Abolition of Prostitution held in 1880 issued an appeal for the suppression of public prostitution and this cause was taken up by the Tokyo Women's Moral Reform Association — *Tokyo Fujin Kyôfu-kai*. The name was later changed to *Nihon Kirisuto-kyô Fujin Kyôfu-kai*, Japan Christian Women's Moral Reform Association which, in assimilation to similar foreign organisations, was usually called Women's Christian Temperance Union. This association, founded in 1886, based the claim for the abolition of prostitution on the demand for monogamy.

The discriminatory attitude of the Japanese authorities to women appeared in the infamous Security Police Law of 1900 which, in Article 5, prohibited women, minors and the members of certain professions, to belong to political organisations, attend political meetings and engage in political debates. Article 17 enabled the police to suppress attempts to organise labour unions and socialist parties. The activities of the women engaged in the Democratic Society (*Heimin-sha*) founded in 1906 who intended to promote the participation of women in politics were a complete failure.

In 1911, Raichô (Haruko) Hiratsuka convened a meeting which resulted in the foundation of the Blue Stocking Society (*Seitô-sha*) and the publication of a magazine called *Seitô* (Blue Stocking). The name was adopted from a social club formed in London around 1750 by Mrs Elizabeth Montague. The magazine advocated a liberation movement, including free love, individualism and woman's self-realisation. The magazine folded after less than five years but thanks to the efforts of Noe Itô and her collaborators, it developed from a periodical concerned only with feminine thought, literature, refinement and art to a publication playing a leading role in the campaign of enlightenment on the problems of women and prepared the ground for the women's movement in the twenties.

Japan's industrialisation in the Meiji period opened job opportunities to women, but working conditions were hardly attractive. Girls, mostly from the country, worked in cotton spinning mills and filatures for a number of years before getting married, often as indentured workers. The mills worked day and night shifts which allowed them to make full use of their equipment and gave them a compititive advantage in world markets. The girls, therefore, lived in dormitories and were not allowed to go out. Due to overwork and malnutrition, tuberculosis was rampant. The protest actions of these women against their inhuman treatment were to no avail. The opening of the telephone service offered more favourable employment conditions and telephone operator became a prestige occupation.

In 1901, women workers in the textile industry constituted half of the total number of workers in manufacturing, and 11.4 per cent of the female workforce were under 14 years of age. Conditions were particularly atrocious in match factories where the majority of the workers were young girls aged between ten and fifteen although it was not unknown for children as young as six or seven to work there.

Among the eleven who were hanged together with Shûsui Kôtoku in 1911 for an alleged plot to assassinate Emperor Meiji was a woman, Suga Kanno, whose concern was not limited to the specific issues of women but who was opposed to the political oppression by the authoritarian bureaucracy and the atrocious social injustices.

The women's movement took on real significance after the First World War. With the maturity of Japanese capitalism and the progress in the country's industrialisation, the number of women in the labour force increased while compulsory education enabled women to assert their rights. Everywhere, women's associations were organised which advocated the advancement of women and the abolition of prostitution. In 1920, Raichô Hiratsuka, Fusae Ichikawa and Mumeo Oku formed the New Women's League (*Shin-Fujin Kyôkai*) which formulated a comprehensive political and social action programme including participation of women in politics, freedom to take part in political meetings, women suffrage, peace, protection of mothers and abolition of prostitution.

In 1921, Kikue Yamakawa and Noe Itô set up the Red Wave Society (*Sekiran-kai*) which proclaimed the struggle against the intellectual enslavement of women and their subjection to male domination. It also supported socialism, and other associations, such as the Proletarian Women Movement and the Kanto Women Federation established in 1927 pursued similar aims. Like most socialist organisations, the Federation was suppressed by the police. With the Manchurian and China 'Incidents,' associations based on nationalism and promoted or directed by the government became the only organisations allowed to exist. Japan's defeat and the political changes in the post-war period brought nominal equality to women but their actual situation remains far from real equality.

Changes in the Status of Women

There is still an enormous gap in the perception of the requirements for full equality of women in official policies and in the thinking of women leaders. This gap was very much in evidence in the United Nations Ten-Year Interim World Conference on Women held in Copenhagen in July 1980. The official representatives of the 145 countries which signed the Convention on the Elimination of All Forms of Discrimination Against Women were chosen by their respective governments and their declarations showed that each government treats problems relating to women according to its own national priorities. Although women form the majority of the human species, no nation in the world is governed by women despite a few female heads of state and heads of government who as exceptions prove the rule. Besides the official Copenhagen Conference, a semi-official NGO (Non-Governmental Organisations) Forum was held where women without official credentials discussed problems as women themselves saw them.

In a report entitled 'Women: A World Survey,' economist Ruth Leger Sivard examined the changes in the status of women since World War II. Her conclusion: 'There is no major field of activity and no country where women have attained equality with men.'

Women have achieved least recognition and influence in politics. In 10 of the world's 11 oldest democracies, women were given the right to vote only in the twentieth century, and women held no more than 10 per cent of the seats in national legislatures. Women's social and economic position remains far from satisfactory. Women account for a disproportionally large percentage of the poor, the illiterate, the unemployed and the underemployed. Women's average life expectancy ranges from a high of 80 years in Iceland and Japan to a low of 40 years in Afghanistan and Chad. Nutritional anaemia afflicts half of the women of childbearing age in developing countries where the average number of children per woman is 7.9 but infant mortality may be as high as 20 per cent.

Nowhere are women's earnings equal to those of men. In a few countries, such as Australia and Sweden, women's salaries and wages come to about 90 per cent of those of men, but in many countries, including Japan, women may earn only half of the corresponding earnings of men. Moreover, women's employment is generally limited to occupations considered 'women's work' and entry into professions such as law and medicine is limited to a relatively small number. Women have achieved most progress in education. Although two-thirds of the women over the age of 25 have never been to school in developing countries and 10 per cent more boys than girls are enrolled in schools and universities worldwide, girls' enrolment has risen from 95 million in 1950 to 390 million in 1985.

In their book 'Women in History,' Susan Raven and Alison Weir portray women and discuss feminine achievements in over 35 countries in ten fields: the written word, performing arts, visual arts, politics and power, science and medicine, religion, education and social reform, sport, travel and exploration, and business.

While the feminine qualities of women are essential for their role in the family, the cooperation of men and women outside the home usually requires sex-indifferent attitudes and operations. This often causes uncertainty in mutual relations. On account of the prevalence of male-oriented problems and solutions, there is little room for and no recognition of the specific contributions of women while in competition with men, quantitatively and qualitatively higher demands may be made on women. Men may feel threatened by the competence and intelligence of women and try to block their advance out of fear for their position.

Progress Achieved by Women

Nevertheless, women have succeeded in breaking into many occupations and professions traditionally considered exclusive preserves of men. Recently, a mother of a six-year-old boy became Mexico's first fully-fledged woman matador. In Paris, a woman headed the Metro Security Force and a woman graduate of France's Naval Academy became the first woman officer to serve on board a ship at sea.

Seven US Air Force members were the first all-women crew to make a trans-Atlantic flight, flying a C141B Starlifter from McGuire Air Force Base to Frankfurt, West Germany. In July 1984, the first two women received regular assignments as captains of Boeing 747 jumbo jets.

Because of a sharp drop in the pool of eligible males, the American military has been forced to rely increasingly on women in order to maintain the all-volunteer army. More than 200,000 women now serve in the combined forces, roughly 10 per cent of the total. Women were also needed to boost the quality of personnel. A considerable number of the male recruits had abilities ranked 'below average' and the armed forces have been losing their top male technicians to the better-paying private sector.

An unsolved problem is the combat role of women. US federal law prohibits women from combat duties but the top echelons know that the enforcement of this prohibition in war-time would cause inextricable muddle. Military women think that the objections against women's combat duties are irrelevant and feel frustrated. 'Don't train me for a job and then tell me I can't do it because I'm female. That's a waste of taxpayers' money and a waste of my time,' said a woman officer.

Another citadel of exclusively male employment fell when US courts held that cities such as New York, Buffalo and Dallas violated the law by refusing to hire women as firemen. In 1982, 450 women worked side by side with 180,000 male fire fighters despite the warning of experts that women have a 20 per cent strength deficit in emergency situations. Fire fighting is one of the most hazardous civilian occupations; in 1981 over 100 US firemen lost their lives on the job. More outspoken than the protests of the unions has been the opposition of the wives of firemen who are wary of the proximity of their husbands to female colleagues during nightshifts and are concerned about their safety in dangerous situations.

A policewoman won a sex discrimination battle against London police chiefs who had ruled that she was 'too pretty and attractive' to share a patrol car with a married policeman. She protested to an industrial tribunal which recommended that she should return to work with police traffic teams.

In the United States, the Census Bureau reported that the proportion of women in traditionally male-oriented executive, managerial and administrative occupations rose from 18.5 per cent in 1970 to 30.5 per cent in 1980. The ratio of women among public

administrators and officials increased from 21.7 per cent to 33.6 per
cent, the percentage of women financial managers went up from 19.1
per cent to 31.4 per cent, and that of personnel and labour relations
managers from 21 to 36 per cent. The proportion of women in accounting and auditing rose from 25 to 38 per cent. In the professions, the
percentage of women showed notable gains: judges and lawyers from 5
to 14 per cent, architects from 4 to 8.3, engineers from 1.7 to 4.6,
doctors from 9.6 to 13.4, veterinarians from 5.3 to 13.3, mathematics
and computer scientists from 16.7 to 26.1, natural scientists from 13.6
to 19.9 and college teachers from 29.1 to 36.6. Women accounted for a
larger share in the category of writers, artists, entertainers and actors,
42.1 per cent compared with 32.5 per cent a decade ago. In this category, women writers and editors made up 49.3 per cent.

Some business women enjoy national recognition. Among them is
Mrs Katharine Graham, Chairman of the Washington Post Co., the
only woman to head an enterprise on *Fortune's* list of the 500 leading
American companies. She is one of the women executives who took
over the business when husband or father died. Others are Christie
Hefner of Playboy Enterprises and Moya Lear, chairman of Lear Avia.
But there is also a growing number of women who reached the top by
their own efforts.

Nevertheless, in 1983, the average yearly wages of full-time, year-
round female workers in the United States were only 66.5 per cent of
those of men. One reason is that women on average work fewer hours
than men, another that new women entrants to the more highly paid
jobs are beginners with low salaries.

Even more impressive than the entry of women into the male-
dominated worlds of labour and politics are the roles played by women
in guerilla and terrorist movements, as leaders of criminal gangs,
bandits and drug syndicates. While in many countries, including Japan,
women have been active in terrorist organisations, they are usually
excluded from combat roles in regular military forces. In some
countries, women are subject to compulsory military service. Recently,
several hundred women in the German Democratic Republic (East
Germany) sent a letter to Erich Honecker, the country's head of state,
demanding the right to refuse military service (the GDR's Conscription
Law makes women subject to conscription in case of a national emergency) and perform social duties instead.

In November 1983, Lady Mary Donaldson became Lord Mayor of
London, the first woman elected to this office since it was established in
1215. Her term of office expired on 9 November 1984.

Britain was the first country to make a woman commander of a
NATO installation when Captain Joan Hopkins was appointed to
command a Royal Air Force base. In May 1982, Anne Krueger,
professor of economics at the University of Minnesota, became the first

woman vice-president in the 36-year history of the World Bank (International Bank for Reconstruction and Development).

French women worked for the election of François Mitterand as president. He made the minister of women's rights a cabinet post, increased the budget for this ministry ten-fold, officially recognised 8 March as Women's Day in France and appointed a record number of women cabinet ministers. They were no longer relegated to what was called the 'female ghetto' — departments of health, the family or education. In the cabinet of Prime Minister Laurent Fabius, women held important posts in the fields of economics, defence, social affairs and the environment.

A farmer's daughter who had to drop out of school because of poverty was elected governor of the Chinese province of Jiangsu, the first woman governor in the history of China. In Malaysia, a 42-year-old London-trained lawyer was appointed the first woman judge.

In the United States, a woman has to be more competent than a man to get the same job at less pay in higher executive positions and she has to prove her competence more often. But women have made significant progress in the higher civil service, local administration (including state governors and city mayors), the judiciary (a woman, Sarah Day O'Connor, has been appointed to the Supreme Court) and in technical professions. The 98th Congress had only two women senators and 22 women representatives, but 12 per cent of the representatives in state legislatures were women. The nomination of Geraldine Ferraro as the Democratic Party's candidate for vice-president in the 1984 election acknowledged the decisive role American women play in the country's voting pattern. The defeat of the Mondale-Ferraro team was seen by many as a setback for women in politics but Mrs Ferraro insisted that Ronald Reagan's election by 62 per cent of the men and 54 per cent of the women voters confirmed the existence of a gender gap. However, many other women candidates were defeated. Of ten women running for the Senate, only the incumbent, Kansas Republican Nancy Kassebaum, was successful. Madeleine Kunin was elected governor of Vermont and the 20 incumbent House members gained reelection, but of the 41 women seeking new House seats, only two made it. At the state level, 939 of the 1,756 women running for legislative seats won election.

Women have been equally or even more successful than men in entertainment, but not as directors or producers.

A formidable obstacle to the advancement of women has been the fact that political and economic organisations have been built up by men and take no account of the women's way of thinking and working. A society with strong emphasis on public life and economic activities beyond the family creates a dominant role for men and lowers the status of women. Education and career opportunities are generally

unrelated to the family and the role of woman in the family but to the
social and political system. The tendency to a one-sided, male-oriented
society was already strong in ancient Greece and Rome. The
prominence of military activities reinforced the male bias in the feudal
system and in Japan's *bushidô*.

Ideological and institutional dominance of women is evident
throughout modern history and has been stronger in Japan than in most
western countries. The discrimination against women starts at the top.
Article 1 of the Imperial House Law (*Kôshitsu Tenpan*) reads: 'The
Imperial Throne shall be succeeded to by a male of the male line of the
Imperial lineage.' Japan was going to ratify the Treaty Against Sexual
Discrimination and in the budgetary committee of the House of Councillors, the question was raised whether this would necessitate a revision
of the provisions on the Imperial succession. Reijirô Tsunoda, director
general of the Cabinet Legislative Bureau, said that the government had
no intention of amending the law and he contended that traditionally
only males had succeeded to the throne. This, of course, is in direct
conflict with historical fact because there have been as many as ten
empresses who reigned in their own right and an eleventh empress
(historically prior) who ruled as regent for her infant son. But
bureaucrats have a way of disregarding inconvenient facts.

Like many other things in Japan, male succession was taken over
from the West, in this case from Prussia, and put into the Meiji
constitution (Art. 2). Women leaders like the late Indira Ghandhi,
Margaret Thatcher or Iceland's president, Vigdis Finnbogadottir, the
divorced mother of a 9-year-old adopted daughter, are unthinkable in
Japan while even Switzerland, though slow in granting women political
equality, has elected a woman, Mrs Elizabeth Kopp, to the Federal
Council which places her in a position to take a one-year turn as
Switzerland's chief executive. Malta has a woman president, Mrs
Agatha Barbara, and Dominica a woman prime minister, Mrs Mary
Eugenia Charles. Yugoslavian Prime Minister, Milka Planinc, is the
first woman head of government in the socialist bloc. The remarkable
campaign of Mrs Corazon Aquino rallied the majority of Philippine
voters and succeeded in ousting strongman Ferdinand E. Marcos in
February 1986.

In Bangladesh, Sheikh Hasna Wajed, eldest daughter of the mur-
dered president Sheikh Mujibar Rahman, assumed the leadership of the
Awami League, and Begum Khaledka Zia, whose husband, president
Ziaur Rahman, was also assassinated by military rebels, became leader
of the Bangladesh Nationalist Party.

In Sri Lanka, Chandrika Kumaratunge, daughter of two prime
ministers, Solomon Bandaranaike, who was assassinated in 1959, and
Sirimavo Bandaranaike, who succeeded him and became the world's
first woman prime minister, founded her new party, challenging her

younger brother chosen by their mother as leader of the opposition after she was stripped of her own civil rights.

Women's Educational Opportunities

Most women leaders agree that the practical political, social, legal and economic equality of women depends on the equality of their education and professional training. In many countries, women's access to education is legally guaranteed but this does not mean that equality in education has been achieved.

In pre-war Japan, women were only admitted to women's colleges which were inferior to higher institutions of learning for men. People regardless of class considered higher education of women unnecessary. Also upper-class women were restricted in their social activities. A sharp break came with the Second World War. Women had to take charge of many functions; they worked in factories, as nurses at the war front, in neighbourhood associations and as air-raid wardens. After the war, women gained new educational opportunities but employment remained restricted, particularly by administrative policies and business practices.

Japan's Fundamental Law on Education (*Kyôiku Kihon-ho*) states: 'All people must be given an equal opportunity to receive an education corresponding to their ability and there shall be no discrimination because of race, creed, sex, social status, economic position or family origin' (Art. 3, Par. 1). This provision which has been lifted almost verbatim from the constitution (Art. 26 and 14), lays down a norm to which reality does not attain. The fact of the matter can be seen from a single example. Tokyo University, Japan's most prestigious (though overrated) university was opened to women in 1946. In that year, 19 women passed the entrance examination which was 2.0 per cent of total admissions. In 1981, 230 women qualified, equal to 7.5 per cent of all admissions.

Equality is hampered by the fact that the educational system was set up by men whose thinking was dominated by the educational requirements of men. The learning abilities of girls and their specific learning needs are taken into consideration only haphazardly and superficially. Although coeducation may have significant advantages, it also has serious flaws, not the least being the impossibility to adapt curricula to the differences in development and the sex-specific requirements in educational contents and methods.

Although there is no great difference in the percentages of Japanese boys and girls going on to senior high school after finishing the nine years of compulsory education, an enormous divergence appears at the higher levels of secondary education. Since 1969, the percentage of girls entering senior high school has been higher than that of boys; 92.8 per cent of the boys and 94.9 per cent of the girls graduating from junior high school in 1985 went on to senior high school. But more boys than girls continue their education beyond high school, and while boys prefer a four-year college, girls generally go to junior college. In 1984, 20.8 per cent of the girls who finished junior high school three years ago entered junior college after graduating from senior high school and only 2.0 per cent of the boys did so but 36.6 per cent of the boys went on to a four-year college while the percentage was 13.7 for girls.

Lately, the rate of high-school graduates enrolling in four-year colleges has declined and more young people are entering higher vocational schools. A college diploma alone no longer guarantees a job and employment prospects are better for technically-trained people, especially if they obtain some kind of state licence. The difference in pay no longer seems to justify the costs of a college education.

An educator wrote the following condemnation of today's education in Japan: 'The truth is that schools aren't giving anyone the basic skills they need in later life. They are preparing girls and boys for a bygone era.'

One reason for the lack of adaptation of school education to the needs of women is the prevalence of men in the direction of schools. This is part of the general problem of the promotion of women to leading positions. It can hardly be expected that school education becomes attuned to the special needs of girls if school principals, university presidents and the upper-echelon bureaucrats of the ministry of education are men.

In 1983, 265,451 (56.0 per cent) of the 473,987 teachers at Japanese elementary schools were women, but of the 23,693 principals, only 509 (2.1 per cent) were women. The situation was even worse in junior high schools where women constituted 33.3 per cent of the staff (91,147 out of 273,703) but only 0.2 per cent of the principals (19 out of 9.920). Of the 252,714 senior high school teachers, 45,828 (18.1 per cent) were women, but they accounted for only 2.4 per cent of the principals (119 out of 4,952). The higher percentage of women principals in senior high schools is due to the relatively larger number of private senior high schools (compulsory education ends with junior high). Many of the private girls schools are managed by religious congregations and their experience shows that women are quite capable of running schools. The situation was similar for junior colleges where 14.8 per cent of the presidents were women (55 out of 364; 39.4 per cent of the staff were women, 6,780 out of 17,202). The teaching staff at universities numbered 109,139 persons, including 9,216 women (8.4 per cent). Of the 440 presidents, 19 were women (all at private universities), a ratio of 4.3 per cent, but among professors, the ratio of women was even lower (4.0 per cent, 1,429 out of 35,915).

The remaining disadvantages of women in education in Japan are partly attributable to their weak political influence. A survey of the Prime Minister's Office conducted in 1982 found that 46 per cent of local residents hardly discussed social or political issues with their neighbours. The percentage was 34 per cent for men but 56 per cent for women. To the question whether they would like to contribute to the well-being of society, 50 per cent of the male respondents said that they were interested and 44 per cent said they were not; the percentages were 38 and 53 per cent, respectively, for women.

Women in Politics and Government in Japan

Japan has the reputation of being one of the world's most male-dominated societies and Japan's political establishment is the most representative segment of this realm of male ascendancy. Women are practically excluded from all positions of any importance in Japan's public life. In Japan's first post-war election (April 1946), 39 women were elected to the House of Representatives. This high-water mark has never been reached again. In September 1984, only eight of the 508 members of the House of Representatives were women (1.6 per cent of the membership) and 19 of the 249 members of the House of Councillors (7.6 per cent; there were vacancies in both houses).

This difference does not reflect any concern for women in the selection of candidates for the upper house but purely and simply party strategy. Formerly, half of the members of the upper house were chosen nationwide as individuals (which was called the national constituency; the Election Law has been changed and a system of proportional representation with voting for party lists has been adopted). Parties nominated well-known women entertainers and leaders of women organisations as candidates for the national constituency because they were sure vote-getters. The Liberal-Democratic Party chose these women merely for the sake of publicity and the Communist Party tried to gain the support of women's organisations. The Socialists were least inclined to nominate women candidates because the party is dominated by the labour unions which are among Japan's most rabid anti-women organisations. Chances are almost nil that women will become executives of political parties. The highest post given to a woman is director of the women's bureau.

Women are even less prominent in prefectural and local assemblies which are all under the control of local bosses. As of December 1983, the national average of female representatives in local assemblies was 1.2 per cent of the membership of prefectural assemblies, 2.9 per cent of city assemblies, 0.7 per cent of town and village assemblies, and 7.5 per cent of the members of the assemblies of Tokyo's city wards.

Only two women have been mayors, Tomo Matsuno of Hotsumi in Gifu Prefecture and Masue Fujita of Tamakura in Fukushima

Prefecture. This, of course, cannot compare with the position of women in the United States where women have been mayors of such large cities as Chicago, San Francisco and Houston. Very few women hold important posts in Japanese local governments. One of the reasons is the increasing number of bureaucrats from central government agencies, above all the home ministry and the ministry of construction, being employed in leading local government positions after retirement. As of February 1980, 717 former central government officials held posts in prefectural governments, including 21 prefectural vice-governors. The majority of the doctors in the Tokyo health centres are women but the directors are all men. More women are section chiefs of preventive medicine because preventive medicine is considered less attractive by male doctors.

Of the 283 members of the boards of education, 39 (13.8 per cent) were women (June 1984) As of August 1982, the agricultural committees counted 65,123 members of whom 60 were women (0.09 per cent), an indication of the backwardness of the public position of women in agricultural communities.

At the highest level of government, the same situation prevails. In the entire post-war period, only three women have held cabinet posts. Masa Nakayama served as minister of health and welfare in the first Ikeda cabinet which lasted not even five months. In 1962, Tsuruko Kondo became state minister in charge of the Science and Technology Agency and chairwoman of the Atomic Energy Commission in the second Ikeda cabinet; she lasted one year. After a lapse of 22 years, Miss Shigeru Ishimoto became the third woman to get a cabinet post; she was appointed director general of the Environmental Agency in the third Nakasone cabinet in 1984. The climate and style of Japanese politics seem uninviting for women.

The first woman ambassador was Mrs Nobuko Takahashi who was appointed ambassador to Denmark in 1980. Mrs Takahashi had had a distinguished career in government service; she had been director of the Women's and Minors' Bureau of the Ministry of Labour and served as deputy director of the International Labour Office from 1976 to 1978. That she was the only woman among 113 ambassadors (including temporary ambassadors and ambassadors to the United Nations and its organisations) was clear proof of the discriminatory treatment of women by official Japan. Mrs Takahashi's ambassadorship ended in 1983 and the second woman to fill such a position was Mrs Ryôko Akamatsu who was chosen as ambassador to Uruguay in November 1985. She was a graduate of the Department of Law of the University of Tokyo and had been posted as minister to Japan's Permanent Mission to the United Nations from 1979 to 1982 after serving as director of the Women's and Minors' Bureau of the Ministry of Labour.

Access of Women to Government Service

In 1938, Yoshiko Mibuchi became the first woman to pass the Japanese national law examination, but at that time, nomination to courts of law was restricted to males of the Japanee empire, and the only legal career open to her was to become a lawyer. In 1949, however, she became Japan's first woman judge and she also was the first woman to be appointed presiding judge when she was posted as presiding judge at the Niigata Family Court. She died in 1984. Up to 1982, only one other woman had been presiding judge, Mrs Aiko Noda, who served at the Shizuoka Family Court. On 1 June, 1983, Mrs Mitsuko Terazawa, who had been associate judge at the Tokyo High Court, was appointed presiding judge of the Tokushima District and Family Court. No woman has ever been appointed to the Supreme Court or has been chief judge at a high court. Women have also failed to advance in the public prosecutor service. No woman has held the post of chief public prosecutor or superintendent public prosecutor, to say nothing of prosecutor general (equivalent to attorney-general in the United States).

The first woman instructor at the Research and Training Institute of the Ministry of Justice was appointed in 1976. All aspirants for a legal career must pass through this institute, and some time ago, several of its instructors and officials came under fire for disparaging remarks on women trainees. For the first time in the 86-year history of the National Tax Administration Agency, a woman was appointed head of a district office in 1982, and in the same year, Japan got her first women detectives as distinguished from uniformed police women. As of 1 April, 1983, Japan had 215,138 police officers of whom 3,818 (1.8 per cent) were women.

In 1922, Kikue Yamada took up the post of director of the Women's and Minors' Bureau of the Ministry of Labour and this is the highest position women have ever held in the regular civil service. Of the 139 bureau chiefs in the central government, only two were women in 1982. No woman has ever been vice-minister in any ministry (a few women have served as parliamentary vice-ministers). Michiko Ariga was the first woman to become a member of the Fair Trade Commission (1967) in which she had served as an official. In 1976, Sadako Ogata was appointed minister to the United Nations, the first woman to fill such a post.

Particularly scandalous is the situation in the government's advisory councils. Although many of these councils deal with problems of special interest to women, such as prices, food, markets, health, labour, education and youth, the percentage of women members as of June 1984 was 5.2 per cent. Not a single woman was among the members of 92 of the 204 councils (45.1 per cent). In a council organised at the initiative of Prime Minister Nakasone in 1984 to develop guidelines for the reform of education, only three of the 25 members were women. The Japan Teachers' Union refused to parti- cipate in the deliberations of the council because most of its members were government officials and representatives of the business world while parents, teachers and experts on education had been excluded.

In the civil service, women are discriminated against in recruitment as well as promotion. Fewer women than men take the examination required for government employment and only a small percentage of the women who qualify are actually employed. Women have been barred from many qualifying examinations under the pretext that the job category was not suitable for women. When women pass the examination for a job category open to them, government agencies refuse to accept their applications on the basis that 'no woman has been hired before.'

The class A examination for the senior grade of government offi- cials is divided into two large categories, administrative officials and technical officials. Candidates who pass this examination must then submit to further scrutiny by the ministry or agency for which they want to apply. In the administrative category, women applicants are much fewer than men. In 1984, 94 young women passed the examination for the senior grade administrative category. They were 5.7 per cent of the 1,658 men and women who took the examination. Most women choose the technical field where psychology and pharmacy are considered as 'women specialties.'

The administrative positions of government officials which range from apprentice to deputy bureau chief are divided into eight classes, presumably based on the level of difficulty of the work, and each class is subdivided into up to 39 pay steps. Entrants start with some step in class 8 and each year move up one step; it is, however, possible to advance by more than one step. This, although often achieved by men, is difficult for women. There is a congestion of women employees in the sixth class because advancement to class 5 (chief clerk) is seldom approved for women. In fiscal 1982, 94.4 per cent of the female administrative personnel was in the fifth class and below. In the first class of administrative personnel, only eight of the 1,447 officials were women, and in the second class, only 32 of 5,180 (0.6 per cent). In the highest class of Japan's civil service which is made up of 'specially appointed officials' and comprises permanent vice-ministers, presidents of state universities and directors-general of government agencies, only two of the 1,600 officials were women.

In 1984, 493 of the 17,900 senior grade officials were women (2.8 per cent). First among the ministries in which women holding senior grade positions was the Ministry of Justice (62) because, different from ministries such as the Ministry of Finance for which examinations are limited to administration and economics, they include fields such as psychology, sociology and education. Women fill positions in institutions such as women prisons, reformatories and juvenile classification offices. In the Ministry of Labour (51 women in senior posts), the director of the Women's and Minors' Bureau and four of the five section chiefs were women.

As of June 1984, 47 of the 2,174 judges (2.2 per cent) were women but women accounted for 6.2 per cent of the associated judges (38 out of 609). Women were even less represented among the public prosecutors. Of the 537 class 1 public prosecutors (out of whom the chiefs of the district public prosecutors are appointed), only three were women (0.6 per cent), and out of the class 2 public prosecutors, 3.4 per cent (23 out of 686) were women. Assistant public prosecutors numbered 870, but only one was a woman.

In 1983, the higher officials (section chief and above) in Japan's prefectural administration numbered 13,581, of whom 100 were women (0.7 per cent). In the large cities, 143 of the 5,522 management positions were occupied by women (2.6 per cent). The total number of local employees was 3,228,484 (1983) of whom 1,089,297 were women (33.7 per cent). Of the nurses and other health workers, 98.2 per cent were women, as were 49.3 per cent of the pharmacists and therapists.

In recent years, women have been admitted to some government careers so far closed to them. In 1981, women were allowed to take all civil service examinations except post offices requiring working after 10 p.m. A total of 35 women passed the examination for prison officials, 3 for the immigration service and 184 for employment in tax offices. Until then, the examinations for immigration officers and prison officials (both under the Ministry of Justice) had been restricted to males between the ages of 17 and 33. Women who were employed in these sectors (immigration service 35, 5.1 per cent of the entire staff, prison service 495, 3.4 per cent of the total) had been recruited by special selection without competitive examinations. The National Tax Administration had so far limited its recruitment to men and of its 54,000 employees, only 4,600 were women. The reasons given were that the tax business was not suitable for women, and that the rate of quitting jobs was high. Women were first admitted to examinations in 1980 when about 14,000 people of whom 573 (4.1 per cent) were women, applied for 1,159 positions. The first examination reduced the number of women candidates to 51, and after the second screening (interviews), 32 were left.

In 1979, two women passed the foreign service examination, the first in 20 years. In 1980, out of 1,213 applicants, 466 were admitted to the preliminary examination out of whom 54 passed. Among the 27 who qualified in the final test, three were women, one of whom was the first person ever to pass the examination after having studied only at a foreign university (Oxford) without graduating from a Japanese college. In 1976, the first woman was appointed section chief in the Foreign Ministry; in 1980, a total of 97 women were working at Japanese embassies abroad.

Out of the 23,950 candidates who took the state law examination in 1984, only 453 (1.89 per cent) were successful. Among them were 52 women.

A record 1,274 candidates of whom 155 were women took the examination for the foreign service in 1984. Among the 30 successful candidates was one woman, the 22-year-old daughter of a professional golfer who was studying law at the University of Tokyo. In 1984, 494 candidates of the 1,148 applicants were admitted to the foreign service examination but only 29 were successful. Of the 149 women candidates, only one passed the examination, the fourteenth woman to enter the diplomatic service.

Of the successful candidates who passed the first-class national service examination in 1985, 25 were chosen for the Ministry of Finance. Among the 25 were 22 students of the University of Tokyo, including the only successful woman candidate. She will become the ministry's sixth woman career official.

In 1979, the Transport Ministry allowed women to take the examination for six sectors that so far had been restricted to men: air control officers, Aeronautical Safety Academy, Maritime Safety Academy, Maritime Safety School and Meteorological College. Of the 25 students who completed the basic training at the Aeronautical Training College in 1980, five were women. In the same year, the 1,415 applicants for air traffic controllers included 102 women; of the 31 successful candidates, six were women. Also in 1980, the first woman candidate was admitted to the Maritime Safety Academy. As one of the last government institutions that had been closed to women, the Kobe Mercantile Marine Academy accepted five women candidates, including a Thai student, in 1982. The first woman lighthouse keeper was appointed in 1984. Until then, all 270 lighthouse keepers operating the 91 major lighthouse installations had been men. 2,552 lighthouses are completely automated.

In 1986, the Civil Aviation College admitted the first woman. At present, there is no woman among the 3,000 pilots serving in Japan's civil aviation industry and there are no female military pilots.

In 1976, a woman passed the first-grade navigation officer examination but under current laws, she cannot obtain a captainship because this requires a one-year experience as a crew member on an ocean-going merchant ship. The Seamen's Law prohibits women from working at night on ships.

After completing six months of ocean-going training with 66 men in August 1984, the first two women to graduate from the Tokyo University of Mercantile Marine were unable to find seafaring jobs and had to be satisfied with working on land, but in December, one of the women, Miss Ayako Hayashi, embarked on a Danish containership as third officer and cargo coordinator for a three-month training period.

The medical school of Japan's defence forces was opened to female candidates in 1985. In all, 537 women, 12.5 per cent of all applicants, took the entrance examination in the autumn of 1984 and of the 16 successful candidates, eight actually entered the Defence Medical College in April 1985. The college trains medical officers for the three services of Japan's Self-Defence Forces. The school charges no admission fees or tuition and the students have the same status as other Defence Agency personnel. They receive a monthly stipend (at present ¥60,000), three bonuses equivalent to 3.8 months' pay each year and are provided with clothing and meals by the school. Besides the military drill during the six years of medical education, the students, who are appointed to sergeant upon graduation, must complete a six-month officer candidate course. They are then promoted to first lieutenant and are obliged to work as military surgeons for at least nine years.

A survey of the Ministry of Home Affairs published a few days after the enactment of the Equal Employment Opportunity Law revealed that one-third of the 47 prefectural and 11 municipal governments discriminated against women in recruiting. Discrimination was particularly rampant in the hiring of senior high school graduates. Rules for the screening of candidates contained provisions such as 'males only' or 'mainly males.' The ministry refused to announce the names of the offending bodies and a ministry official offered the explanation that women graduates did so much better than men in qualifying tests that female applicants would win the entire quota of new entrants if no discriminatory measures were taken. Better hire incompetent males than competent females!

Employment opportunities are also unfavourable for women in public corporations. The Japan National Railways (JNR) used to hire women only as switchboard operators and secretaries and as nurses in the JNR hospitals but not for station duties (except during the war years). If women are hired, men will have relatively more night duty because women are not allowed to work after 10 p.m. (with the exception of nurses, telephone operators and hostesses in bars and night clubs). Male workers, therefore, were opposed to the hiring of women. Fear of competition was another factor. In 1977, JNR hired 50 women for railway station duty. Of these women, 28 took the examination for promotion and 15 passed after slightly more than a year. It takes male employees about four or five years to pass this examination.

Japan is a prime example of the discrepancy between the norms laid down in legislation on the status of women and reality. In the case of Japan, this discongruity is not the result of ideological prejudice but of historical inertia which perpetuates the male predominance of the feudal system. But it is also due to the upbringing of women which fails to foster any strong interest in public affairs and trains them to devote their energies to the immediate concerns of family life. There are numerous women organisations for an enormous variety of purposes but until now, no broadly-based movement for asserting women's rights and gaining equality in public life has emerged. The relatively few women active in local or national politics are largely beholden to the existing male-oriented and male-dominated parties which will be the last to help women secure the position required for the well-being of society.

Women and Crime

The greater exposure of women to social life has resulted in a higher female crime rate. In 1980,, 74,225 women were arrested in connection with crimes, 19 per cent of all arrests. Of the minors arrested for criminal offences, 28,322 (18.9 per cent) were girls. Theft accounted for 88.3 per cent of the crimes for which women were arrested; the largest part involved shoplifting. The number of women was also relatively large in the arrests related to prostitution. Other crimes committed by women which attracted public attention included infanticide or abandonment of new-born babies, killing of lovers and embezzlement for supporting their lovers. Also frequent were suicides of mothers who took their children along. In 1983, when suicides numbered 24,970, the number of men over 50 committing suicide was three times that of women. Other phenomena indicating some unsavoury kind of women's emancipation were the 'host clubs' and 'sex tours' for women.

Although there are exceptions, organised crime continues to be dominated by men, and notwithstanding the infamous Bonnie and Clyde crime duo, about 80 per cent of the male criminals would not choose women as partners in crime.

Criminality is one of the fields which show that the social environment influences women in about the same way as men. In the United States, blacks are more likely to come into conflict with the law than whites. Between 1974 and 1979, about 3 per cent of black males in their 20s were in state prisons on any given day, compared with four-tenths of one per cent of white males of the same age. In the years from 1978 to 1982, black women were eight times more likely than white women, and six times more likely than other females, to be serving prison sentences.

7

Women in the Labour Market

THE INFLUX OF WOMEN into the labour market has been one of the most noteworthy recent social phenomena in the industrial countries. The changes in the American labour market have been so sweeping that they have been called a work revolution. More women are working, men are dropping out, women are assuming leading positions in many sectors of the economy and they are advancing into professions considered male preserves not long ago. It is, therefore, not just a matter of numbers; much more important has been the push of women into jobs hitherto regarded suitable only for men and their ascent into leading posts. In the last two aspects, Japan has been behind the United States and the advanced European countries but the impact of these trends on the country's labour situation cannot be overlooked.

Population Growth and Women Workers

As far as the number of women workers and their proportion in the labour force are concerned, the situation is different in each country, due to differences in traditions but also on account of demographic factors, above all differences in birth rates. Women constitute nearly half of the 4.8 billion world population and account for 34.6 per cent of the world's labour force of 1.96 billion. Although the birth rate has declined in almost all advanced countries in the post-war era, the rates of decline and the time sequences have been different.

In Britain and in the Federal Republic of Germany, the post-war baby boom came relatively late in the five years from 1960 to 1965, when the birth rate was already declining in the United States and Japan. As a result, substantial generations are now coming into the German and British labour markets, aggravating the unemployment situation, while in both countries, the birth rate has already declined below the reproduction level.

In Japan, the proportionally largest increase occurred in the five years immediately following the war. In the period from 1945 to 1950, the population grew by 15.6 per cent; in the years after 1950, the largest five-year increases were registered in the years from 1951 to 1955 and from 1971 to 1975 (7.3 per cent in both periods). In the five years from 1976 to 1980, the population grew by 4.4 per cent. Japan's highest post-war birth rate was reached in 1947 with 34.3 births per 1,000 popula-

tion. It came down to 19.4 per 1,000 in 1955 and this rate emerged
again as two peaks in a generally downward trend in 1967 and 1973.
The rate fell to 13.0 in 1981, 12.87 in 1982, 12.7 in 1983 and 12.5 in
1984.

(By way of comparison average yearly growth rates of population
in per cent for the United States, the United Kingdom and West
Germany were as follows: United States, 1950-1960, 1.9; 1975-1979,
0.8; 1975-1982, 1.0; United Kingdom, 1960-1965, 0.77; 1975-1979, 0.0;
1975-1982, –0.2; West Germany, 1960-1965, 1.36; 1975-1979, –0.2;
1975-1982, –0.1; birth rate per 1,000 of population, United States, 1955,
24.7; 1980, 16.2; United Kingdom, 1964, 18.8; 1980, 13.5; West
Germany, 1963 and 1964, 18.5; 1980, 10.0.)

As of April 1984, Japan's population numbered 119,316,468; it was
composed of 58,811,417 men and 60,505,051 women. Young people
(0-14) numbered 26,907,000 and accounted for 22.5 per cent of the mid-
year population (119,483,000); the percentage had been 24.3 per cent in
1975. There were 80,904,000 people in the productive age classes (15-
64), making up 67.7 per cent of the population (almost the same as in
1975), and 11,672,000 people were 65 years and older (9.8 per cent;
1975: 7.9 per cent). Despite the sharp post-war increase, the population
pressure has been relatively weak; the sharpest dislocations were caused
by the enormous influx of people from the country into the cities which
resulted in the depopulation of the rural areas and the huge
concentrations in the industrial belts (1980: Tokyo-Yokohama, 18.54
million; Nagoya, 6.22 million; Osaka-Kobe, 13.62 million; Fukuoka,
4.55 million).

Even in the post-war recessions, Japan's unemployment rate
remained low which is partly the result of computing the number of
jobless; the rate does not include people who worked more than one
hour in the week preceding the count. In June 1984, the unemployment
rate reached a high of 2.81 per cent (actual number of totally
unemployed: men 990,000, women 680,000). The rate was highest, 5.1
per cent, for women 15 to 19 years old; it was 4.9 per cent for the 20-24
class, 4.2 per cent for the 25-29 group and dropped to 2.9 per cent for
the 30-34 group. The low average was due to the low rates in the
higher age brackets (40-44, 2.2 per cent; 45-49, 1.8 per cent; over 65,
0.9 per cent).

In 1984, Japan's working age population (15 years and older)
numbered 93.47 million of whom 45.44 million (48.6 per cent) were
male and 48.04 million (51.4 per cent) female. The 59.27 million strong
labour force comprised 35.8 million men (60.4 per cent) and 23.47
million women (39.6 per cent of the labour force and 48.9 per cent of
all women over 15).

The proportional increase in the female labour force has remained
below the increase in the female population aged 15 and over. In 1984,

the female working-age population was 42.6 per cent larger than in 1960 and 18.3 per cent larger than in 1970; the growth of the female labour force in the period from 1960 to 1983 was 26.4 per cent and from 1970 to 1983 14.8 per cent. As a percentage of the female working-age population, the female labour force declined from 54.5 per cent in 1960 to 49.9 per cent in 1970 and further to 45.7 per cent in 1975 when women constituted 37.3 per cent of the labour force.

The proportion of women in the labour force was high in Scandinavian countries (1983: Sweden 46.6 per cent, Denmark 45.4 per cent, Norway 42.9 per cent) but also in Thailand (1980: 47.0 per cent). In the United States, the labour force comprised 64,580,000 men and 48,646,000 women (1983) so that women accounted for 43.0 per cent of the labour force. Of the women over 16 years of age, 51.0 per cent were in the labour force and working women have outnumbered those who stay at home since 1977. Only 5 per cent of American households consist of a working father, a stay-at-home mother and children. The largest numbers of the women in the labour force were in the 20-to-44 age groups. Of the 20-24 age group, 70.0 per cent were in the labour force, and the percentages were nearly the same for the following age brackets (24-29: 69.0 per cent; 30-44: 67.4 per cent) which shows that many women continue working after marriage. On the other hand, only 42.0 per cent of the 16-19 age group were in the labour force because many young women were going to school.

The proportion of women in the labour force in Great Britain was 39.1 per cent with 10,515,000 women working together with 16,034,000 men (1980). Women in the labour force accounted for 35.9 per cent of the women of working age. The percentage of employed women, 41.8 per cent, was slightly higher than the ratio of women in the labour force which seems to be mainly due to the small number of women working in family enterprises. Compared with other industrial countries, the ratio of young women in the labour force was high (54.6 per cent of the 15-19 age class) which may indicate that fewer girls were going to school.

In West Germany, the labour force was composed of 17,450,000 men and 11,092,000 women (1983), making the proportion of women in the labour force 38.9 per cent. The percentage of women over the age of 15 in the labour force was 41.0 per cent and women made up 38.6 per cent of all employees. By age groups, the percentage of women in the labour force dropped from 70.5 per cent of the 20-24 age class to 63.5 per cent of the group 25-29 and 58.6 per cent for the classes from 30 to 44. Young women prefer going to school; only 38.6 per cent of the 15-to-19-year-olds were in the labour force.

Structure of Japan's Labour Force

In Japan, the ratio of women in the labour force to the number of women of working age was highest for the 20-24 age group with 72.4 per cent (1984); it was sharply lower for the age classes 25-29 (53.9 per cent) and 30-34 (50.6 per cent). The percentage rose again for the higher age brackets (35-39: 59.6 per cent; 40-44: 68.1 per cent; 45-49: 67.1 per cent). The share of women between the ages of 15 and 19 in the labour force dropped from 49.1 per cent in 1960 to 17.2 per cent in 1982 (1984: 18.5 per cent), a sign that most girls attend school beyond the age of compulsory education (15). Actually, the proportion of women not in the labour force going to school rose from 21.6 per cent in 1960 to 39.1 per cent in 1984.

By marital status, the composition of Japan's labour force was as follows. Of all married women (30.53 million), 51.1 per cent (15.61 million) were in the labour force, so were 53.6 per cent of the unmarried women over 15 and 32.9 per cent of the widowed and divorced women (1984). Of the women in the labour force, 15.32 million were at work, with 2.02 million working in agriculture and 13.3 million in the non-agricultural sector. Couples living together numbered 29.84 million (1984); the husband was working in 21.54 million of these households, the wife was also working in 13.33 million. Couples employed in non-agricultural work numbered 7.21 million. There were 12.58 million wives who did not work; in the 3.78 million households in which the husband did not work, the wife worked in 780,000 households while neither husband nor wife worked in 3.01 million households. When both husband and wife were working, they were most frequently in the middle age groups (wife 35-44 groups: 57.4 per cent of working wives; wife 45-54 years: 54.7 per cent of working wives). Of all employed women (15.08 million), 8.93 million (59.2 per cent) were married, 4.75 million (31.5 per cent) were single, and 1.4 million (9.3 per cent) were widowed or divorced.

In a five-class division of the incomes of the household heads, the wife was working as well as the husband in 53.0 per cent of the lowest income class; 49.9 per cent of class II, 45.8 per cent of class III, 45.1 per cent of class IV and 34.8 per cent of class V. The share of the wife's earnings in the family income was generally 8.2 per cent; it was 13.7 per cent if the wife's age was below 24 and 9.9 per cent for the 45-49 age group.

Structure of Female Work Force in Japan

In 1982, the proportion of working women in the number of women living together with their husbands was lowest in the 25-29 age class (29.9 per cent); it was only marginally higher in the 15 to 24 group

(30.9 per cent) but much higher in the older age classes (30-34, 38.3 per cent; 35-39, 52.2 per cent). There were sharp differences within the same age class depending on the presence and number of children. In the lowest age bracket, 15-24, 47.2 per cent of the women without children were working, but the ratio was 14.9 per cent if a woman had one child, 17.9 per cent if she had two, and 25.0 per cent if she had three children. The differences were much smaller for the higher age groups (35-39 years: no child, 59.6 per cent working; one child, 50.5 per cent; two children, 52.3 per cent; three children, 51.1 per cent).

In three-generation households, the percentage of women holding outside jobs was generally high. It rose from 44.5 per cent when the last child was born to 81.9 per cent when the last child was 14 years of age. In nuclear families, the ratio of women working outside the home was lowest, 18.4 per cent, when the last child was born, and reached 64.5 per cent, when the last child was 13.

Women working in primary industries numbered 2.46 million in 1984, 10.8 per cent of the 22.82 million women at work; 6.47 million (28.4 per cent) worked in secondary industries and 13.82 million (60.6 per cent) in tertiary industries which provided work to 42.4 per cent of all Japanese workers.

Women employees numbered 15.18 million. 66.5 per cent of all working women and 35.6 per cent of all employees. Women managing their own businesses numbered 2.96 million (13.0 per cent of all working women) of whom 2.52 million were engaged in non-agricultural sectors and 440,000 in agriculture. Another 4.63 million women (20.3 per cent of all working women) worked in family businesses. Of 15.08 million women actually employed, 12.17 million (80.7 per cent) were regular employees, 2.27 million temporary employees and 640,000 day labourers. Regular employees are covered by minimum wage laws and cannot be dismissed unless they commit a felony, because of other legally recognised reasons or on grounds specifically stated in the enterprise's employment regulations. Temporary employees are those employed for a time exceeding one month but shorter than a year. They do not enjoy the same job security as regular employees and can be laid off or dismissed more easily. Day labourers are hired on a day-to-day basis for less than a month, mainly as construction workers, dock workers or sweepers. Statistically, work is classified as part-time if the weekly working hours remain below 35 hours.

The number of women employees by age classes showed the same structure as the women labour force. Women employees were most numerous in the 20-24 year class with 2.55 million (16.8 per cent of all women employees). Their numbers declined in the following age classes (24-29: 1.68 million; 30-34: 1.61 million), but rose again in the 35-39 class (1.87 million) and reached a peak in the 40-44 group (2.05

million). Only 710,000 girls between the ages of 15 and 19 were employed (4.7 per cent of women employees). Women employees accounted for 31.6 per cent of the women over 15 years of age; the employees in the 20-24 class constituted 65.1 per cent of the women in that age group, those in the 25-29 class 42.7 per cent. The ratio was also high in some of the higher age classes (40-44: 44.2 per cent; 45-49: 42.4 per cent; 50-54: 35.2 per cent). It was only 16.6 per cent for the 15-19-year-olds.

In 1984, the number of women employees (15.18 million) for the first time exceeded the number of women exclusively engaged in housekeeping (15.16 million). Women employees were most numerous in services (4.23 million; 29.8 per cent of all women employees), 4.23 million worked in manufacturing (27.9 per cent), 4.03 million were employed in wholesale and retail trade (26.5 per cent) — these three branches employed 84.2 per cent of all women employees. The percentage of women in the total number of employees was highest in services with 49.0 per cent; it was also high in banking, insurance and real estate (45.5 per cent; 910,000 women employees), wholesale and retail trade (44.2 per cent), manufacturing (34.9 per cent) and agriculture (32.1 per cent). It was considerably lower in government (16.9 per cent) and in industries in which women usually perform only auxiliary functions (utilities 14.3 per cent, construction 13.9 per cent, fisheries 13.3 per cent, mining 12.5 per cent, transportation and communications 12.1 per cent).

Part-time Employment

Women were largely used for office work (1984: 5.0 million, 32.3 per cent of women employees), operatives in production processes numbered 3.41 million (22.5 per cent) and 1.83 million were sales personnel (12.1 per cent). Women constituted 52.4 per cent of all employees performing office work, 26.5 per cent of all operatives, 47.0 per cent of the employees engaged in specialised work and 31.3 per cent of the sales personnel.

In the professions, women accounted for the largest part of the personnel in the field of health care (1983: 904,000 of 1,309,200; 69.1 per cent); other fields in which women were strongly represented included the performing arts (musicians, singers, dancers) and professional athletes (80,300 out of 130,400; 61.9 per cent), teachers (570,000 out of 1,324,800; 43.1 per cent) and formative artists, designers and photographers (44,000 of 170,700; 25.8 per cent). The percentages of women were small in professions such as technicians (2.4 per cent), scientific researchers (6.4 per cent) and the legal professions (9.2 per cent).

By size of enterprise, the structure of female employment in the non-agricultural sector was as follows: 5.8 million (38.5 per cent) worked in enterprises with 1-25 workers, 2.5 million (16.6 per cent) in enterprises with 30-39 workers, 2.19 million (14.5 per cent) in those with 100-499 workers and 2.89 million (19.2 per cent) in enterprises with over 500 workers; 1.67 million (11.1 per cent) were public employees.

Women holding part-time jobs numbered 3.28 million (22.1 per cent of all women employees). Part-time workers numbered 1.18 million in sales (36.6 per cent of part-time women employees), 900,000 in services (27.4 per cent) and 770,000 in manufacturing (23.5 per cent). Part-time women workers constituted a large portion of the women employees in sales (29.6 per cent), utilities (25.0 per cent), construction (23.2 per cent), transportation and communications (20.5 per cent) and services (20.3 per cent).

Operations for which women part-timers were often employed included packaging, canvassing for life insurance, door-to-door sales of cosmetics, cleaning and other maintenance work.

Part-time women employees were most numerous in small enterprises. Establishments with 1-29 workers employed 1.71 million women working part-time (52.1 per cent of all part-time women employees and 29.9 per cent of the employees of these enterprises). In enterprises with 30-99 workers, part-time women employees numbered 440,000, in those with 100-499 workers, 330,000, and in those with over 500 workers, 540,000. There were 260,000 women working part-time in government offices.

According to a 1983 survey of the Prime Minister's Office, 55.2 per cent of all women want to find a job, leave on account of marriage and childbirth and resume working thereafter; 19.5 per cent want to work only until marriage or childbirth, 16.6 per cent want to continue working until retirement age and a mere 2.2 per cent are not interested in finding outside work. Of the women who wanted to reenter the labour market, 55.2 per cent preferred to start again in their forties and 32.4 per cent in their fifties.

Some enterprises (7.0 per cent of all enterprises) have adopted a special system for rehiring women workers who quit for marriage or childbirth. The reasons for the arrangement were: to cope with labour shortages (50.5 per cent), smooth replacement of vacancies (34.8 per cent), to secure specialised or skilled workers (42.4 per cent), reputation of the enterprise; to attract talented women (28.1 per cent).

Of the women working part-time, the vast majority, 78.1 per cent, did not want to become full-time employees. Their reasons were: they would have to work at less convenient hours (64.4 per cent), they intended to work only for a short period of time (8.5 per cent), they would no longer be exempt from taxes and social dues (6.7 per cent), their work would involve greater responsibility (5.6 per cent), they did not want to work overtime (3.9 per cent). (The ceiling on earnings of housewives working part-time exempt from income tax was raised from ¥790,000 to ¥900,000 a year in 1984.) Part-timers who wanted to become regular employees were motivated by the following considerations: they would have more stable jobs (46.6 per cent) higher pay (27.1 per cent), more responsible work (10.1 per cent), they could make better use of their potential (6.8 per cent) and their time (5.2 per cent).

One of the drawbacks Japanese companies encountered in hiring part-time workers was the high incidence of petty pilfering (not confined to women). Theft seems to be a problem not only in the retail trade but also in the restaurant and hotel business where the filching of kitchen stores and items such as soap, towels and slippers or even blankets and bed sheets adds up to considerable losses.

The government has set up special employment agencies for part-time workers to facilitate the hunt for part-time jobs and eliminate jobs with poor working conditions. As of August 1984, such so-called 'part banks' had been organised in 24 different localities.

Among the special measures taken by the government for creating employment opportunities are the 388 government training centres which provide training for about 330,000 trainees. Women accounted for about 12.5 per cent of the training applications and for 37.9 per cent of those for retraining. Subjects taught included western and Japanese sewing, dress making, typewriting and sales. Private enterprises operate about 300 institutions and industrial organisations about 800 training institutes. Women constituted 21.2 per cent of the trainees in private institutions. For women with children who are hired through public employment agencies, the state pays one-quarter (small enterprises one-third) of the wages. Enterprises providing training receive ¥17,000 a month per trainee. Women with children who participate in training courses organised by public employment agencies can receive government subsidies (average monthly allowance ¥106,750; travel allowance up to ¥1,470 a day).

Enterprises use part-time workers for a variety of reasons. Some of the reasons are obviously related to the employment conditions of part-timers: wages are low, easy adjustment to the work load, particularly seasonal and hourly fluctuations in business, replacement of regular workers before or after regular working hours or during absences, and to fill vacancies when it is difficult to hire régular workers. Some companies put employees who want to continue working after reaching retirement age on a part-time basis. Enterprises find it more economic to assign certain types of work to part-timers and it seems that automation has created some kind of part-time work.

Women in the US Labour Force

In the United States, the advance of women into many manual jobs formerly considered exclusively male occupations has created considerable resentment among males. But women are protected by the Equal Pay Act of 1963, Title VII of the 1964 Civil Rights Act and the 1975 Equal Employment Opportunity Act. They cannot be stopped from competing in 'untraditional' occupations which has resulted in a large increase in the number of women performing outdoor jobs and doing work requiring bodily strength.

Nevertheless, more than half of all women remain in the 'pink-collar ghetto,' working in service industries and 'helping professions.' Ninety-nine per cent of all secretaries are women, as are 95 per cent of the nation's registered nurses, 87 per cent of the restaurant workers and 83 per cent of the elementary school teachers. Of all women at work (1983: 48,009,000), 93.4 per cent were employees, only 5.6 per cent were self-employed and 1.0 per cent were family workers. Of all women employees (44,821,000) 42.8 per cent worked in regional, social or personal service industries, 22.6 per cent in wholesale and retail trade, restaurants and hotels, 16.2 per cent in manufacturing and 11.5 per cent in banking, insurance, real estate and corporate services.

In the job structure of female employees (1982), secretaries accounted for the highest percentage with 35.2 per cent, 19.8 per cent had service jobs and 17.0 per cent performed specialised and technical work. The proportion of women in managerial positions, 6.5 per cent, was higher than that of sales personnel (6.2 per cent), and only in Canada was the relative number of women in managerial posts higher (1984: 8.4 per cent). (These figures are given by the International Labour Office. According to other sources, the number of women in managerial positions rose from 1.4 million in 1972 to 3.5 million in 1983 which would make the ratio of women in managerial posts to all women employees 7.3 per cent.)

A study by the Rand Corporation concluded that the turnover rates of young women working in jobs traditionally held by men were not higher than those of their male counterparts. The assumption that women leave their work prematurely — to get married or to bear children — and that their training for skilled positions goes to waste is erroneous, the report asserted. It also noted that girls aged 14 to 17 who had been raised in single-parent households headed by women were much more likely to settle into traditional male jobs than girls who grew up in two-parent homes. The findings appeared to apply to Anglo and Latino women but not to blacks — perhaps, the report surmised, because female-headed households have been an established fixture in black societies. The study, which dealt mainly with blue-collar occupations rather than professions, observed that the brightest, most intelligent girls were most likely to take up jobs in male-dominated fields while the less bright girls were more attracted to home-making and occupations with which women were traditionally associated.

The proportion of women engaged in better-paying jobs had increased considerably prior to the 1981-1983 recession. Between 1970 and 1979, the ratio of women in managerial positions rose from 10.2 per cent to 24.6 per cent, women in professional occupations from 24.6 per cent to 35.9 per cent, and women in technical jobs from 26.4 per cent to 39.3 per cent. But a representative of a working women's group said that '80 per cent of the nation's 43 million employed women are trapped at the lowest-paying, lowest-status jobs in America.' Considering the working conditions of many illegal immigrants in the United States, this may be an exaggeration, but women constitute an increasingly larger part of the American population living below the poverty line and head about half of all poor families. In 1983, 35.3 million Americans lived in poverty, an increase of more than 9 million since 1979. The proportion of Americans living in poverty, 15.2 per cent, was higher than at any time since 1965.

International Trends in Female Labour

In West Germany, of the 10,425,000 women at work in 1983, the vast majority, 87.9 per cent, worked as employees; family workers accounted for 7.3 per cent and self-employed women for 4.8 per cent. The concentration of women in the service industries was almost the same as in the United States, with 35.7 per cent of women employees working in social and personal services, 27.3 per cent holding jobs in manufacturing industries and 20.8 per cent employed in wholesale and retail trade, restaurants and hotels. Although the percentage of secretaries was almost as high as in the United States (1982: 34.5 per cent), other occupations were more evenly represented, services 17.6 per cent, specialised and technical professions 16.1 per cent, operatives 15.7 per cent, and sales personnel 12.8 per cent. But only 1.4 per cent of the women held managerial jobs. Nine-tenths of the West German wives working in their husbands' businesses are covered by 'spouses' labour contracts' which assure them the benefits of social legislation.

The proportion of self-employed women was high in some developing countries; it was 27.0 per cent in the Philippines, 23.5 per cent in South Korea, and 11.4 per cent in Thailand. The situation was somewhat similar in Italy (16.0 per cent) and Spain (14.9 per cent); it was 10.7 per cent in Australia, considerably higher than in other advanced countries. A similar phenomenon was the large number of women working in family enterprises. The percentage of family workers in the number of women at work was 65.7 per cent in Thailand, 36.4 per cent in South Korea, 30.6 per cent in the Philippines, while it was 16.2 per cent in Spain and 11.1 per cent in Italy.

A relatively high proportion of women working in family businesses and of self-employed women characterised the female work structure in countries such as France (7.5 per cent and 9.3 per cent), Belgium (7.2 per cent and 8.6 per cent) and Austria (8.8 per cent and 8.9 per cent), whereas the percentage of self-employed women was small in Britain (3.8 per cent; the percentage of family workers did not appear in the ILO statistics).

In a report released in 1985, the OECD (Organisation for Economic Cooperation and Development) noted that despite improvements in the employment opportunities and conditions of women in the industrialised countries during the last ten years, women continued to earn less than men, about 20 per cent to 40 per cent in the OECD member countries. Wage differentials were relatively small in the Scandinavian countries, and in Britain, Ireland and Australia, women's wages experienced a proportionally larger increase than those of men. But incomes of women grew only slowly in West Germany and France.

The percentage of women in the labour force in the OECD countries rose from 49.2 per cent of the women of working age in 1975 to 54.7 per cent in 1983 while the percentage of men declined from 87.0 per cent to 84.3 per cent. Inequalities in education, training, employment and the tax and social security systems have combined to perpetuate occupational segregation and make women more vulnerable to poverty and dependence. Women remain crowded in a narrow range of occupations and into jobs requiring little skill or training. The share of women in public sector employment varies greatly from country to country. In Scandinavian countries, as many as seven out of ten public employees are women but there are two men to every woman in Japan and Australia.

Part-time work of women has grown rapidly in the last ten years. In 1981, part-timers accounted for 53.6 per cent of the work force in Norway, 46.4 per cent in Sweden, 45.2 per cent in the Netherlands and 43.6 per cent in Denmark. The share of part-timers in the women work force was high in most advanced countries; it amounted to 94.3 per cent in Britain, 93.8 per cent in West Germany and 92.0 per cent in Denmark, but was only 64.1 per cent in Italy.

In the Third World, women are sometimes made to participate in futile development projects. Mrs Shobita Jain, director of the programme for women's development of the Indian Social Institute, recently stated that funds meant for the socio-economic uplift of women were dissipated in impractical ventures while more deserving schemes languished for lack of funds. She maintained that the commercial viability of projects aimed at the economic rehabilitation of women was never considered and that women were directed into programmes based on work patterns that were traditionally considered suited for women like cooking or embroidery. Women should be trained to make products that were in demand in village markets. As in industrial countries, the traditional segregation of jobs according to sex prevents women from taking up jobs in which a shortage of trained workers exists and which would enable women to advance into better paying occupations.

Access to the Labour Market

Women still face considerable discrimination over access to the labour market. In private industry, Japan's traditional employment and wage system has been a great obstacle to the employment of women. Life-long employment and salaries based on seniority are rapidly changing but still remain the main features of employment in large companies. For other than technical personnel, Japanese enterprises do not base their recruitment on special skills or qualifications. They provide the training required for the work in the company through on-the-job training, special courses and the rotation of employees. On account of the practical impossibility to dismiss regular employees, enterprises restrict their recruitment to graduates of institutions (universities, junior colleges and senior high schools) which seem to guarantee a certain degree of reliability.

As a rule, new employees in Japan are inducted only once a year, after graduation, so that all new entrants start their work on 1 April. Recruitment during the year occurs only in exceptional cases. The recruitment process, however, begins many months before the actual hiring. Most schools have special officials in charge of placement who contact the personnel departments of the firms with which the school has placed graduates in the past. Armed with the recommendation of the school, the prospective graduates visit the enterprise they want to join — some years ago, a date was set for the beginning of these interviews so as to prevent recruitment starting before the summer holidays. Depending on the state of the economy, students have to bestir themselves and call at a number of enterprises before finding a job; on the other hand, when business is brisk, enterprises vie with one another in snatching the best students.

Employment and School Education

Employment prospects influence educational decisions only in a very general way. For fields such as medicine, engineering or the arts, preparation limits the choice of a school, but otherwise, the scramble to get into the 'right' school is unrelated to the profession or kind of work young people intend or hope to do. Graduation from senior high school is a must for any kind of 'decent' job so that 92.8 per cent of the boys and 95.0 per cent of the girls graduating from junior high school go on to senior high school. Relatively few girls intend to pursue a life-long business career. Graduation from junior college gives them a certain advantage in the job market but accounts for very little in the employment opportunities of boys. The difference in career intentions also explains the differences between the sexes in attending college and in their studies. In 1984, 1,328,157 males and 405,923 females were enrolled in four-year colleges (called university in Japan). Fields of study preferred by boys were social studies (which include law and economics) (46.4 per cent), and technical sciences (24.9 per cent) while other fields attracted relatively little interest (humanities 7.7 per cent, health care 5.9 per cent, education 4.9 per cent, agronomy 3.9 per cent, sciences 3.7 per cent, arts 1.2 per cent). Humanities were the favourite field of girls (35.5 per cent), followed by education (17.1 per cent) and social sciences (14.7 per cent). Subjects formerly considered typically feminine played a minor role (health care 9.4 per cent, domestic science 7.8 per cent, arts 7.1 per cent) and typically male subjects came last (sciences 2.6 per cent, technical sciences 2.1 per cent, agronomy 2.1 per cent).

Employment by Sex

In 1985, 288,343, 77.2 per cent of the 373,302 graduates of four-year colleges found employment. The rate was somewhat higher for men (78.8 per cent) than for women (72.4 per cent of 92,370 graduates), but it was the second year in a row that over 70 per cent of the women graduates found employment. Women graduates of junior colleges numbered 162,056 of whom 131,709 (81.3 per cent) could find jobs. In 1984, 280,712 boys graduating from senior high schools (56.6 per cent of the male graduates) and 326,525 girls (60.0 per cent of the female graduates found work. The placement of women graduates by industrial sector in 1984 was as follows. Of the senior high school graduates who found employment, 30.8 per cent took jobs in manufacturing, 30.4 per cent in sales, 21.2 per cent in services and 9.6 per cent in finance and insurance. The largest field of employment for women graduates from junior colleges was services (37.0 per cent of those being hired), 19.5 per cent were employed in manufacturing, 17.3 per cent in finance and insurance and 13.7 per cent in sales. The employment distribution of women graduates from four-year colleges by industry was: services 52.7 per cent, manufacturing 16.7 per cent, sales 14.0 per cent, government 6.2 per cent, finance and insurance 4.7 per cent, transportation and communications 2.1 per cent, and construction 1.9 per cent. By job categories, 31,864 (49.3 per cent) found specialised technical and professional jobs (instructors 17,474, technicians 6,245, health care 4,280, other 3,865), while 26,200 (40.5 pere cent) were hired for office work.

For graduates of both junior and senior high school, the number of job openings far exceeded the number of job seekers. For junior high school graduates, job offers amounted to 43,249 for female and to 40,577 for male graduates. Girls seeking employment numbered 20,901 and boys 24,821; 20,793 girls and 24,630 boys were actually hired. For senior high school graduates, vacancies amounted to 387,739 for female and to 412,228 for male graduates. There were 290,439 female and 216,121 male graduates wanting employment and 287,845 jobs for young women and 219,367 jobs for young men were actually filled.

About half of all enterprises hire male as well as female senior high school graduates and of these enterprises, half apply the same standards for hiring men and women while half attach different conditions. College graduates are recruited by about one-third of all enterprises; of these firms, one-quarter hire male as well as female graduates, about 70 per cent only male and 5 per cent only female graduates. About 70 per cent of the enterprises recruiting senior high school graduates hire men and women for different types of work, and the same applies to about 50 per cent of the firms employing university graduates. There is some variation in the type of work not assigned to women among the different industries. On account of legal restrictions, night work is not assigned to women, as is work involving much overtime. Certain positions were not assigned to women if the work involved frequent negotiations with clients or much travel or required good judgement, high technical skills or great bodily strength. Other firms hired women only if they could produce a recommendation. Men were assigned to positions nationwide while women were only employed in the locality where they lived. In a similar arrangement, men were recruited by the head office whereas women were hired locally by each branch office.

Many companies have dormitories for single male employees and provide company housing to their married staff, but women are required to live at home and applicants living alone in apartments are often not hired. (Dormitories for women workers were common in pre-war times in the textile industry.) Some enterprises do not hire married women, others have different age limitations for men and women.

Employment Situation for Young Women

According to some girls (college graduates) who have tried to find employment, many enterprises do not take the trouble to examine women's applications seriously. In particular, they attach no importance to the girls' scholastic records. In the girls' view, among the factors helpful for getting a job, looks rank first, connections second and the scholastic record comes last. At a trading company, an official told a gathering of women who had applied for employment: '. . . in our company, your performance at college is quite inconsequential. On the contrary, those with too excellent a record are undesirable because they tend to be cheeky. We are not looking for women who try to compete with men but for women willing to serve as assistants, women who can serve tea well and who are healthy, cheerful and cute.' No comment needed.

Hospitals administering plastic surgery reported that the number of students having their eyes, noses, lips and chins reshaped increased when the job market grew tight. When jobs are scarce, good looks often can help in getting hired. The Jujin Hospital, one of the leading Tokyo hospitals specialising in remodelling facial features, gave facelifts to about 10,000 students in 1983. The proportion of student patients rose from about 15 per cent in 1972 to almost 45 per cent while that of housewives dropped from about 40 per cent to less than 20 per cent. A girl wanting to become a stewardess remarked that the statement in Japan Air Lines' recruiting pamphlet that personal appearance didn't count was just pretence. 'In choosing between two girls of equal ability, it's evident that the better-looking girl will be preferred.' To the assertion of the personnel officer of a trading company that it is not the shape of the eyes that they look at but the gleam in the eyes that reveals the inner person and the individual's potential, a plastic surgeon countered: 'If those companies don't take appearances into consideration in hiring, as they claim, why is it that they conduct individual interviews after grading written examinations? The first impression that a person makes comes from face and posture. That's why male students from Tokyo University come to us for facial operations because they know that they cannot win by just being smart.'

A recent study, however, asserted that good looks, while a positive factor in hiring decisions, may become a liability when a woman seeks a managerial post. The relationship between beauty and seeming competence of a manager appears to be contrary for men and women. Men with good looks are seen as more masculine and capable but attractive women, because they are viewed as more feminine, are judged less capable for masculine-type jobs. Unattractive women were considered more reliable than their beautiful sisters.

A poll among young women asking them to list the most desirable employment conditions showed the following order of preferences: stability 63.8 per cent, high wages 58.2 per cent, good atmosphere 49.3 per cent, growing enterprise 49.2 per cent, convenience of commuting 44.9 per cent, opportunity for advancement of women 37.9 per cent, many holidays, little overtime 35.7 per cent. While 59.0 per cent wanted work involving responsibility, 3.0 per cent did not want responsible work.

Women seniors in four-year colleges expecting to graduate in 1986 indicated IBM Japan as their first choice in seeking employment, a private recruting company reported. The firm's large size, its stability, future prospects and high wages were given as reasons for the preference. In second place was the Japan Travel Bureau, followed by Fujitsu Ltd, Suntory, Japan's largest liquor producer, fell to fourth place after having been number one for two consecutive years. Eight electronics-related firms, such as Canon Inc., Nippon Digital Equipment Corp., Sharp Corp. and Ricoh Co., were among the top 30 firms appearing in the survey. A 1984 survey of 1,200 prospective women graduates of junior colleges showed that the most sought-after employment was with Japan Air Lines. Stewardess remains a glamour job and a popular television drama about stewardesses may have given it additional attraction. Women's prospects for employment were somewhat better in 1985 than in the preceding year. About 990 of the 1,800 listed companies intended to hire about 3,000 women graduates of four-year colleges and 890 firms planned to employ about 9,300 girls graduating from junior colleges.

Relatively few girls seeking employment with a private company are seriously contemplating a life-long career. A 1982 survey covering 10,000 young women in the last year of college or junior college found that 92 per cent of the students wanted to find a job after graduation but only 34 per cent of the college and 14 per cent of the junior college students intended to work until retirement age. The others wished to quit when they got married or had children but about 40 per cent of them wanted to work again when their children had grown up. The average girl seems to regard the independence connected with their work primarily as an opportunity to throw off society's restraints for a while, to smoke in public, to go on overseas trips and to indulge themselves in every selfish way for a few years before they revert to type and become concerned about finding a good marriage partner. (As regards overseas trips, in 1981, 6.5 per cent of the women aged 20 to 24 and 5.2 per cent of those in the 25-29 group had been abroad. In 1982, young women between the ages of 20 and 29 accounted for 43 per cent of the women who went on overseas trips.)

Of the college graduates who started to work in 1983, 26.4 per cent wanted to work until marriage or until they had children, 32.3 per cent intended to work until retirement age, and 40.8 per cent wanted to resume work after their children had grown up. In the same year, 14.2 per cent of the women who quit working had worked less than one year, 24.6 per cent left after one or two years of work, 16.8 per cent after three or four years, and 22.3 per cent after five to nine years. But the percentage of women with ten or more years of service rose from 14.8 per cent in 1976 to 22.0 per cent in 1983. Of women college graduates who were working, 73.4 per cent had less than five years of service and only 11.8 per cent had worked for more than ten years. Of male employees, 36.4 per cent had worked less than five years but 41.1 per cent had over ten years of service. The earnings pattern of women who re-enter the job market after having interrupted their careers show that they never catch up with their original potential. Usually, their real wages are lower than what they received when they left. They suffer from an erosion of skills that hampers their future progress. The longer the hiatus in a woman's career, the greater the impact on her future earnings.

In the lower age brackets, the ratio of 'standard workers' (workers who joined the enterprise immediately after graduation from school and continued working for the same enterprise) is higher for female college graduates than for their male counterparts. In the 20-24 age group, the ratio was 93.5 per cent for women and 88.9 per cent for men, in the 25-29 group, it was 60.6 per cent for women and 56.8 per cent for men. The relation changed for the following age classes: 30-34, women 36.3 per cent, men 48.6 per cent; 35-39, women 19.1 per cent, men 45.9 per cent.

Actually, the attrition rate for female employees is quite high. Department stores expect to lose 50 per cent of their new sales girls in 12 months, trading companies count with the loss of 50 per cent of their newly hired female staff in two years, banks in three and insurance companies in four years. So far, enterprises have failed to develop a system to screen women employees and differentiate between those who want to work only until they get married and career-oriented women who really want to work. Because girls do not intend to stay, they have little interest in advancement and positions although they hope for wage increases. Nevertheless, despite a large expansion of part-time work, the average length of service has increased. But employers do not want to invest much time and money in training if they cannot count on a reasonable return which is the main reason for much of the discrimination in assignments, training and positions.

Job Training

Training for new entrants is usually given in three fields, etiquette, general orientation and basic information, and training for special work assignments. In the last category, 67.7 per cent of all enterprises provide this kind of training to newly hired employees; in 72.1 per cent of these firms, the training is the same for men and women, 14.2 per cent give it only to men, 1.4 per cent only to women and training is different for men and women in 12.3 per cent of the enterprises. General information on the company and its activities is given to new employees in 58.1 per cent of the enterprises; this orientation course is the same for men and women in 84.3 per cent of the companies providing such informa-

tion. If education in etiquette is carried out (54.6 per cent of all enterprises), men and women receive the same training in 75.8 per cent of
the firms; this kind of education is limited to women in 13.9 per cent of
the enterprises.

Training directed to workers in the course of employment has
various purposes: improvement of performance in the present job,
preparation for transfer to a different, particularly a more difficult job,
preparation for transfer to a different position involving the handling of
subordinates or instruction after such transfer. Except for the training
aiming at improvement in the present job (66.1 per cent of all enterprises), only a third of the enterprises have institutionalised this type of
training; if it is given, it is either the same for men and women or
limited to men; about 10.0 per cent of the enterprises give women a
different type of training. Only a third of the enterprises prepare their
employees for assuming management positions, and in over two-thirds
of the firms, only men receive this kind of training.

In the aptitude tests of vocational schools, girls' ability of spatial
imagination was inferior to that of boys. They had greater difficulty in
working out three-dimensional objects on the basis of a two-
dimensional sketch. In Soviet vocational schools for watchmaking,
boys and girls were initially trained together but the results were
unsatisfactory. The two sexes were then trained separately; male
apprentices were instructed in repair work and the girls were shifted to
assembly operations.

In West Germany, the training of young women in technical
occupations has produced a number of beneficial results. Where young
women work, the atmosphere of the place improves, and in mixed
training groups, conversation and behaviour become more civilised. In
metalworking and electrical appliances, the performance of young
women is at least equal to that of young men, and the women's
dexterity and zeal make up for their lack of strength. In the Federal
Republic of Germany, women are by law excluded from only 30 of the
451 apprentice training sectors.

Nevertheless, the chances of girls to receive training that will
qualify them for a future career are not very promising. In view of the
impact of marriage and childbirth, the legal employment regulations
and the possible withdrawal from the labour market, employers remain
sceptical of the economic sense in hiring and training women. Working
class families tend to take the education and training of girls not
seriously enough. They expect the girls to get married or neglect the
long-range earning prospects in favour of a quick addition to the family
income. Girls, therefore, come into monotonous, unhealthy and
insecure jobs and drop out as soon as they get married.

The number of women who, after graduation from college or
junior college, work in engineering or technical research and

development has increased but in these fields, traditionally regarded as male preserves, women face great difficulties in assignments and promotion.

Historically, women have not been as interested as men in the fields of mathematics and sciences. Because far fewer girls and women are learning to use computers than boys and men, women may be locked out of jobs and miss opportunities for advancement in the future because many jobs will be directly related to computers. This may wipe out part of the gains made by women during the past decade in business and industry.

Part of the training given by Japanese enterprises consists in rotation so that the employee can become familiar with different aspects of the company's business. Regular rotation was the custom in 65.7 per cent of all enterprises; rotation was restricted to men in 50.4 per cent and extended also to females in 49.6 per cent of the enterprises. Many firms consider the rotation of women employees unnecessary because women perform only supplementary work, others contend that women themselves did not want to be rotated.

Japanese Enterprises and the Employment of Women

Japanese employers often state that women are not interested in their work because they quit when they get married or become pregnant. What kind of work do these women quit? Most women are hired only for uninteresting, dead-end jobs with low pay and no prospect of promotion. These women are not stupid. They realise that their jobs have no future and gladly accept marriage as a more satisfactory alternative.

Japanese girls proficient in English think that they have better chances abroad than in Japan. A Japanese company would utilise their linguistic abilities but they would always remain in subservient positions without possibility of advancement.

The first and only Japanese woman to obtain a doctorate from Harvard University, Yôko Ishikura, took a job as a consultant with McKinsey & Co. After graduating from Sophia University with a degree in English, she worked five years as a translator but then used her savings to go to the United States and study because she saw no prospects of advancement in Japan. Women have better opportunities for advancement with an American company than with a Japanese firm, she said. Japanese firms have no role for MBAs or PhDs.

The use Japanese firms make of their female employees explains the qualities they expect in the women they hire. Ninety-five per cent of the companies want cheerful and obedient girls, 92.7 per cent cooperative individuals, and 86.7 per cent girls with a sense of responsibility. Very few companies look for leadership ability, specialised knowledge, creative or analytical powers. For much the same reasons, women remain largely in occupations that have traditionally been regarded as women's jobs: office work, salesgirls, waitresses, nurses and teachers in elementary schools.

The higher a woman's education, the more difficult it is for her to find suitable employment. The industries that welcome graduates from four-year colleges are sectors that women do not like, such as wholesaling, retailing, banking, insurance and real estate. Fields in which women want to work are government, press and publications, television, trading companies and services. Department stores and supermarkets are particularly unpopular with college graduates. Publishing, in which women want to work, is typical for the treatment women must face. They are denied the chance of moving from one type of job to another in contrast to their male counterparts who are able to learn the various phases of the business. There are, however, women's magazines (1981: 27 with a total circulation of 90 million) many of which are edited by women. Dentsu, Japan's largest advertising agency, established a wholly-owned subsidiary staffed entirely by women.

Women are often excluded from conferences although such meetings may be important for performing their duties. They are left behind to take care of telephone calls or other minor chores. Even if women attend conferences, their opinions have less chance of being heard or adopted than those of men.

Management's attitude that women can be used for any kind of 'unimportant' job surfaced in a case in which a woman employee sued the Japan Iron and Steel Federation, asking the court to confirm her position as a librarian and to order the association to pay her a solatium. The court agreed that her transfer from the post of librarian, a professional occupation, to general office work constituted discrimination and ordered her reinstatement.

A large company which operates one of Tokyo's leading book-stores as well as a chain of supermarkets has been accused of discrimination in hiring female employees. The firm's labour union published two memos which laid down the guidelines for hiring. Management contended that these guidelines were only a collection of views expressed in staff meetings during training sessions in 1972 and 1973 and did not represent company policy. Below is the gist of the contents.

1. Females not to be hired: (1) ugly, (2) short, (3) country bumpkins (these three are colloquial expressions often used in derogatory remarks: *busu, chibi, inakamono*), (4) wearing glasses, (5) dull-witted, (6) quick-tongued, (7) interested in law, (8) suffering from chronic illness, 2. Females for whom caution is required if considered for hiring: (1) supporting progressive parties (left-wingers), (2) with

links to political or religious organisations, (3) not Japanese nationals (Koreans), (4) having changed jobs twice or more often, (5) having quit a four-year college before graduation, (6) complicated family situation, (7) father university professor, (8) person held in esteem is a teacher. 3. Applicants for part-time work requiring caution: (1) divorcees, (2) husband is teacher or writer, (3) persons living as boarders, (4) persons with professional qualifications such as kindergarten teacher or nurse, (5) persons who have been changing jobs, (6) persons who have been living at home without definite aim. The case was taken up in the Diet but the firm claimed that the discriminatory practices had been discontinued.

Japan's Wage System

The relatively low wages of women are one of the distortions in the system of remuneration that can be found in practically all countries. In Japan, the system is also biased in favour of senior employees; salaries and other forms of remuneration are unreasonably high for the higher echelons in government as well as private industry. Monthly salaries of up to ¥5 million and retirement allowances of ¥200 million are completely out of proportion to the contribution of such individuals to an enterprise or government agency. That salaries of executives are much higher in the United States is no justification.

Japan's industrial wages and salaries are determined by a number of factors which have little to do with the type of job or individual merit. The main factors are the size of the company, education and length of service. Large companies pay considerably higher wages and salaries for the same type of work. The starting wage or salary is different for employees joining a company upon graduation from junior or senior high school or from college. Since about 90 per cent of all graduates from junior high school (age 15, equivalent to 9th grade; end of compulsory education) go on to senior high school, the number of workers with only a junior high school education has become relatively small. Most manual workers start working after graduation from senior high school (age 18, 12th grade).

Girls constitute the largest proportion of the students of junior colleges (usually two-year course, generally of a practical orientation). In addition to base pay, regular monthly wages and salaries may include dependents or family allowances, housing and living allowances, seniority pay, efficiency pay, special pay and responsibility or grade pay. Women ordinarily are not household heads and therefore do not receive family allowances or similar extras. In the case of white-collar or clerical workers, overtime pay seldom corresponds to the actual overtime hours worked. Most companies pay a transportation allowance or provide commuter passes (which, up to a certain amount, are tax-exempt). Many companies issue free uniforms. For men, overalls or uniforms are only provided to service personnel and technical staff, and part-time women workers are usually given smocks. Very important are the semi-annual bonuses (June or July and December), usually computed as a multiple of the monthly wage (for example, five monthly wages). Most salaried workers are paid once a month, and most firms transfer the wage or salary (minus withholding tax) to the bank account of the employee.

Under a bank's pay regulations, family allowances were paid to male employees irrespective of the income of their spouses but were not paid to a female employee if her husband's income was so high that she was not entitled to a deduction for dependents from her pre-tax income. A woman who had supported her husband and her daughter had been paid a family allowance of ¥18,000 a month but a year after her husband, an official of a political party, was elected to a seat in the city assembly, the bank stopped payment and demanded repayment of the allowances paid during the period her husband received a salary. The Morioka District Court decided that the practice of not paying family allowances to a female worker whose husband earned an income constituted discrimination and offended against Article 4 of the Labour Standards Law (the court did not rule on the violation of Article 14 of the Constitution alleged by the plaintiff). The bank has appealed the decision.

The remuneration of executives (company presidents, directors) remains outside the regular wage scale. In the latter half of fiscal 1982 (October 1982-March 1983), the average monthly salary of company presidents was ¥1.53 million, their summer and year-end bonuses averaged ¥5.78 million. In large companies, the president's monthly salary averaged ¥2.48 million, in small firms, ¥950,000. The average pay of other executives ranged from ¥990,000 for vice presidents to ¥630,000 for ordinary directors.

A survey undertaken by *Fortune* magazine estimated that the average yearly earnings of Japanese division heads (*buchô*) in 1983 amounted to ¥9.56 million, which made them the lowest-paid managers of this rank among twelve industrial countries (including Brazil and Mexico). Their average income was not even one-third of that of their Swiss counterparts (¥32.1 million) and only slightly higher than one-third of that of American managers of the same class (¥27.4 million; conversion rate $1=¥245). The average yearly remuneration of section chiefs (*kachô*), ¥7.25 million, ranked in eleventh place, just above Mexico with ¥7 million.

Writing in a Japanese magazine, Mr Akira Hasegawa, who works in the United States for the Bell company, opined that the remuneration of Japanese middle management should be doubled and expressed the view that the present state of affairs, the result, he thinks, of post-war egalitarianism, was a socialist system at best and, at worst, a modern slave system. Both his assertions are poppycock.

It may be possible to' compare managers holding the position of division head, but such a comparison inevitably puts aside basic differences in the structure of Japanese and foreign companies and the work of their personnel. American companies hire managers for their competence and performance; Japanese managers arrive at their positions because they survive the attrition inherent in the promotion process. American managers have to prove their worth by results and are fired if they fail; Japanese managers have to fit into the company pattern and last until retirement to get a substantial retirement allowance and/or a pension. There are other differences that make a comparison difficult but I think that, in general, the structure of remuneration in the so-called capitalistic countries is incompatible not only with the most elementary principles of justice but also with economic rationality.

Although Japan's economic system can be called dirigism, ideology inspires neither the gerontocratic oligarchy which controls it nor the bureaucrats who manage it. They only want to wield power while in office and land a plush sinecure upon retirement.

Wage Differentials

In 1984, the monthly wages paid by establishments with over 30 workers averaged ¥368,775 for men and ¥191,143 for women, so that women's wages were only 51.8 per cent of those of men. The differential was somewhat smaller in basic wages (men ¥272,714, women ¥144,407, 53.0 per cent) but greater in special earnings (overtime, bonuses; men ¥96,061; women ¥46,736; 48.7 per cent). These differences varied by age, education, length of service, size of the enterprise and branch of industry. The differences between the starting wages of male and female graduates narrowed in 1985. Based on the average of 723 firms, starting wages of male university graduates were ¥142,471 per month, those of female graduates ¥135,865, 95.4 per cent of men's wages. Male graduates of senior high schools received an average of ¥116,095, female graduates ¥113,103 (97.4 per cent).

Between 1960 and 1975, women's wages rose faster than those of men so that the ratio between the two improved from 42.8 per cent in 1960 to 56.2 per cent in 1978 but thereafter, the ratio declined. The difference between the wages of women and those of men tends to grow with the higher age of the workers. In the higher age brackets, the wages of production workers continue to rise but white-collar employees who stay on after reaching retirement age often receive lower salaries. As of June 1984, the average basic wages were (in ¥1,000) ¥237.5 for men and ¥139.2 for women. Men's wages ranged from ¥102.3 a month for workers under 17 to ¥300.0 for the 45-49

group. Women's wages were ¥96.0 for those under 17 to ¥153.6 for
the 55-59 group. If wages for the 20-24 age group are put at 100, the
index of the age differential came to 71.1 for male workers under 17
and 208.5 for the 45-49 group. For women workers, the index was 75.8
for young women under 17 and 121.3 for the 55-59 group. The index
for the sex differential (men=100) was highest for young workers
(under 17: 93.8); it declined gradually until the 25-29 group (80.2), then
fell rapidly 30-34: 66.5; 35-39: 57.4) and reached a low of 48.2 for the
45-49 group; it was up to 59.8 for the 55-59 group.

Men's wages or salaries rise sharply with the years of service while
the increase is relatively smaller for women so that the wages of women
with long years of service tend to be proportionally lower than those of
men. Another factor affecting the wage and salary levels of long-
serving employees is the preponderance of men in higher posts whereas
few women are promoted to leading positions. The wage index of
junior high school graduates with 30 years of service (20-24=100) was
198.0 for men and 176.7 for women; the wages of women which had
been 94.0 per cent of those of men for workers under 17 were only 71.4
per cent of those of men with 30 years of service. For senior high
school graduates, wages of workers with 30 years of service were
¥392,210 for men and ¥280,200 for women; the index (20-24=100) was
278.2 for men and 221.5 for women.

For workers who are not recruited after graduation, wages are
generally lower, and the difference between the wages of men and those
of women is rather large. In 1984, the average monthly wages of junior
high school graduates not hired at the traditional term were ¥163,900
for men and ¥101,700 for women. The difference was small for
workers under 17 (men ¥100,500; women ¥92,700) but was already
considerable for the 20-24-year-old (men ¥156,100, women ¥106,000).

The difference between the wages of men and women also depends
on the kind of industry. In 1984, the difference in the average monthly
wage based on sex in establishments with over 30 workers was largest
in foods and tobacco manufacturing where women's wages were only
40.8 per cent of those of men (men ¥328,382, women ¥133,892). For
the entire manufacturing sector, the ratio was 42.8 per cent; it was 45.7
per cent for finance and insurance, 47.8 per cent for construction, 60.5 per
cent for services and 68.1 per cent for transportation and communications.

Women are more numerous in low-paying industries and there are
also relatively more women than men in small enterprises in which
wages as well as special allowances are low. If wages and special
allowances paid by large enterprises (with over 1,000 workers) are
assumed to equal 100, wages of enterprises with 100-999 workers were
83.9 and their allowances 67.0; wages of enterprises with 10-99 workers
were 79.3 and their allowances 48.7. In 1983, 24.7 per cent of the
women and 30.5 per cent of the men worked in establishments with

over 1,000 workers, 33.7 per cent of the women and 33.0 per cent of the men in enterprises with 100-999 workers, and 41.6 per cent of the women and 36.6 per cent of the men were in firms with 10-99 workers.

A survey undertaken by the Ministry of Labour in July 1985 and covering about 89,000 enterprises employing four or fewer workers found that the monthly pay of male workers averaged ¥204,144 and that of female workers ¥106,396. This was 62.5 per cent of the average wages of male workers in enterprises with over 1,000 workers (¥326,860) and 60.7 per cent of the average pay of female workers in such enterprises (¥175,143). Compared with enterprises employing from five to 25 workers, the pay of the small enterprises averaged about 80 per cent. The average bonus of small enterprises was ¥398,099 for men (equivalent to 1.99 monthly wages and 27.2 per cent of the average bonus of male employees of large companies — ¥1,461,419) and ¥178,247 for women (1.68 monthly wages and 22.4 per cent of the average bonus of female workers of large companies — ¥796,733). The average working time was 7.6 hours a day and 24.5 days a month. Of the 8,198,000 workers employed by the small enterprises in 1981, 52.7 per cent were women and female part-time workers accounted for 31 per cent of the entire labour force. Female workers were particularly numerous in small eating and drinking places and other establishments in the service industry.

Low Pay of Women Workers

In the United States, the average pay of women workers in the non-agricultural sector was 65.0 per cent of the average pay of men in 1982. But the Census Bureau found that in 1981 six million American women — about one out of eight — earned more money than their husbands. Nearly one-quarter of these women had completed four or more years of college and 38 per cent had more schooling than their husbands. On the average, however, women earned only 40 per cent of their husbands' pay. The husband was the sole earner in 29.6 per cent of all households, the wife the sole earner in 3.9 per cent, both were earners, but the husband earned more in 44.5 per cent, both were earners, but the wife earned more in 8.2 per cent, neither husband nor wife worked in 13.8 per cent of the households.

In a case that dragged on for nearly a decade, a federal judge ordered Northwest Airlines to pay $52.5 million in backpay and interest to 3,364 stewardesses who had charged that they had been paid less than male pursers. Northwest maintained that the pursers' position involved greater responsibility and duties justifying a higher salary and appealed the verdict.

In many cases, the classification system perpetuates old work concepts which are generally disadvantageous to women. According to the job classification of the City of Denver, for example, tree trimmers, painters and tyre service assistants were paid more than nurses working in the intensive care unit of the city hospital.

In West Germany, the average male white-collar worker in 1980, earned about $500 a month more than his female counterpart, and blue-collar workers were paid 60-75 cents an hour more than women. In 1982, the ratio of the average earnings of women to those of men was 72.7 per cent. In a special case, the basic salary was the same for men and women but men were given bonuses denied to their female colleagues.

In Britain, men earned considerably more than women on the same jobs. The gap narrowed between 1971 and 1976 but there has been little change since. The greatest improvement has been in the salaries of women with a university education; their earnings rose from 60 per cent of what similarly qualified men received in 1971 to 75 per cent in 1980. But the average pay of women was only 69.1 per cent of the average of men.

In 1981, the average wage of women engaged in non-agricultural work ranged from 44.8 per cent of that of men in South Korea to 92.8 per cent in Australia (1982: 91.9 per cent).

There are indications that a sharp increase in the number of women entering a certain job category or profession causes that occupation to lose status. Men shun those jobs and the salaries drop, making the problem of equality of pay academic. This is said to have happened in the United States in jobs such as insurance adjuster and examiner, bill collector, real estate agent and broker, checker, inspector and production-line assembler.

Salaries of Japanese Civil Servants

The data below on the salaries of government officials in Japan will allow a comparison with the salaries and wages in the private sector. In addition to the monthly salaries, government employees receive the customary semi-annual bonuses, a variety of allowances and retirement allowances. The salaries quoted are for officials of the national government; some local bodies pay considerably higher salaries and some of the bonuses paid by local governments triggered severe criticism. Torazo Ninagawa, who stepped down as governor of Kyoto Prefecture in April 1978 after seven terms as governor received a cheque for ¥126 million (after tax) and the Tokyo Metropolitan Government paid an average of ¥49.9 million to 15 bureau chiefs who retired in July 1984. Because bureau chiefs had received retirement allowances as high as ¥65 million, an amount of 77 times the last monthly salary of the retiree was fixed as maximum.

National government pay scale, effective 1 July, 1985 (in ¥1,000):

prime minister, chief justice of the Supreme Court ¥1,725; cabinet ministers, prosecutor general, chief of the Board of Audit, head of the National Personnel Agency ¥1,258; head of the Fair Trade Commission, head of the Imperial Household Agency ¥1,202; permanent vice ministers, presidents of Tokyo and Kyoto universities ¥1,025; bureau chiefs (buchô) ¥397.8; section chief (kachô) ¥352.1; head of group (kakarichô) ¥221.7; clerk ¥132.1; chauffeur ¥212.7; janitor ¥185.8; professor at state university ¥402.0; assistant professor ¥301.3; graduate assistant ¥225.3; head of medical department at state hospital ¥322.1-¥395.9; medical officer ¥234.7; chief head nurse ¥351.4; head nurse ¥250.4; nurse ¥198.9; assistant nurse ¥148.4.

In view of the country's fiscal indebtedness, the prime minister and the cabinet ministers have declined salary increases since 1982. Prime Minister Nakasone, therefore, will actually receive a monthly salary of ¥1,395,000, and the 20 cabinet ministers one of ¥1,017,000.

Working Hours

Women generally work fewer hours than men and the difference is particularly great in overtime. The number of days worked per month is also usually lower for women. Some women forego overtime work and promotions that might interfere with domestic obligations and more than half quit working at least once for family reasons. Because of these interruptions, women generally have fewer years of service. In 1984, the average monthly working hours in enterprises with over 30 workers were 164.4 hours for men and 157.4 hours for women. Monthly overtime came to 17.9 hours for men and 6.8 hours for women. Men worked an average of 22.0 days a month and women 21.8 days. The longest regular working hours were in woodworking (men 178.4 hours, women 173.9 hours) where the monthly days worked were also most numerous (men 22.9 days, women 22.4 days). The highest average of overtime worked came to 23.0 hours for men in manufacturing and to 7.8 hours for women in finance and insurance. These figures, however, are only for overtime stated explicitly on the pay slip; employees customarily work much overtime without being paid.

Wages of regularly employed part-timers were calculated on an hourly basis in 77.4 per cent of all enterprises and on a daily basis in 20.9 per cent; they were computed on a daily basis but paid monthly in 17.7 per cent and on a monthly basis in 2.1 per cent of the enterprises. The average hourly wage of women part-time workers was ¥572, with differences depending on age, type of industry and size of enterprise. The average hourly wage of women aged 18 or 19 was ¥554; it was ¥623 for the 20-24 age group, ¥554 for the 30-34 group and ¥586 for the 50-54 group. The average was ¥540 in manufacturing, ¥573 in sales and ¥640 in services. Enterprises with over 1,000 workers paid ¥601, those with 100-999 workers ¥557. The special allowances paid to part-time women workers are considerably lower than those paid to full-time regular workers. In 1983, the bonuses paid to part-time women employees averaged ¥78,800; they were higher, ¥91,000, in manufacturing, but lower, ¥73,000, in sales and ¥60,300, in services. Establishments with over 1,000 workers paid an average of ¥120,000 but bonuses were much lower in smaller enterprises, ¥75,000 on average in firms with 100-999 workers and ¥63,700 in those with 10-99 workers.

Part-time women employees worked an average of six hours a day and 23 days a month. Overall, part-time workers were covered by unemployment insurance in 45.3 per cent, by health insurance in 43.5 per cent and by old-age pension systems in 41.1 per cent of the enterprises employing part-time labour. The wage system was different from that of full-time employees in 69.6 per cent and allowances were different in 46.0 per cent of the enterprises. Regular wage increases were given in 54.7 per cent and bonuses in 62.7 per cent of the enterprises but only 9.6 per cent paid retirement allowances. Of the large enterprises, (over 500 workers), 94.2 per cent had a different wage system for part-time workers but 75.0 per cent had unemployment insurance, 74.4 per cent health insurance and 72.1 per cent old-age insurance for part-time workers. Retirement allowances were paid by 19.8 per cent.

Actual conditions of women workers are much worse than reported in official surveys. Recently, a group of working women in Kumamoto Prefecture compiled a booklet giving examples of the inequitable and sometimes illegal treatment of women. In a garment factory employing about 40 housewives, the women have to work overtime until midnight when the deadline for the shipment of merchandise draws near. The firm's president is quoted as saying that he would only have to write an apology if found to have violated the law. In another factory, women were compelled to work four to five hours overtime per day without any extra pay. The monthly wage at this shop amounted to about ¥70,000, less than the starting wage of a senior high school graduate. Because the owner maintained he would go bankrupt if he had to pay higher wages, the women agreed to work overtime without compensation.

Women working on a take-home basis are even worse off. Minimum wages have been fixed for only four categories of work and the compensation fails to provide even a subsistence income.

The majority of the women do not belong to unions, work for low wages and put in overtime hours without extra pay. They receive only small bonuses and retirement allowances. The booklet describes employers as 'tyrants who make their employees work like slaves.'

Holidays

Nearly half of all enterprises with more than 30 workers had a weekly holiday, but these enterprises employed only 22.1 per cent of the workers. The largest percentage of workers (27.0 per cent) is given two days off each week, two free days are given to 16.7 per cent of the workers every other week, to 14.7 per cent once a month and to 7.7 per cent three times a month. Part-time workers were given paid holidays in 31.8 per cent of the enterprises; 81.0 per cent gave holidays to workers who had been working over a year, in 71.7 per cent, part-timers received six days of vacation; 17.8 per cent gave holidays also to workers who had worked less than a year.

According to a union survey carried out in June 1982, 54.1 per cent of the women employed part-time actually worked 6 to 8 hours and 11.1 per cent over 8 hours. Sixty-five per cent worked 20 days a month — almost the same number of days as those worked by full-time women employees. Although 61.7 per cent of the respondents had been working continuously for the same employer over a year, only 21.8 per cent were given paid holidays. (Article 39, Paragraph 1 of the Labour Standards Law stipulates that a worker reporting for work continuously for at least 80 per cent of the workdays during a period of one year must be given six workdays of paid vacation, and one workday must be added for each additional year up to 20 days of paid vacation.)

The 1980 national census included questions on time spent on various activities. For this purpose, activities were classified as primary activities (eating, sleeping, personal care), secondary activities (work, school, household work, child care), and tertiary activities (study unrelated to school education, hobbies, sports, recreation and amusement). In hours and minutes per day, married women in nuclear families spent 10.32 h on primary, 8.30 h on secondary (work 2.58, household chores 2.36 h) and 4.58 h on tertiary activities. For working women, primary activities took 10.28 h, secondary 9.33 h (work 5.54 h, household chores 2.36 h) and tertiary 3.59 h. Working men required 8.26 h for secondary activities of which 7.20 h were taken up by work.

Similar statistics have been compiled by the Prime Minister's Office ('Basic Survey on Social Life'). Of women employees, 60.7 per cent worked between 35 and 48 hours a week. On weekdays, they spent 10.17 h on primary activities (sleep 7.29 h), worked an average of 7.51 h, needed 1.46 h for household work and 21 minutes for shopping; they spent 3.09 h on tertiary activities. On holidays, 11.25 h were used for primary activities (sleep 8.18 h), 6.14 h for secondary (work 2.17 h, household chores 2.51 h, shopping 49 minutes) and 6.23 h for tertiary activities.

Homework

A type of work largely related to the system of sub-contracting is work
done at home called *naishoku* (literally inside work). It consists of simple
manufacturing or assembling (very often sub-assemblies) on a piece-
work basis for cottage industries or other intermediaries. Toys and
sundries such as paper flowers used to be typical products of the home
industries, and work such as sewing on buttons used to be done in this
way. But automation has eliminated many operations formerly providing home employment. Of the firms using homeworkers, 96.3 per
cent were medium or small enterprises with a work force of less than
300 workers which were particularly hard hit by the recession.

In a new form of homework, women organised groups of about
five housewives living in the same neighbourhood to operate word
processors for typing jobs. Each woman gets paid in proportion to the
work she does; hourly payment ranges from ¥300 to ¥1,500 and the
daily work from zero to 10 hours or more.

In October 1984, 1,186,500 people of whom 1,107,000 were
women were engaged in homework. It was a full-time job for 75,700
workers, 1,094,200 were housewives and 16,600 were family members.
Most of the women still performed work related to textiles (garments
32.0 per cent, knitting 17.3 per cent). Work on electrical appliances
constituted the second largest category with 17.9 per cent and sundries
came third with 13.8 per cent (paper and paper products 5.3 per cent,
leather goods and printing and related work each 2.3 per cent). The
average age of the women homeworkers was 43.8 years; women between the ages of 30 and 40 made up 36.6 per cent) and those between
40 and 50 33.8 per cent of the workforce. The average work experience
of women was 7 years and 4 months. Women workers averaged 6.1
hours a day and 20.7 days a month; men on average worked 10.7 hours
a day and 24.6 days a month.

Women's pay averaged ¥324 an hour while men earned ¥887. Of
the women, 70 per cent received less than ¥400 and 30.6 per cent
between ¥200 and ¥300; of the men, 60 per cent earned over ¥700 and
31.3 per cent between ¥1,000 and ¥2,000. Consequently, the average
monthly income of men amounted to ¥240,800 whereas that of women
was only ¥39,700, far below the subsistence level. By comparison,
women's wages in small enteprises in the manufacturing industry with
1 to 4 workers were ¥578, an hour, their monthly income ¥95,600,
their working time 7.1 hours a day, 23.3 days a month. In enterprises
with 5 to 29 workers, women earned an average of ¥623 per hour; their
monthly income was ¥106,000, with 7.5 hours of work a day and 22.8
working days a month.

The main reason why enterprises relied on this type of homework
was that the work had to be done by hand (62.9 per cent). Other

reasons were lower costs (18.5 per cent), changes in the volume of work (12.1 per cent), shortage of workers (9.7 per cent), small-lot products (9.1 per cent) and need of great skill (4.1 per cent). Women took up this kind of work because they had free time (38.4) per cent), because they could not go out for work (34.7 per cent), because the income of the head of the household was insufficient (32.7 per cent), because they could spend the income from homework at their own discretion (29.5 per cent), because they needed extra money to pay for land, house, education (25.7 per cent) and because they could make use of their skills or talents (6.2 per cent).

Housewives now have more free time because they have fewer children and electrical appliances make household work easier and faster. The *naishoku* type of work used to be associated with poverty but now many middle-class women work at home, some because they need the money, others because they can combine it with taking care of small children, and still others because it gives them something to do. Usually, however, women prefer part-time work outside the home which is more remunerative.

Many housewives looking for part-time work are being victimised by fraudulent schemes. One favourite ploy is luring them into buying knitting machines at exorbitant prices with the promise — usually broken — to buy the socks or mittens produced. Another trick is to offer courses teaching skills such as colouring animation slides and promising contracts to put the newly acquired skills to use. The lessons are expensive and the contracts, if concluded at all, are soon terminated for 'defective products.'

The *naishoku* work is regulated by the Family Labour Law which provides that each worker should have a 'family worker's card' entitling him or her to a minimum piece rate and compensation in case of illness or accident. But one-third of the home workers do not have such a card. The Ministry of Labour has fixed minimum wage rates for 183 types of work which cover only a small section of the industry.

West Germany enacted legislation for improving the working conditions of part-time workers. The employer is obliged to contract for definite periods of work on a daily, weekly or monthly basis. If no working time is fixed, a period of ten hours is assumed as the weekly work term for which the worker must be paid even if he or she is not called upon to work.

If the labour contract does not lay down any other regulation, the employer can decide on the time the part-time worker must report for work but in case of irregular working periods, the employer must notify the worker at least four days in advance, otherwise, the worker can refuse the assignment (but he will not be paid). If the contract does not specify a definite daily working period, the employer must use the services of the worker for at least three consecutive hours a day; if there

is not enough work, wages for three hours must be paid anyhow. But
employer and worker can agree on other arrangements.

Advancement of Women

That women advance to leading positions is considered exceptional not
only in Japan's public life but also in private business. Internationally,
Japan is the most backward of the advanced industrial nations as far as
the ratio of women in management positions is concerned. A survey of
the Ministry of Labour in 1984 showed that 56.3 per cent of the about
5,200 companies covered had women in managerial posts. Of the enterprises promoting women, 15.9 per cent advanced women up to executive positions, 4.7 per cent up to department head (buchô), 28.3 per cent
up to section chief (kachô), 30.9 per cent up to head of group (kakarichô)
and 20.0 per cent to other leading jobs. The reasons of the companies
not promoting women were based partly on the work for which
women were employed, partly on the qualities of women. Over half of
these companies denied promotions because the work for which
women were employed was only supplementary, over one-third
because women quit work very soon. Some companies thought that
women lacked management and leadership ability and others did not
entrust women with management tasks on account of legal restrictions
on the work of women. According to a 1981 survey of the Ministry,
the companies willing to promote women included 74.2 per cent of the
enterprises surveyed in finance and insurance, 74.8 per cent of those in
services and 64.9 per cent of those in wholesale and retail trade.

Two surveys of the Prime Minister's Office investigated the
involvement of women in policy decisions. The first survey, based on
conditions as of 1 January, 1979, found that in 1,497 listed companies
and special corporations, only 996 of the 361,612 persons responsible
for the formulation of policies were women (0.3 per cent). A second
survey covered 2,416 organisations other than business companies. As
of 1 January, 1981, 642 women were among the 35,820 individuals in
charge of policy decisions (1.8 per cent).

Many Japanese managers continue to oppose the advancement of
women into managerial posts with the old assertion that women's
professional consciousness is low and that they have little leadership and
planning ability. Employers claim that women's abilities do not grow
commensurate with seniority and that women stop improving beyond
the age of 30. Mitsubishi Corporation, Japan's largest trading company,
had a work force of 5,953 men and 3,854 women in 1981 but not a
single woman held an administrative post. The firm hired 89 women
college graduates but only for clerical and auxiliary work. On the other
hand, Meiji Mutual Life Insurance Co. promoted 102 female employees
to management positions in April 1983, the first Japanese enterprise in

which the number of female managers reached three digits.

A survey covering 992 companies in the service sector located in the Tokyo metropolitan area and in the Osaka-Kobe district found that almost one-third of the firms were willing to promote women to managerial posts although 39.9 per cent were reluctant even to hire women.

Responding to a 1983 poll, three out of four women working in managerial positions in major Japanese firms expressed confidence in their ability to perform their duties successfully. Two out of three were proud of their affiliation with the company for which they were working and the majority thought that their positions and salaries were satisfactory.

Sometimes, women do not want to be promoted because they would have to assume greater responsibility which would make it more difficult to keep up with their household work. Many women would reject an opportunity for a career, even if such a chance were available, for the sake of raising children. Women refuse to be transferred and may break into tears when asked to do something difficult. On the other hand, the thought that men cannot be expected to serve under a woman is still strongly held by many Japanese men. A woman who had successfully passed the examination for promotion was asked to pass up the chance to advance in favour of a male colleague. 'It would be a disgrace for a man to serve under you,' she was told.

In Britain, a two-year Manchester University study concluded that women managers cope better with pressure even though they come under heavier stress from the demands of home and work than their male counterparts. The report told companies refusing to break their male-dominated hierarchies that they were missing out on good management material by failing to promote women.

In a landmark decision, the US Supreme Court ruled that Sumitomo Shoki America, Inc., the New York-based subsidiary of a major Japanese trading company, had violated American civil rights laws by discriminating in its employment practices on two counts, sex and nationality. Sumitomo argued that it was entitled to have management personnel of its own choosing under a 1953 US-Japan trade treaty, but the court decided that Sumitomo Shoji America was a company of the United States, not of Japan, and that its employment practices had to conform to American law. Nevertheless, the court recognised that knowledge of language and other cultural and business aspects were necessary skills and constituted bona fide occupational qualifications justifying seemingly discriminatory hiring practices.

Bangkok Bank has two branches staffed entirely by women and the Thai government's savings bank has one. Bangkok Bank established the first all-women branch in 1964 because Thai women traditionally take charge of the family's finances and the bank's manage-

ment thought that women customers would find it easier to discuss
financial problems with members of their own sex.

In Switzerland, the Banque Hypothécaire de Genève opened a new
branch office staffed entirely by women because 45 per cent of its
customers were women.

Obstacles to the Promotion of Women

A serious obstacle to the advancement of women into managerial
positions will be the glut in the promotion process. Because of the
Japanese recruitment system, employees of the same class advance like a
phalanx — at least in large enterprises and the government service. (The
system allows management to discern who is forging ahead and who is
falling behind.) Because positions become fewer in the higher echelons,
the number of those who can be promoted decreases and companies
find it impossible to provide enough jobs for senior employees.
Moreover, the retirement age has been going up and the attrition
process does not sufficiently reduce the number of employees with long
years of service so that the surfeit is becoming more and more
unmanageable. Some companies send their surplus staff to subsidiaries
but this possibility is limited. A few years ago, the expression *madogiwa
zoku* (window tribe) came into vogue. Enterprises created new posts
with management titles (and corresponding salaries) but no real work.
The employees, therefore, occupied 'window seats' (in Japanese offices,
the desks of the managers are arranged along the walls facing the staff
seated in the middle of the office) but they had nothing to do and spent
the time reading newspapers or magazines.

High government ·officials often move into executive positions
with enterprises under the jurisdiction of the respective ministry or
agency (a custom referred to as *amakudari* — descent from heaven) or
are given executive posts in one of the over 100 'special corporations'
(*tokushu hôjin*) created by the bureaucracy to provide sinecures for their
retirees (much to the annoyance of the staff of these corporations whose
chances for advancement are curtailed). Many government agencies
have or had no mandatory retirement age and the growing senescence
of Japan's population makes the problem of how to take care of the
rising number of elderly very difficult. Enterprises, therefore, are
reluctant to steer people into a management career and try to limit
promotions to those from whom they can expect a significant contribution to their business.

Successful Career Women

Women have achieved much more recognition outside government and
industry and have been doing much better as owner-managers of their

own businesses than as employees. In Japan, the first woman doctor to open a clinic was Mrs Ginko Ogino who began to practise in 1885. Women doctors have firmly established themselves, especially in gynaecology, paediatrics, ophthalmology, as nose, ear and throat specialists and as dentists, less in surgery. The number of women lawyers, however, is still limited, mainly because graduation from the Research and Training Institute of the Ministry of Justice is required for a legal career. In 1984, 23,019 women were company presidents (*shachô*), 3.7 per cent of the total number of presidents (619,631). In literature, women have been the recipients of Japan's most prestigious literary awards, the Akutagawa prize (15 women) and the Naoki prize (12 women). Many women have gained recognition as pianists, violinists, singers and actresses but few women have become prominent conductors, composers, painters or architects. Japanese women athletes have been less successful than those of other countries but Japan has had some outstanding women teams, for example, in volleyball.

Among the most successful business women are the canvassers selling life insurance. The Japanese branch of the 'Million Dollar Round Table' has 187 members of whom only 50 are men. The membership qualifications for this organisation include the writing of insurance contracts with an aggregate face value of $2.25 million for at least two years; this record has to be maintained for at least three out of five years. A 42-year-old woman who started selling insurance seven years ago earned about ¥15 million in 1984. In the last four years, she sold an average of 230 contracts a year with a face value of ¥900 million.

Women have displayed their business talent not only in the so-called *mizu shôbai* as 'mama-sans' of bars, snack bars and other eating places, but also as designers, owners of fashion boutiques, ladies' and children's wear and food stores. The highest degree of emancipation has been gained by women in the entertainment world. In these circles, a real women elite can be found, with women earning many times the salary of a company employee, living in luxury apartments and enjoying a life-style completely different from that of an 'ordinary' working woman.

But in the fiercely competitive entertainment world, success and even more survival are a fight against formidable odds. Each year, about 600 young men and women make their professional debut as singers but after two years, only six are still in show business. The average length of the careers of actors and actresses, however, comes to 21.1 years, which is due to the strong traditions in the Japanese theatre.

There is much exploitation of women in the entertainment world and gangsters have a frightful grip not only on prostitution, drugs and gambling but also on otherwise legitimate businesses in amusement and entertainment. In these circles, women find it very hard to escape manipulation by males; on the other hand, lesbianism is not infrequent.

In a move indicating a growing awareness of Japan's establishment attitude to women's role in business, the Japan Committee for Economic Development (*Keizai Dôyûkai*) invited five businesswomen to become members of the organisation. They included Hanae Mori, one of Japan's leading designers. It was the first time in Doyukai's 40-year history that women joined the organisation which counts about 1,200 members.

In the United States, more than a third of all MBA candidates are women. The organisers of a business forum for women found that 1,400 women fitted their criteria for membership: women who are in charge, wholly or in part, of companies whose sales were at least $1 million or managing operations with a budget of that size in large firms.

In the beginning of 1983, women were the sole owners of 2.8 million small businesses in the United States. If partnerships and partially-owned corporations were included, the number of small businesses owned by women came to over 3.7 million, one-fourth of all small businesses. Business ownership by women grew about four times in the last five years. Greater independence of women, the increase in the number of divorced women who must support a family, and a growing number of women whose husbands were out of work were given as reasons for the increase. Women have made their mark as managers and executives in many businesses by their ability, efficiency, perseverance and ingenuity.

In the Federal Republic of Germany, an association of women entrepreneurs has over 1,500 members. Only women heading an enterprise with yearly sales of DM1 million or employing at least 10 workers can join the association. Actually, there are about 100,000 firms led by women meeting these conditions and altogether, half a million enterprises out of a total of 2.5 million are under the direction of women. Most of these enterprises are medium-sized firms, and many of the women took over when their husbands died. This is the main reason why three-quarters of these undertakings are in branches associated with male activities, such as construction, machinery, metal products and plastics. One-third of the women executives are junior high or business school graduates; one-fifth graduated from high school. Their work week averages 60 to 70 hours, with 70 per cent of their time devoted to professional work and 30 per cent to household chores.

The most prominent of German women entrepreneurs is Grete Schickeldanz who succeeded her husband as president of Quelle, Europe's largest mail-order house with 35,000 employees and yearly sales of DM9 billion. She joined the company in 1927 as an apprentice. Christine Princess of Urach studied engineering at Stuttgart Technical College and became one of the first engineers to specialise in electronic data processing. She now heads the Organisation and Data Processing Division of Daimler-Benz and is the only woman on the Control Board (Aufsichtsrat) of the maker of Germany's most prestigious cars.

Transfers

A survey of the Ministry of Labour carried out in August 1984 found that 46.6 per cent of the companies restricted their transfers to the change of positions inside the work-place, only transfers not requiring a change of residence were the rule in 24.3 per cent of the firms and 19.0 per cent shifted workers also when the new assignment necessitated moving to another location. In the last category, 86.6 per cent of the companies ordered such transfers only for men, 7.2 per cent transferred women as well as men, 4.7 per cent instituted these transfers for women only if the employees themselves desired them and 0.7 per cent moved only women in special positions. If the transfers did not require moving to another place, 46.4 per cent of the companies ordered them for women as well as men but 40.1 per cent limited them to men. New assignments inside the plant were handled equally for men and women by 57.5 per cent of the companies, 19.2 per cent limted such transfers to men and 20.3 per cent gave new assignments inside the enterprise only to women in special positions. The transfers of men to distant localities with the men leaving their families behind and living alone at the new place of work (referred to as *tanshin funin*, to proceed to one's post alone) has become a difficult problem which will be discussed in connection with the family.

An agreement between management and labour stipulated that women employees would not be transferred to permanent jobs because the operating conditions of the steel mill made it difficult to provide enough permanent positions for women. The work in shifts and hazardous operating conditions were in conflict with the protective provisions for women in the Labour Standards Law. In a suit brought by women employees, the Kawasaki branch of the Yokohama District Court held that no discriminatory treatment was involved since 'being a woman' was not the reason for the regulation. The case is being appealed.

Transfer on account of childbirth is invalid but if childbirth is not the reason for the transfer, it is not invalid although it occurs after childbirth. A woman hired as an announcer by a TV station cannot be transferred to office work against her will. If the employment contract specifies the type of work, transfer to another type of work without the consent of the employee is invalid.

Voluntary welfare measures instituted by companies for their employees include dormitories for single workers, company housing at low rents, loans for the acquisition of land or the building of a home, short-term loans for household expenditures, subsidies for private insurance and monetary gifts for events such as marriage or death. Dormitories for single workers were provided by 32.7 per cent of all enterprises; 42.9 per cent provided them for male and female workers but 43.8 per cent only to men. Company housing was available in 31.2 per cent of the enterprises, 49.7 per cent made no distinction between men and women but 36.3 per cent gave it only to men.

Health Protection of Women Workers

For protecting the health of women and particularly their function as mothers, the work of women is subject to special legal restrictions. In Japan, minors below the age of 18 and women are not allowed to work underground in mines, to do hazardous jobs or to engage in work involving the handling of heavy loads. Night work, in particular, may have damaging effects on women, causing menstrual disorders and abnormal pregnancies. Only in specified occupations such as nurses, telephone operators and broadcasters, airline stewardesses, hostesses in night clubs and actresses may women work after 10 pm. No woman may work more than two hours overtime on any given day, six hours in any given week, or 150 hours in a single year. Japan's Labour Standards Law stipulates that employers must give leave to women for whom work at the time of the monthly period is very difficult or who perform work that would create hazards (Art. 67). The law also provides for maternity leave and time-out for nursing. Women can ask for maternity leave within six weeks preceding the expected date of confinement and cannot resume work for six weeks following child-birth (this period can be shortened to five weeks if a doctor certifies that it does not constitute a health threat; Art. 65, Par. 1 & 2). Women can also ask for lighter work during pregnancy (Art. 65, Par. 3). Women having babies below one year can take 30-minute breaks in addition to the regular rest period for nursing (Art. 66). Women teachers, nurses and other female personnel in medical, welfare and child care institutions can be furloughed until the child is one year old.

In an ideologically inspired perversion of the principle of equality, the city council of Tanashi (Tokyo Prefecture) amended a city ordinance to give also the husbands of women city employees with babies under one year two 30-minute periods a day 'nursing time.'

A woman employee of a German patent counselling firm in Tokyo asked for permission to take an hour off each day for nursing her baby — reporting to work 40 minutes late and getting off 20 minutes early — for five months. The firm turned down the request but the woman took an hour off each day anyway alleging that this had been the practice in the past. When the firm cut her salary, she filed a complaint with Tokyo's local Labour Relations Commission which ordered the firm to pay more than ¥100,000 in back pay and post an apology at the firm's main office entrance. The case is not yet closed.

In November 1983, the Japanese Supreme Court overturned the verdict of the Tokyo High Court which had found the change in work rules concerning special leave for women employees without the union's consent unreasonable. Prior to the revision, women employees of Takeda System Co. were given paid leave for up to 24 days a year without pay cuts. In 1974, the company changed these provisions, allowing two days of special leave a month but reducing basic daily pay to 68 per cent. Eight women employees went to court claiming that the unilateral change of the work rules was invalid. They lost in the court of first instance but on appeal the Tokyo High Court ruled that the company's revision deprived the women employees of their vested rights and amounted to a *de facto* loss of wages. In its appeal to the Supreme Court, the company maintained that women employees had abused the regulations and the Supreme Court held that the Tokyo High Court had failed to examine whether the company's action had been reasonable or not and remanded the case. I think that the Tokyo High Court was right and the Supreme Court wrong. If the company thinks that there are abuses, it can negotiate with the union to stop them but it has no right to change the rules unilaterally and arbitrarily.

Women workers suffered another setback when the Supreme Court ruled that the Labour Standards Law does not make it obligatory to consider the days taken off for menstrual leave as working days. It depends on the agreement between labour and management whether these days should be counted as working days or days of absence. Unless a labour contract causes 'extreme economic disadvantage' to women workers, it is not illegal. In the case before the court, the basic monthly salary was paid in full to women workers under an oral agreement between labour and management but in computing the diligence allowance, the firm counted the days taken off by four women workers for their menstrual leave as absences. In their suit, the women claimed that the pay practice of the firm discouraged women from taking menstrual leave but the Tokyo District Court and the Tokyo High Court turned down the complaint and the Supreme Court, in July 1985, upheld the lower courts. That women taking leave suffer a certain disadvantage does not necessarily discourage women from availing themselves of this right, the court said.

Childbirth Regulations

In 1981, the actual situation was as follows, Women who gave birth during the year constituted 4.7 per cent of all married female workers and 2.4 per cent of all women workers. The average days of absence from work were 38.5 days before and 48.8 days after childbirth; 21.7

per cent of the women who gave birth quit work altogether. Only 5.7 per cent of the pregnant women were assigned lighter tasks and 27.5 per cent of the nursing women took time out for nursing. In 28.1 per cent of the enterprises, women accounting for 13.4 per cent of the female work force requested leave for their menstrual period. The average for those who took leave was 5.8 times a year for a total of 7.7 days. Only 30 per cent of the women who took pre- and post-childbirth leave provided by law received their full wages while most women were given 60 per cent of their regular pay. In addition to the legal requirements, 25.8 per cent of all enterprises had special arrangements for pregnant and nursing women to visit hospitals, 20.0 per cent had special work relaxations, 18.1 per cent had special vacations, and 1.6 per cent had special in-house child care facilities.

In 1983, child-birth expenses were paid by the government-administered health insurance system in 147,915 cases; the average allowance was paid for an average of 66 days and amounted to ¥157,611 per case. The enterprise-administered health insurance system paid for 96,723 cases; the allowance was paid for an average of 69.2 days and amounted to ¥194.013 per case. Local government employees were paid childbirth allowances in 70,971 cases.

The private health insurance system pays a maternity allowance to compensate for the loss of income from unpaid leave before and after birth if the mother herself is working; she receives six-tenths of her wages for 42 days before and after birth. She is also paid a childbirth allowance of one-half of her standard monthly wage, or a minimum of ¥150,000 for childbirth expenses. If the mother does not work, the husband receives an allowance of ¥150,000 for childbirth expenses. In addition, a child-care allowance of ¥2,000 is paid. Similar payments are provided under the government's insurance system but government employees and teachers receive eight-tenths of their salaries as do teachers under the health insurance plan of private schools.

Some Japanese enterprises have adopted a 'child leave system' under which mothers can take leave of absence for periods ranging from six months to three years. Most enterprises permit the mother to stay away from work until the baby is one year old. By 1981, the system had been adopted by 14.3 per cent of all enterprises (services 42.9 per cent, finance and insurance 3.4 per cent, large enterprises 19.9 per cent). In 90 per cent of the firms implementing the system, the woman is given back the job she held before. Many enterprises pay the full social security contributions (unemployment, health and old-age insurance), that is, employer and employee payments, during the worker's absence, but if the worker quits just before the end of the leave, companies often require reimbursement of the employee contribution. Since fiscal 1975, the government pays a subsidy to enterprises giving maternity leave for longer than three months; since 1 April,

1985, these subsidies total ¥800,000 over two years for large and ¥1 million for small enterprises.

Government employees can be given a one-year maternity leave. While almost all government employees (including teachers at public schools) are given back their old jobs, the same is not the case for all employees in the private sector.

As of April 1984, child-care centres numbered 22,704, including 13,656 public centres (59.5 per cent) caring for 1,075,885 children (56.5 per cent) and 9,268 private centres caring for 804,233 children. The majority of the children cared for by these centres were between 3 and 6 years; the percentage of infants was rather small.

In the United States, the number of women in the work force with children under six has doubled since 1970 and amounted to about 8 million in 1984. Some of these women put off having children until they had established careers and now hold management jobs. Nearly 2,000 companies provide some form of child-care assistance and in addition to running day-care centres at or near the place of work, enterprises offer arrangements such as job sharing, flexible time schedules and generous maternity and paternity leaves. The availability of day-care centres has sharply reduced absenteeism and improved morale and efficiency.

In the Federal Republic of Germany, working mothers are entitled to six weeks leave before and eight weeks leave after childbirth, in case of premature or multiple births, twelve weeks. The health insurance systems pays up to DM25 a day and the employer supplements these payments up to the net wage income of the woman. The total compensation is based on the average earnings during the last three months prior to the six-week leave before childbirth. Mothers not covered by health insurance receive a motherhood allowance of DM400.

Special Safeguards for Women Workers

The special protection afforded to women is not without problems. The regulation of absence for menstruation and leave for pregnancy and child rearing give the impression that these events are considered as some kind of industrial accident interrupting the production process with emphasis on limiting the impact of this interruption to a minimum. The special legal protection of women often has a negative effect on their employment opportunities. The law barring women from nightwork shuts women out from many better paying jobs. In West Germany, the law making 14 weeks of paid pregnancy leave mandatory discourages employers from hiring women of childbearing age.

In 1981, the Soviet Union published rules barring women from 460 jobs, including digging and driving heavy trucks. But two years later, a Soviet newspaper reported that little had changed and that women were still doing heavy manual work on building sites and in factories. Part of the problem was that factories relied on women to do hard, monotonous or dirty work instead of modernising their equipment.

In an American survey, nearly a third, 32.85 per cent, of working women, regardless of the nature of their jobs, experienced stress in their work. The most stressful jobs were those requiring a large amount of work but allowing little control over the work or the environment. Low-level workers, such as clerks, were more likely to experience stress-related health problems. Uncertainty about employment had a more damaging effect on health than certain knowledge of impending unemployment. Most women's jobs involved conditions which contributed to stress: pressure without having power, not being able to decide how to do one's work, unchallenging jobs and the coercion to apologise although being right. More than one in four women working full-time had to put in a 40-hour week or more.

One of the objections against the Equal Rights Amendment was that it would lead to the abolition of the special safeguards for women under present laws regulating family relations, labour conditions, punishment for sex crimes and prison discipline.

The health threat arising from the exposure of workers to noxious substances poses particular problems for women and the application of protective laws has become more crucial with the increase in the number of women working in the chemical industry. The US Safety and Health Administration listed 24 chemical substances that pose potential reproductive problems for women, and employers have responded with policies of 'protective exclusion' which keeps women of childbearing age out of contact with them. Some groups charged that these policies were discriminatory. Their view was that women should not be protected against their will and that safety should not be secured at the expense of equality. They demanded another solution.

When it was detected that lead could have an adverse effect on human foetuses, the American Cyanamid Company in West Virginia decided to exclude fertile women from areas of the plant that could expose them to contact with lead. Four women employees of the company underwent voluntary sterilisation in order to keep their high-paying jobs at a lead pigment plant. In the ensuing public debate, questions were raised as to whether a company should be allowed to discriminate against a woman worker in favour of her unborn child, and whether the practice of excluding fertile women from certain high-paying jobs was just another form of discrimination. The chemical companies argued that there was no choice but to ban women from areas that presented the threat of miscarriage or physical or mental damage to unborn children. Unborn children, the companies said, had legal rights which their mothers could not waive. If they did not act to protect unborn children, they would leave themselves open to claims for damages on behalf of children born with defects.

There can be no doubt that the best solution would to be remove all hazards from places of work but there are cases in which this is technically not feasible. For some chemicals, there is no safe level of exposure. For women, the most dangerous period is in the earliest days of pregnancy. If evidence of potential risks remains after using engineering controls, personal protective equipment and job rotation, the exclusion of women seems to be the only possible course. But opponents maintain that not all women excluded by protective policies wanted children or planned to have them.

Some evidence seemed to indicate that a foetus could be affected through the exposure to chemicals of the reproductive organs of the male but the scientific data are not clear.

A woman who worked as a telephone operator and suffered from arm and shoulder pains, an occupational disease of operators, refused to undergo a physical examination at the hospital designated by the company and wanted to see her own doctor. The company cut her wages by one-quarter on the grounds that she had not complied with the company's order. The woman sued and sought the nullification of the disciplinary action. The Kushiro District Court ruled that individual workers have the freedom to choose their doctors for the treatment of occupational diseases and in August 1983, the Sapporo High Court upheld the decision. But in March 1986, the Supreme Court overturned the decisions of the lower courts and ruled that a company can order an employee to receive treatment for a job-related ailment at a designated hospital if the order is given in accordance with company rules.

The limitations given with women's physiological constitution often cause disadvantages in remuneration. The Japanese courts have held that the provision in the Labour Standards Law entitling a woman to menstruation leave does not mean that the leave must be paid. But if a company's employment regulations stipulate that a woman can have one day of paid menstrual leave, it does not mean one day of leave per pay period but one day for each menstrual period.

Japan Schering, a subsidiary of a West German pharmaceutical company, had an agreement with its labour union providing that employees who worked less than 80 per cent of their yearly working days would not be eligible for wage increases. In calculating the employees' actual days of work, the company deducted not only days of absence or lateness, but also the monthly special leave for women, paid leave and days off due to accident or illness. Twenty-four employees who had been denied wage increases on the basis of the days of absence calculated in this way filed suit. The Osaka District Court declared the practice unfair and illegal and ordered the company to pay a total of ¥21 million in compensation. The company has appealed the decision.

In recent years, the number of 'motherless families' has increased and the father has to take care of the household and the children. In West Germany, the Bremen Labour Court decided that the rule giving a woman who runs a household and must work more than 44 hours a week one extra paid day-off a month, the so-called household day, applies also to men and that a man who acts as housekeeper (for example, a divorced man who has custody of a child) is entitled to an additional day off.

In Britain, a woman went to court claiming that the pay for a nanny should be tax-deductible because an independent woman could not work without such help. She lost in the first instance.

Termination of Employment

Reasons for ceasing to work can be broadly divided into those on the part of the employer and those on the part of the employee. In 1981, Japanese women quit working for the following reasons: expiration of contract period 5.6 per cent, attainment of retirement age 2.0 per cent, dismissal for the convenience of management 4.5 per cent, resignation for personal reasons 83.0 per cent. Death terminated employment in 2.0 per cent of the cases and some workers lost their jobs because the enterprise went out of business and for various other reasons. Marriage and childbirth (included in personal reasons) accounted for 18.8 per cent of the cases in which women quit work but 80 per cent of the women returned to work after childbirth.

A different break-up is presented from a poll in which women were asked to state the main reason why they quit working. The main reason was marriage with 43.9 per cent, health 12.8 per cent, difficulty of combining housework and child rearing with outside work 11.2 per cent, education of children, care of sick or elderly family members 4.5 per cent, transfer of husband 1.8 per cent, dissatisfaction with work 2.1 per cent, human relations in place of work 1.8 per cent, low pay 1.3 per cent. Many women consider work outside the home as detrimental to family life; they mention, in particular, the effect on the rearing of children (65.1 per cent), care of the sick and elderly (35.4 per cent), household work (32.1 per cent), education of the children (30.1 per cent), and the health of the woman (30.3 per cent). Only 1.7 per cent thought that outside work had no influence on their home life. Women quitting work after less than one year considered their work as only temporary; 18.8 per cent said that the work was unstable and 14.6 per cent found that the work did not agree with them. Of the women quitting after one to nine years of work, 41.9 per cent left because of marriage, and 22.4 per cent in order to devote full time to their children. Of the women who had worked longer than ten years, 47.4 per cent quit on account of sickness or old age, and 11.2 per cent because they had reached retirement age.

While companies often complain that women quit after a few years, they generally expect women to leave when they get married and have children. They do not know what to do with women who are looking for life-long employment. The regulations of some companies laid down that women employees had to leave when they entered the sixth month of pregnancy. Japan Air Lines (JAL) grounded stewardesses who became pregnant, and for stewardesses of All Nippon Airways (ANA) and Toa Domestic Airlines (TDA), pregnancy meant the end of employment. The retirement age of female cabin attendants had been set at 40 years by JAL, at 35 years by ANA, at 58 years for single women and at 33 years for married women by TDA. Some companies hired married women only when they had no children.

Retirement

A retirement system had been adopted by 87.3 per cent of all enterprises (1985). The system was the same for all workers in 80.5 per cent of these firms, different for men and women but the same for all men and all women in 15.6 per cent, and different according to the type of work in 2.9 per cent of the enterprises. All utilities companies had retirement systems and in 90.6 per cent of these firms, it was the same for men and women. In manufacturing, 90.6 per cent of the companies had retirement systems but it was uniform for men and women only in 75.3 per cent of these firms. Different retirement ages depending on the type of work had been fixed by 12.5 per cent of the companies in transportation and communications with retirement systems. In companies in which the retirement age was different for men and women, the retirement age of women was below 45 in 2.8 per cent of the firms, at 45 in 6.6 per cent, between 46 and 49 in 1.1 per cent, at 50 in 23.6 per cent, between 51 and 54 in 8.6 per cent, at 55 in 44.3 per cent, between 56 and 59 in 81.1 per cent, and at 60 or over in 4.9 per cent. The retirement age for men was considerably higher in these companies; in nearly half, 49.4 per cent, it was 60 per cent, in 26.0 per cent between 56 and 59, at 55 in 17.2 per cent and lower than 55 in only 0.1 per cent.

The courts have ruled that a provision in the labour regulations requiring a women to quit upon marriage is invalid. 'Voluntary' retirement extorted by an alleged custom of quitting at the time of marriage is invalid. Retirement regulations fixing the retirement age of men at 55 years and that of women at 30 were ruled invalid because unreasonable and against Article 90 of the Civil Code ('Legal actions having as their objective matters contrary to the public order and good morals are invalid'). In 1971, the Tokyo District Court decided that the retirement regulations of Nissan Motor Co. fixing the retirement age of

men at 55 and that of women at 50 were valid, and the decision was
upheld by the Tokyo High Court in 1973. But in a later suit involving
the same company, the Tokyo District Court ruled in 1973 that a
difference in retirement age based solely on the difference in sex was
irrational and against Article 90 of the Civil Code. The Tokyo High
Court upheld this ruling in 1979 and it was substantially confirmed by
the Supreme Court in 1981. The decision of the Supreme Court has
been followed by the Sendai District Court in 1982 (retirement age of
men 55, of women 45 invalid) and by the Hiroshima District Court in
1984 (retirement age of men 62, of women 57 invalid).

In 1968, the Morioka District Court decided that regulations
requiring the voluntary retirement of married women and women over
30 were invalid because they constituted discrimination contrary to
Article 14 of the constitution and Articles 3 and 4 of the Labour
Standards Law. But in 1971, the Sendai High Court overturned the
decision and held that notification of a dismissal was an offer to rescind
the labour contract and that the resignation was an acceptance of this
offer. Thus, the court 'reasoned,' it was a voluntary cancellation of the
labour contract.

Dismissal

Facing the necessity of reducing its labour force, Furukawa Mining Co.
decided that the dismissal of married women was the most practical
way of doing it, and the courts, up to the Supreme Court, sanctioned
this method. The Tokyo District Court, however, ruled that to make
the dismissal of married women and women over 27 years of age the
general standard of any personnel adjustment was contrary to the
constitution and to the spirit of the Labour Standards Law and that
dismissals based on this rule were invalid. The same court decided that
personnel adjustment based on a rule providing for the dismisssal of
women with two children was invalid. Also held invalid was a
procedure calling for the voluntary retirement of married women and
women over 25. But the action of a hospital requiring retirement of
men over 60 and women over 55 in order to solve the difficulties of the
hospital was held reasonable in the light of the circumstances.

In the personnel adjustment necessitated by rationalisation, the
Nagoya District Court ruled, part-time workers cannot be dismissed
simply because they have been designated by this term. An employment contract making the employment of men over 30 and of married
women temporary did not obstruct the freedom to marry and dismissal
at the end of the term is valid. This decision of the Tokyo District
Court was appealed but the case was settled by composition. The
Osaka District Court found that dismissal under a temporary
employment contract had actually been used to enforce early retirement

and constituted an abuse of power. If a monthly employment contract has been automatically prolonged over a period of three years, the contract is not changed into an unlimited contract but a part-time worker can expect that the contract will be renewed. Dismissal without any reason for not continuing the former practice is invalid. This 1983 decision of the Akita District Court is being appealed.

A woman teacher who always took leave on the day before Sunday or holidays claiming to have her period went to court to have her dismissal rescinded. But the court decided that she was obviously unfit as a teacher and upheld the dismissal.

In a suit against Air France, the refusal to renew an employment contract because of the personal appearance of the employee (no longer attractive) was held to be an abuse of power. A woman cannot be fired because she refuses to serve tea to her male colleagues. Serving tea, the court found, was no obligation under the employment contract.

In a case that attracted wide attention, US television anchor-woman, Christine Craft, was awarded $375,000 in actual and $125,000 in punitive damages in a sex bias suit against a television station whose executives had demoted her, she claimed, for being 'too old, unattractive and not deferential to men.'

The Tokyo District Court ordered Japan Air Lines to cancel a disciplinary pay cut against a stewardess who had refused to change her flight schedule. The stewardess was to serve on a flight leaving at 3 pm but shortly after noon was ordered to work on a plane leaving in 15 minutes. She asked the manager to talk to the union first and eventually somebody else was picked for the flight. But in March of the following year, the stewardess's pay was cut on the grounds that she had refused to comply with a company order. The court found that a change of the duty schedule on the very day of duty was extremely disadvantageous for the employee and that such a change was neither covered by a labour-management agreement nor by accepted labour practices. Management, therefore, had no right to change the duty schedule in this way and the stewardess's refusal was not a rejection of a company order. In addition to cancelling the disciplinary action, JAL had to pay a solatium of ¥200,000 for mental suffering.

Pensions

In an important decision, the US Supreme Court ruled 5 to 4 that it is illegal for a company to provide lower retirement benefits to women employees than to men after both sexes have made equal contributions to a pension plan. The court rejected the argument of the employers and the insurance companies that smaller monthly pension payments did not constitute sex discrimination because actuarial tables showed that women tend to live longer and thus collect benefits over a longer period of time. 'An individual woman may not be paid lower benefits simply because women as a class live longer than men,' Justice Thurgood Marshall wrote.

The decision does not affect insurance contracts but bills pending in Congress would prohibit sex discrimination also in life, auto, disability and health insurance as well as in individually purchased annuities. Unisex insurance, however, may be a mixed blessing for women. As things stand, a woman pays less for life insurance than a man of the same age because the odds are that she will live to pay premiums longer, and the insurance company's payout will be at a later time. Young men pay higher auto insurance premiums than young women because statistics show that they are more likely to be involved in accidents. Under unisex insurance, women as a group would pay more for insurance. But the existing system, which may be fair to men and women as members of groups, is definitely unfair to many individuals. The National Organisation for Women claimed that, on balance, discrimination in insurance actually cost a woman $15,700 more than a man over a lifetime.

Most British insurance companies charge women more than men for health coverage but less for life insurance on the grounds that women are more prone to sickness than men but tend to live longer. In a sex discrimination suit brought by a London dentist whose insurance company charged her 50 per cent more than a man in the same circumstances, the court ruled in favour of the insurer. 'There is overwhelming evidence that a substantial loading is justified,' the judge said. But he also opined that there was no satisfactory evidence that women needed more sick leave.

A woman employed by a municipal government claimed that male employees with the same number of years of service had been promoted and their salaries raised and that, according to the practice of the municipality, her salary, too, should have been increased after certain years of service even if she were not assigned to a post with greater responsibility. The Tsu District Court ruled in favour of the woman but the Nagoya High Court, in April 1983, overturned the verdict because being a woman had not been the sole reason why the pay of the woman had not been increased. The woman has appealed to the Supreme Court.

In a recent ruling, the Supreme Court upheld the verdict of the Tokyo High Court which had increased the damages granted to the parents of an 8-year-old girl killed in a road accident because the computation of the Tokyo District Court involved sexual discrimination. The High Court calculated the compensation for 'lost income' on the assumption that the girl would have worked from the age of 22 to 68 after graduation from college with her remuneration based on the average annual wages of both male and female workers. (The awarding of damages for 'lost income' of a child to the parents is completely absurd but established Japanese practice. It is one of the instances in which Japanese courts reach what they consider socially desirable decisions by preposterous legal reasoning. The assumption that the girl would have graduated from college and would have worked to the age of 68 is entirely gratuitous.) The Supreme Court supported the basic thinking of the High Court but rejected the plaintiff's claim for 'complete equality in compensation' for both sexes.

A restructuring of the old-age pension system amalgamated the welfare pension systems managed by private associations established by large enterprises and the national pension system run by the government. The new system, scheduled to go into effect on 1 April, 1986, will pay a basic pension to everybody over the age of 65. Salary and wage earners will receive an additional amount proportional to their earnings during the years they contributed to the pension system. Under this arrangement, housewives who did not work outside the home will have an independent right to the basic pension. The revision left intact the inordinately advantageous pension system for government employees and the even more outrageous pensions for former members of the Diet.

Labour Unions

In June 1984, the number of Japanese labour unions amounted to 74,579 with a membership of 12,358,075 of whom 3,411,925 (27.6 per cent) were women. An estimated 22.2 per cent of all female workers were unionised compared with 32.6 per cent of male workers. The largest percentage of women members were in unions in finance and insurance (57.6 per cent; 584,478 out of 1,014,259), services (44.5 per cent; 833,869 out of 1,872,277), sales (36.7 per cent; 355,828 out of 968,269) and government (35.5 per cent; 487,514 out of 1,382,048). As a percentage of union membership, women unionists were most numerous in manufacturing and services (both 24.4 per cent), finance and insurance (17.1 per cent) and government (14.3 per cent).

Eliminating Discrimination

The most controversial issue in labour relations of working women is discrimination. Discrimination has been and is notorious in recruitment, hiring, training, work assignment, renumeration, promotion, dismissal, retirement age and retirement benefits. To end discrimination, women have demanded equality but the application of the principle of equality laid down in Japan's constitution (Art. 14, Par. 1) to labour relations is far from being achieved. In 1980, Japan signed the UN Convention on the Elimination of All Forms of Discrimination against Women, and the Diet had until 1985 to ratify this convention. Ratification, however, required equal treatment of women which was not the case in Japan. The government intended to pass a law, tentatively named Equal Employment Law, and a subcommittee of the Women's and Youth's Problems Council was entrusted with submitting recommendations. Three sides were represented on the committee, management, labour and the public interest, but they failed to reach agreement on a proposal. The report drawn up by the committee proposed a ban on discrimination 'without rational reasons' at all stages of employment, from recruitment to retirement, and removal of all restrictions on the positions and the promotion of women to management and special positions.

Labour demanded a legal ban on all discriminatory treatment, punitive measures against violations, and the retention of the protective provisions of the present labour legislation prohibiting, with a few exceptions, night work, excessive overtime work and work in dangerous occupations and assuring maternity leave. Management, represented by Nikkeiren (Japan Federation of Employers' Associations) was opposed to the legal enforcement of equality in employment. Nikkeiren maintained that the Japanese employment system was incompatible with equality. Employers do not hire qualified personnel to fill job openings but train their employees and place them in various posts depending on their talents and the needs of the enterprise. Since women usually quit after a few years, management would run too great a risk if it made the same kind of investment in women workers that it makes in men. (Nikkeiren's argument assumes that the life-long employment system is universal which is far from the real situation.) Nikkeiren also wanted to have all protective measures for women abolished because they conflict with equal treatment.

The members of the committee supposedly representing the public interest proposed a ban on discrimination in promotion, retirement and dismissal but opposed punitive provisions. They also recommended abolition of protective measures except those concerning pregnancy and employment in specific industries. For recruitment, employers should provide equal opportunities to men and women without being forced to do so.

Women charged that the employers were trying to trick them into choosing between 'equality' and 'protection.' The attitude of management can be seen from a remark of Mr Bunpei Otsuki, president of Nikkeiren, who rejected the proposed law on the grounds that women's primary role lies in housekeeping and childbearing.

Based on the recommendations of the committee, the government submitted a bill to the Diet in May 1984. In an obvious attempt to downplay the importance of the measure, the government did not propose a new law but an omnibus bill amending existing legislation such as the Working Women's Welfare Law of 1972 and the Labour Standards Law.

The bill was passed by the lower house but was stalled in the upper house and carried over to the next session of the Diet. The House of Councillors approved the government's bill with an amendment on 25 April, 1985, and the House of Representatives passed the measure on 17 May, 1985. The 'Law Concerning the Revision etc. of Laws Related to the Ministry of Labour for Securing Equal Opportunity and Treatment of Men and Women in the Field of Employment' went into effect on 1 April, 1986.

Equal Opportunity Law

The law contains two main sections, supplementary provisions of the Employment Security Law and the Family Labour Law as well as the review provisions added by the House of Councillors. The first section represents a complete revision of the Working Women's Welfare Law, the second section is a partial amendment of the Labour Standards Law. The main provisions are as follows. Employers must endeavour to give women equal opportunity with men in recruitment, employment, job assignment and promotion and provide equal treatment for men and women in job assignment and promotion, but failure to do so is not punishable. Discriminatory treatment in retirement age and dismissal is forbidden. Specifically, marriage, pregnancy and childbirth cannot be made a reason for the discharge of women. Discriminatory treatment is also prohibited in job training and welfare measures (such as home loans).

The provisions of the Labour Standards Law limiting overtime work, work on holidays and night work have been abolished for supervisory personnel and specialists. The two-hour limit on overtime work has been rescinded for industrial work. For non-industrial work (such as services), monthly ceilings will be set by administrative order for each sector within the limits of 6 to 12 hours a week and 150 to 300 hours a year. Monthly ceilings will also be fixed for holiday work. Night work will be allowed for certain occupations for which the employers get permission from the administrative agencies. The provisions concerning dangerous and harmful work have been abolished except for pregnant women. Maternity leave has been extended to 10 weeks before and 8 weeks after childbirth for women pregnant with more than one foetus (for others, the regular leave of 6 weeks before and after delivery remain in force). Pregnant women cannot request overtime work, work on holidays and night work. Government agencies will promote the reemployment of women who quit working for childbirth and the education of their children, and the government will encourage the adoption of the 'child leave system' by enterprises.

Local governments are to establish arbitration committees which will solve disputes over sex discrimination in employment.

The law falls far short from enforcing equality of men and women at the workplace as understood in the UN convention and does not affirm equality as a human right of women. It even avoids the word commonly used in the discussions on equality (instead of *byôdô*, the law uses *kintô*).

The effect of the law will largely depend on its implementation. The guidelines drawn up by the Ministry of Labour eased the restrictions on overtime work of women in the service industry and non-industrial sectors. All restrictions were removed for women managers and 14 categories of professionals. In the Diet proceedings, the term 'specialist' used in the law was interpreted to comprise physicians, dentists, pharmacists, journalists, reporters, lawyers, certified public accountants, tax accountants, architects, designers, system engineers and researchers. Industry wanted to have programmers and sales engineers included.

The ceiling on overtime work of women in non-manufacturing industries has been set at 24 hours during a four-week period or 150 hours per year. For female nurses and women working in hotels, inns, restaurants and entertainment establishments, the ceiling has been fixed at 12 hours during a two-week period or 150 hours per year. The exemption of women tour guides and postal workers from the prohibition of night work has been revoked. The guidelines require at least one day off every four weeks.

The work of women on board ship is regulated by the Seamen's Law. In connection with the measures for the promotion of equality in employment, this law was also amended. As a rule, pregnant women cannot be employed on board ship, but service for a special voyage can be allowed if, at the request of the woman, a doctor certifies that there is no objection to the work. A medical certificate is also required if the woman wants to resume work six weeks after delivery instead of the regular eight weeks of maternity leave. During pregnancy and one year after delivery, a woman cannot do work categorised as harmful under the regulations for the protection of mothers. During the same period, a woman cannot perform overtime, holiday or night work. For other women, the prohibition of night work has been abolished but work harmful to a woman's reproductive system remains prohibited.

Equal Pay for Equal Work

Legally, the principle of equal pay for equal work has become almost universal. Art. 119 of the Treaty of Rome which went into effect in 1959 directly obliged all member states to enforce equality of remuneration. The premise of equal pay is equal work. Work is equal if the operations have the same characteristics. Basically, the principle means that the pay rate should apply to the job and not to the worker so that workers doing the same job should be paid at the same rate. In accordance with this principle, the European Court of Justice ruled that a woman succeeding a man must be given the same salary as the man; also, in 1982, the court held that Britain had failed to establish a system guaranteeing equality of pay of men and women.

It is extremely difficult to push the principle of 'equal pay for equal work' against deeply ingrained social prejudices. In local communities, a strong bias against the ability and aptitudes of women remains and discriminates against women in the form of social customs. For compulsory common labour or corvees in Japanese rural communities called 'kaeki' or 'fueki,' such as clearing underbrush, dredging rivers or repairing roads, the assessment of the work of women is lower than that of men although usually women do the work more steadily and efficiently. Old men and boys are treated as full workers whereas women's work is discounted at a rate of 50 to 80 per cent and a difference ranging from ¥50 to ¥3,000 is made. In the agricultural and fishing cooperatives men constitute the majority of the full members and although they do the same work, wives or widows have no right to vote or to participate in the management. The situation is not dissimilar in the cities. Neighbourhood (district) associations are run by the local bosses and their cronies although women do much or most of the work. Women busy themselves with the affairs of the PTA's but the presidents usually are men proposed by the school principals. The first 'White Book on Women' issued by the Prime Minister's Office in January 1978 blandly acknowledged that 'socially' male superiority had remained unchanged despite the legal equality of the sexes but contained no suggestions for rectifying the situation.

The adjustment of women's pay scale cannot be accomplished by a quick fix. If women's pay is raised, men also demand higher wages. The climb of women will obstruct the rise of men or will push them down. Higher wages of women will mean higher production costs which may result in shifting production to low-wage countries and thus reduce jobs. The ILO thought that a large differential between the wages of men and women would best secure jobs for women.

In 1955, the West German Federal court prohibited so-called 'women labour groups' because they discriminated against women. In their place, industry organised so-called 'light wage groups' but much of the supposedly light work was far from easy whereas some of the male operations were less heavy than the wage schedule suggested.

Comparative Worth

In recent years, the opinion has been voiced that the principle 'equal pay
for equal work' is inadequate because many women do not do the same
work as men. Instead, the principle of 'comparative worth' (also called
'pay equity') has been advocated. It means that women's pay should be
based on a comparison of the work performed by women (for example,
as secretaries or nurses) to various kinds of work ordinarily done by
men comparable in worth. For this comparison, various criteria such as
educational and training standards associated with the work should be
used for arriving at an appropriate pay level. In practice, the comparison postulated by this concept seems very difficult. It is easy to detect
glaring inequities but it may hardly be feasible to make a comparison
the basis of a wage standard. It seems not only more logical but also
easier to measure the remuneration of women not by a comparison
with men but by the economic worth of the work of women in and by
itself.

In May 1985, the city of Los Angeles agreed to adjust the wages of
3,900 women holding traditionally low-paying jobs on the basis of the
idea of 'comparable worth.' Pay increases were to bring the wages of
secretaries, clerks and librarians of whom at least 70 per cent were
women, close to wages paid for jobs of similar skill levels dominated
by men such as gardeners, garage attendants, drivers and maintenance
personnel. The settlement with the city was negotiated by the American Federation of State, County and Municipal Employees which, in a
1982 survey, had found sex discrimination in the city work force, with
82 per cent of all women earning less than $25,000 and 65 per cent of
the men earning more than $25,000. City officials stated that 'fairness
and equity' had been the only issue in the negotiations, but without a
negotiated settlement, the city might have been forced to pay back
wages from as far as 1978. In a case in Washington state, a federal judge
ordered the state to make retroactive salary adjustments which would
have cost more than $500 million. The ruling was appealed and in
September 1985, a three-judge panel of the 9th US Circuit Court of
Appeals overturned the verdict. The American Federation of State,
County and Municipal Employees which had brought the suit intended
to go to the Supreme Court and Eleanor Smeal, president of the
National Organisation for Women (NOW) vowed to fight for the
acceptance of comparable pay for women. The Reagan administration
and its supporters are opposed to this concept. In 1984, the 9th Circuit
Court rejected a comparable-pay suit brought by state nurses and the
Supreme Court refused to hear the case.

The Employment Opportunity Commission has held that failure
to pay comparable wages does not constitute discrimination in the sense
of the Civil Rights Act of 1964.

Persistent Discrimination

A report of the International Labour Organisation based on a comparison of women's earnings with those of men in 1977 and 1981 in the non-agricultural sectors of 15 countries and in the manufacturing industries of 19 countries concluded that in some countries, men earn more than twice as much as women working in the same sector but that 'it is difficult to say to what measure the inequality in earnings reflects wage discrimination, and how much it arises because women predominantly occupy jobs that are lower paid.' In 1981, the average wage of women working in manufacturing industries in Japan was 43.3 per cent that of men (down from 46 per cent in 1977) while their Swedish sisters were paid 90.1 per cent of their male counterparts. In the United Kingdom, the earnings of women compared with those of men rose from 80.1 per cent in 1977 to 83.7 per cent in 1981.

In France, equal pay for equal work has been the law since 1972 but French women, who make up 40 per cent of the country's work force, earn only two-thirds of the salary of a man doing the same work. Women face great obstacles in promotion and elite positions are generally reserved for men. In July 1983, the French Parliament adopted a law aimed at reducing discrimination against women. Any mention of sex or family status in job advertising is prohibited except for jobs where the sex of the employee is a determining factor. (The Council of State was to draw up a list of such positions.) Preferential treatment on the basis of sex is likewise banned, except in the case of maternity benefits (which include four months of maternity leave).

The law abolished a clause in the 1972 legislation under which employers could justify discriminatory hiring and firing by citing 'legitimate motives.' In the future, the employer will have to prove that there is no discrimination if employees complain of discriminatory practices.

Discrimination is found not only in the basic wage rates of men and women. In many companies, promotion depends on qualifying examinations from which female employees are often excluded. Because women are not promoted, their wages rise only slowly, and because their standard monthly wages (on which the amount of the old-age pensions is based) remain low, their pension benefits are low so that the effects of the discrimination reach beyond the time of work.

Discrimination against women has also been rampant in the transfer, dismissal and layoff of women and in the retirement regulations. A growing number of firms rehire women who leave on getting married or for other reasons on a part-time or piece-work basis. In the United States, a court held that Eastern Airlines discriminated against female flight attendants by requiring them to transfer to ground positions and lose seniority when they became pregnant. In May 1981,

India's highest court ruled that stewardesses serving with Air India, the government-controlled international airline, and Indian Airlines, the domestic carrier, can work until they are 45. The court struck down as discriminatory provisions that required stewardesses to get yearly extensions to continue service beyond the retirement ages of 35 and 30, respectively. The late Indira Gandhi had expressed the view that 40 was too old for an air stewardess because Indian women keep their looks and figures only in very exceptional cases. The court, however, branded the government's argument that 'young and attractive stewardesses can better cope with delicate situations more effectively than older women' an 'open insult to the institution of our sacred womanhood.'

Image and Performance of Women

A great obstacle to the acceptance of women as equals in all spheres of society is the image of women created by the mass media. According to a UNESCO study, the media tend to portray women either as perfectly good or as totally evil, innocent or corrupt, 'mother or whore, virgin or call girl.' Women are depicted as economically and psychologically dependent, incompetent, indecisive, foolish and ineffective. Decisiveness, independence, forcefulness and tenacity are represented as good in men and bad in women. Women are covered by the media primarily as wives, mothers or daughters of men; they are given prominence in their own right only in fashion and entertainment. This study contains a great deal of truth. Although the achievements of women are recognised by the media also in fields such as literature and sports, the accomplishments of women are still regarded as something special and extraordinary and treated differently from similar attainments by men.

In a poll commissioned by Virginia Slims Cigarettes questioning 3,000 women and 1,000 men, 51 per cent of the women said that in a choice between family and a career, they would opt for working outside the home. On another question, 42 per cent of the women wanted housewives to receive a weekly salary from their husbands for staying home but 65 per cent of the men were opposed to that idea. The survey found that 49 per cent of the women and 51 per cent of the men thought there were more advantages to being a man than being a woman, compared with 31 per cent of the women and 42 per cent of the men who held that view in 1974.

Surveys show that middle-aged women in paid labour seem in better physical and mental health than homemakers in spite of the problems of low pay and ghettoisation.

Generally speaking, women are much cleverer than men in initiating social contacts. They are also more accurate in their work. In actual experience, women have shown themselves equal to and often superior to men in many occupations. In Yamaha's production of motorcycles and Fuji Heavy Industry's production of engines for farm equipment, the rate of defective products was consistently lower on all-women assembly lines than on mixed lines so that the all-female lines achieved higher productivity and lower wage costs. For complex repair work, however, which requires a certain degree of imagination, men seem more qualified than women, and in mechanical industries, such as watchmaking, women almost always perform tasks requiring less qualifications.

In Japan, sales and design strategies have responded to the growing economic clout of women. Enterprises have transferred women employees to work on designing and marketing products to appeal especially to women. In the auto market, the number of women car owners has risen three times as fast as male owners since 1981. Fuji Heavy Industries organised an all-female project team to modify the firm's 1000cc car for women drivers. Men ignore the practical requirements of female drivers, Yukie Okano, the head of the team, asserted. What women fear most, she said, is engine stalling. Since automatic transmissions are expensive and not fuel-efficient, the team decided on a clutchless manual transmission. It chose specially designed non-stain soft fabrics to replace vinyl seat covers. Three hundred of the redesigned cars were experimentally put on the market and were sold out in three months, and the same happened to a second batch of three hundred cars.

When the electric appliance market became saturated, manufacturers turned to women for the creation of products that would appeal to women buyers. Besides proposing ideas on design and colour, women developed a TV set which could function as a source of lighting for illuminating a room in various colours.

Many housing companies have employed women to advise clients on interior decoration and sell them the necessary materials. While husbands provide the money, the actual decision-making on interior decoration lies with the wives or daughters. Women are better equipped to deal with female clients. They have the patience and sensitivity required for this business.

At Suntory, women have invented drinks with a low alcohol content appealing to women who finish their working day by dropping in at a bar or small restaurant. But their successes have not helped women to advance to managerial positions.

Women Workers in China

In the People's Republic of China, women workers number 40 million, accounting for 36 per cent of the urban labour force, compared with 7.5 per cent before the Communist takeover. Over 150 million are in the rural labour force. Legally, women are entitled to eight weeks maternity leave which results in a high rate of absenteeism when mothers go back to work without recovering from childbirth. Equality for women is still elusive. Girls make up 35 per cent of the high school students but only 24 per cent of those studying at universities. Only 5.35 million of the 20 million cadres in the Communist Party are women, and women seldom become high-ranking government officials or managers. The 25-member Politburo included only one woman, 79-year-old Deng Ying-chao, widow of Zhou Enlai, and only three ministers in the government were women (1983). Female lawyers numbered 1,200, 10 per cent of all lawyers or one for every 8.33 million women in China.

At the Shanghai Academy of Sciences, 445 males were engaged in advanced research in 1983 but only 76 women. Household chores, lack of space at home and poor health were some of the hardships women scientists had to bear. The average woman scientist spent four hours a day on household chores and in addition coached her children for entrance in special schools. Families lived in cramped quarters and as it was impossible to put more than one desk in a room, the women had to sacrifice their study in favour of husband and children. With low pay, household expenses had to be kept down and women scrimped on their own food to have enough for husband and children.

Women in Silicon Valley

Many economies have been a rich man — poor woman economies. This description fits today's high-tech sector. In California's Silicon Valley which has the fastest-growing and wealthiest economy in the United States, the average yearly income per family is over $26,000. One out of every six people in California with a PhD lives in the Valley. But the working population has two distinct tiers. At the top are a few highly trained and highly skilled people, engineers, scientists and designers who are predominantly male, white, and wealthy. The lower level comprises production workers who are generally female, with nearly half from ethnic minorities. It also includes janitors, clerks-secretaries, food-service workers and hospital attendants, traditionally low-paid, dead-end occupations likely to be filled by women. The upper tier has to endure long working hours, fierce competition and a high-pressure life-style. Many people live beyond their means and sometimes turn to crime if they see no other way out. The divorce rate is enormous, higher than in California as a whole where it is already 20 per cent higher than the national average. Living conditions of the workers in the lower-tiered jobs involve the same problems of poverty as in the other parts of the country.

In a group of 30 professional women working in the Valley

described in a study, two-thirds worked more than 40 hours a week. One-third was divorced or separated, and many of the women with children were so taken up by their jobs that they had little time to spend with their offspring. About 70 per cent thought that the traditional values of home, family and community did not apply in Silicon Valley. Although most of the women felt that the advantages of living in the Valley outweighed the drawbacks, the victims of Silicon Valley are at least ten times more numerous than the winners.

A congressional study on the employment situation in the US Department of State in the years from 1970 to 1981 found a 'general apathy' towards equal employment opportunities for women. The proportion of women foreign service officers remained the same — 26 per cent — during this period but in 1982, 34 per cent of the new foreign service officers were women. Only 3 per cent of the senior department jobs were held by women and ambassadors, who can choose their own deputies, have been 'consistently reluctant' to place a woman in the Number 2 position at their embassy.

Male chauvinism may have played a role in the famous confrontation between Herbert von Karajan and the Berlin Philharmonic Orchestra in January 1983, but it was not purely a case of sex discrimination. The orchestra which engaged its first woman only in 1982 refused to accept Sabine Meyer, 23, as clarinetist. Miss Meyer had been performing with the Bavarian Radio Orchestra and von Karajan, impressed by the purity and gentleness of her playing, wanted her to come to Berlin.

The exclusion of males from becoming kindergarten teachers prompted the charge of 'reverse' discrimination. The enforcement ordinance of the Japanese Ministry of Health and Welfare restricted the application for the qualifying examination for kindergarten teachers to women. The all-female Preschool Teachers Society objected. Due to the rapid growth of kindergartens, day-care centres and institutions for handicapped children, many unlicensed male teachers have been hired.

The old superstition that the presence of women invites disaster because women are unclean survives until this day among men working on ships or in the mountains. This superstition is very strong among tunnel workers and the Japan Railway Construction Company allowed no women into tunnel construction sites. It was only for a ceremony commemorating the workers who lost their lives in the construction of the undersea Seikan tunnel connecting Honshû and Hokkaido that the widows of 22 workers killed in working on the tunnel were invited to the site accompanied by 80 other women. It was also the first time journalists were allowed into the tunnel. How strong this superstition is can be seen from an otherwise trivial incident. When posters promoting a safety campaign featuring a woman model were put up inside the tunnel, they were torn down, apparently by older workers.

Sexual Harassment

Besides discrimination, sexual harassment has caused much distress to working women. Sexual harassment is commonly associated with secretaries having to defend themselves against their bosses, but according to an American study, sexual harassment of blue-collar working women is not only more frequent but also more brutal than that of office workers. In the Detroit auto plants, 36 per cent of all women workers on the line were subjected to some form of harassment ranging from vulgar remarks to outright physical attacks. In the office, the harasser usually is the boss but on the factory floor, women are also molested by their co-workers. The most common kind of harassment was sexual propositioning, but it also included abusive language, verbal innuendo, sexual bribery and social derogation such as spreading rumours that women who resisted were lesbians.

A British report on sexual harassment in a Liverpool office listed 43 per cent of men and women as complaining of being touched up, brushed against and grappled by the opposite sex at work. Other complaints were to be stared and leered at, sexual remarks and teasing, and direct requests for sex. Of the complainants, 70 per cent were women but a surprising 28 per cent were men.

Three women who had filed a complaint under Britain's 1975 Sex Discrimination Act alleging sexual harassment obtained a legal undertaking by the union and the *Daily Mirror* not to discriminate against them. The women had charged that their male colleagues had conducted a war of nerves against them by assailing them, swearing and making obscene phone calls because they threatened what had been considered as exclusively male jobs in Fleet Street.

A West German study found that every fifth working woman had been sexually harassed at her place of work at least once and that most women preferred not to talk about it because this would only result in more difficulties. But in some cases, leading officials had to quit because they had molested women subordinates, and a parliamentarian belonging to the Green Party had to renounce his seat on account of his behaviour towards women party members.

In November 1982, the US Navy ordered commanders to crack down on sexual harassment of women sailors with swift and appropriate disciplinary action. An anti-harassment policy had already been adopted by the Navy in 1980 and the new order intended to ensure that every instance of sexual harassment would be dealt with swiftly, fairly and effectively.

Hollywood has been called the 'city of the predators' because only too often, access to work in the entertainment industry depends on a woman's readiness to submit to the demands for sex by the purveyors of jobs.

Working women are not the only ones threatened by sexual harassment. A questionnaire sent out by the women's committee of Oxford University's student union to the university's 3,000 undergraduate women brought 300 replies, including 41 complaints alleging that women suffered verbal abuse and physical assault, from touching, groping, kissing and propositioning of sex to rape. In 22 cases, tutors were involved.

In a case of 'reverse' sexual harassment, an American male employee sued a female supervisor alleging that he had been demoted because he had refused her sexual advances. A Wisconsin court awarded him $196,500 in damages but the decision has been appealed.

Women at the UN

The United Nations Organisation has often come under attack for its treatment of women. It has been stated that there is no equal opportunity for women in the international civil service. Governments seldom nominate competent female candidates for senior job vacancies. There has been no female undersecretary-general and few women have held the sub-cabinet post of director. The organisation had set the goal of filling 25 per cent of its staff positions with women by 1982 but admitted that the goal had not been reached. However, since his appointment in 1981, UN Secretary-General Javier Perez de Cuelar has appointed several women to higher posts, and since February 1982, six women have held posts of the third-highest rank, that of assistant secretary-general, and a Filipina was nominated secretary-general of the world conference to review the results of the UN Decade for Women. Of the 148 executives at the top three levels of the secretariat, only 7 are filled by women. There are no women among the 27 undersecretary-generals. Women fill only 23 per cent of the 4,000 professional jobs in the secretariat. In recent years, the situation has deteriorated and the percentage of women recruited has been considerably lower than the percentage of women already in the organisation. The Secretary-General set a new goal of filling 30 per cent of all professional appointments during the biennium 1986-1987 with women.

'It is a real feudal system here,' Susan Marham, a UN information officer told the New York Times. 'The women are looked down and treated like serfs.' Many women have complained of sexual harassment. Superiors seek sex from women staff in return for promotions and job security. Women in clerical, typing and junior professional jobs are constantly pressured into going to bed to advance or secure their jobs. Because many of them are aliens who do not have visas to work in the United States except at the United Nations, they will often take employment at a level below what is appropriate to their education and their skills just so they can stay in New York.

Mrs Jeane J. Kirkpatrick, who served four years as US Ambassador to the United Nations, told a breakfast meeting of the Women's Forum on 19 December, 1984: 'I think sexism is alive in the United Nations, in the Secretariat and among my colleagues at the UN, alive in the United States government, alive in American politics.' High politics, she said, and in particular the upper levels of foreign policy, diplomacy and defence are male bastions, and the same is true for the upper levels of foreign policy in all countries. The only difference between men and women in high politics, Mrs Kirkpatrick thinks, is the difference in attitudes about the use of force. In view of Mrs Thatcher's role in the Falklands conflict, the difference may be more a matter of personal convictions than of gender preferences.

A report of the women's committee of the Writers Guild of America, West Coast Chapter, charged that women writers were discriminated against in Hollywood and offered statistical evidence covering the 1980–1982 seasons to prove their charge.

Discrimination against women may have practical reasons. In Tokyo, the proprietor of a small restaurant did not admit women during lunch hours. His explanation: 'Women tend to get engrossed in chatting after eating and occupy tables longer than men. They simply ignore the people lined up outside waiting for a table.'

In a time of global recession, male workers feel doubly irritated by the entry of women into the labour market. On the other hand, women have found that work outside the home has other attractions besides the financial remuneration. They feel independent, capable of taking care of themselves, and playing a useful role in society. Their work gives them a feeling of belonging. In Japan, work is done almost always by a group, and working women form part of the team responsible for the work. They are counted upon to do their share of the work which heightens their self-respect. Whereas household work is usually taken for granted, their contribution, though not essential, is required for the smooth and effective performance of the work of the group. This gives them a sense of commitment and responsibility, provides experience and opens areas of interest beyond the confines of the family.

In Japan, some career women complain that the attitude of other women to professional careers constitutes a great obstacle. Many women still think that a woman's place is in the home, that women should take care of household chores first and foremost, and that working mothers are liable to rear delinquent children. The generations of girls who took a job only a few years and were not interested in a business career have created the unwillingness of employers to consider women as candidates for serious jobs. Women feel incompetent to do the sort of dealings and negotiations that men do and many are averse to travel and to be stationed abroad.

Women and Automation

There has been much discussion on the effects of automation on the employment opportunities of women, particularly as office workers. According to Siemens, 43 per cent of all office work can be automated, and stenotypists will be mainly affected. On the other hand, a qualified secretary can make her work more efficient because she can free herself of much of the routine work. The International Federation of White Collar Workers estimated that technological development affects typists, general administrators, draughtsmen, accounts clerks, data preparation staff, accountants, salesmen, technicians, middle management and shopfloor supervisors. One of the main results is the elimination of commercial office jobs mostly held by women and the creation of new technically qualified jobs which will be handled by men. The machinery that will have the most widely felt impact includes data and word processors, laser scanners and computers. While some commentators emphasise that computers and word processors are complex machines whose handling requires special training, others think that even little qualified workers can learn to operate them in a relatively short time. Many women seem to fear computers as something strange and related to mathematics which girls and women often dislike. But this fear disappears after a short while. Office girls have quickly learned to handle computer terminals and similar devices.

Office automation greatly reduces the work load but does not make the entire office staff superfluous. The increased use of microcomputers and the use of industrial robots in manufacturing have had a noticeable effect on employment. Major Japanese companies reported a decline in their female personnel in 1981 while their male work force increased. In the following year, older male workers were assigned to affiliate firms or moved to simpler work and hiring plans for women were cancelled.

A survey of the Ministry of Labour on the use of office automation equipment undertaken in October 1983 showed that 46.7 per cent of the male and 60.1 per cent of the female work force in Japanese enterprises used office automation equipment. The proportion was highest (65.4 per cent) for women below 30 years; it was 25.1 per cent for the women and 19.1 per cent for the men over 50 years of age. The ratio of the use of automated equipment was highest in enterprises with over 5,000 workers and for information processing (92.2 per cent). It was 60.4 per cent for ordinary office work. 34.4 per cent of the men and 27.5 per cent of the women found that the equipment had made their work easier, 17.8 per cent of the men and 19.8 per cent of the women thought that their work had become more difficult. The companies had arranged training for 50.2 per cent of their male and 72.4 per cent of their female employees, and 47.4 per cent of the men and 23.5 per cent of the women had also studied manuals and other literature.

A study of the American Bureau of Labour Statistics predicted that nine out of every ten new jobs will be in the service sector and that the main growth will be related to computers, telecommunications, health and business services.

The progress in electronics constitutes a challenge to women. The information age will bring the computer into the home and women must learn to handle it. Computers will replace the typewriter and to a certain extent telephone and mail. Electronics makes it possible to do work at home instead of the office and thus could some day make it easier for women to combine homemaking and childrearing with a professional career.

The computer gives management an almost unlimited capability to assess each worker's productivity. The time-and-motion studies of Frederick W. Taylor which initiated the modern concept of scientific management have been refined to an accuracy and comprehensiveness unobtainable by Taylor's stopwatch observations. Efficiency experts measure employees' movements in TUMs (time-measurement units; one TUM is 0.036 seconds); computers can time and record every movement, from the number of times the employee leaves the work site to the number of keystrokes per hour hit by a typist.

Computer monitoring has been adopted as an effective means of timing a worker's speed, efficiency and accuracy, thus improving productivity, speeding the flow of information and giving customers faster and better service. Computer-generated performance reports can be used to structure piece-rate pay systems or work out merit pay, but also for disciplining, demoting or even firing the slow or underskilled employee. The computer has brought a degree of supervision which has dramatically increased stress in the workplace. Opponents of computer monitoring assert that workers, constantly watched and evaluated by a sometimes unseen superviser, suffer from illnesses such as hypertension, heart disease, migraine headaches and stomach troubles. Employees under 'technostress' often provide poorer, slower and less courteous service. Computer monitoring has been denounced as an 'electronic straight jacket' which creates a dehumanising work environment because the worker feels controlled by the machine. Defenders of the system assert that computer monitoring is not necessarily repressive or intimidating. 'A person is more intimidating than a machine. A person can fire you, a machine can only report your scores.'

Technostress resulting from the worker's inability to adapt to new technologies is becoming a problem in connection with office automation. It is said to occur in two forms; fear of and over-involvement with computers. The director of a Tokyo clinic found that 35 per cent of 250 women working in computer-related jobs showed signs of nervous disorders. A survey conducted by Sohyô, Japan's largest federation of labour unions, found that 77 per cent of 6,900 men and women working with display terminals suffered from eyestrain and 46 per cent had become nearsighted or developed a stigmatism. Furthermore, 56 per cent complained about stiffness in the shoulder and 41 per cent of physical fatigue while 37 per cent said working with VDTs made them irritable. American labour unions have expressed concern over the possible radiation emissions from VDTs which may cause reproductive abnormalities.

In the other form of technostress, computer operators, especially programmers, tend to isolate themselves from others and their ability to handle human relations is impaired.

In a related inquiry, Dômei, another federation of labour unions, canvassed 5,000 workers on the effects of operating robots, personal computers, word processors and other devices incorporating microelectronics. While 41.6 per cent were little affected by the new equipment, 43.7 per cent complained of eye-strain, headaches and mental stress. Some adverse effects were experienced by 53.4 per cent of the men and 69.8 per cent of the women responding to the survey.

Sexual equality constitutes a goal for which women all over the world will continue to work. In most industrialised countries of the West, the position of women has changed dramatically in the course of the twentieth century. This does not mean that women enjoy all the rights and the status to which they are entitled nor that all women have profited from the improvement in conditions. But the oppression of women is no longer protected by law and tolerated by the authorities. The debasement of women is no longer the general effect of the social environment although there remain innumerable cases of battered wives, socially disadvantaged women, women forced to live by prostitution or reduced to poverty by divorce. Despite many real problems, women are no longer stigmatised as inferior as a class. In Japan, women enjoy real freedom and real security although the achievement of true equality in all spheres of life is still a dream.

The most important task of the women's movements will be the liberation of women in the countries of the Third World. The hardest nut to crack will probably be the abolition of polygamy.